Jon Drake

By Robert B Hayek

Acknowledgements

Thank you to my friends and family for supporting me over the years. This is the first of many books in the same universe, or as I call the Hayekverse. Thanks to my wonderful cover designer and all the people that helped prepare this book. It's the first of many adventures.

Part 1

Chapter 1: Sins of the Past

January 1st, 2016, near a dive bar in Brasilía, Brazil.

Jon needed cover to get out of the monsoon that drenched his face. His head bobbed back and forth, looking for a place to shelter. His eyes lingered on a bar in the distance, one he recognized, O'Reilly Pub, the one Irish bar in Brasilía. He hurried toward the venue and entered frantically.

His arrival caused a stir as eyes glued on him. At six-foot-two inches, with drenched brown hair and a disheveled beard, Jon Drake could not maintain a low profile even if he wanted to.

The exterior of the bar was green headstones, to resemble Ireland, with brown doors to allow guests inside. The interior of the bar was far simpler. There was a bar with all the drinks on tap and even a little stage area next to the bar area, where the nightly band would perform.

He saddled his way down to the bar where a bartender cleaned the glasses. He took a stool out from the adjacent table and parked it in front of the bar area, where his bartender stared at him.

"God damn man, it is a shit show out there," he said bluntly. He realized what he said and just chuckled to himself. The bartender did not look amused.

He was an enormous man, big enough to hold his own. He had long flowing hair and a beard to match, similar to what Jesus Christ looked like. The bartender also looked unassuming. Jon looked at the bartender and figured he was a Pardo. The bartender looked like he was from several countries all at once.

"What do you want?" asked the bartender in Portuguese. Jon smiled as the bartender asked this.

"You should know me by now, João, I roll with your sister, we're homies."

"I know you, Jon Drake," João answered in English. He continued in his native language.

"That's why I am asking you what you want. I am cool with you and would serve you anything here. But some men do not feel the same appreciation for you. And I do not want that shit in my bar."

"Obviously not," said Jon in English, which João understood. "But it's pouring like a bitch out there. Come on, João, give me a drink."

As he said this, two men appeared from the background, and they looked unhappy. One was a scrawny little man named Yan. The other was a bigger man named Xoán. They approached Jon as he sipped his beer as they stared him down.

"Can I at least finish my beer before I kick your ass?" he asked them.

They did not look amused. Yan stepped up. João wiped the bar clean, despite it already being clean.

"Where's my car, Jon?" asked Yan.

"I think I crashed it somewhere down the street, check the nearest bush."

"You messed with the wrong guys, Jon Drake."

"I have taken down cartel members and you expect me to be afraid of you? Bitch, please!" Jon replied.

"You should be afraid," Yan spoke up. Jon sipped more beer. The beer trickled down his tongue, refreshing his dry throat. He took foot of his surroundings, noticing that others looked at them.

"And if I don't?" Jon challenged them. They looked at one another and both smiled.

"Then we will leave you broken," Yan replied. Jon smirked, and then took another sip of the beer.

The taste wore off. He held the beer in his hand, frowned, and then quickly unleashed a beer bottle over Yan's head, breaking it into many pieces as the man fell to the ground from the impact.

"Is that all you got?" Jon grew bored.

Xoán stared at his fallen partner in disbelief, and then grew angry. He grabbed a bottle of his own and cracked it against the bar. He swung ferociously at Jon, who ducked each swipe.

He bit Xoán's arm, and the thug yelped in pain, then pressed his hands around the man and threw him right across the bar. Xoán slipped down the bar like it was a slip and slide and collided with all the beer glasses and plates. Everyone looked at him now. João just looked exasperated. Jon glanced at him.

"I promise you I will pay for all that," said Jon. Other patrons stood up and surrounded him. "I also will pay for everything else that is about to happen."

A massive bar fight ensued. Several men charged Jon. He leaped over the bar counter and took cover.

He searched for anything that could be a weapon and found a bottle of vodka. With quick reflexes, he grabbed it and smashed it over some guy's head. Another man rushed him, and Jon nailed him with a bottle of whiskey.

"You made me waste good alcohol," he lectured the fallen man.

The rest of the bar was in disarray, but Xoán and Yan kept their gaze on Jon. Realizing this, Jon quickly thought of an action plan.

His fingers blindly found cool glass as he wrapped them around the neck of the bottle, swinging it over his head. It broke across Xoán's skull with a sickening crunch.

Yan hurled himself into him, both tumbling onto the floor. The man's big sweaty body lumbered over him and Jon blindly swung his arms in the air, attempting to haul him away. He stretched his body out and unleashed a right elbow to Yan's head, causing him to yelp and peel over. Two more men charged at Jon and he sidestepped them and rolled toward the stage. His right hand reached for something and he unleashed a drum set against their heads, knocking them both out.

Chaos ensued as sirens roared in the background and the police stormed the place with their guns drawn. They surrounded Jon, who put his hands up. Jon looked back at João.

"Put this on my bar tab. Just don't tell your sister. She'll kill me, even though she's like tiny."

Two cops grabbed Jon and held him down against the table. His head squeezed against the table, his face looking puffy.

"Easy on the face," he yelped.

The cops lifted him up aggressively and hauled him out of the bar. They placed Jon into handcuffs and took him into their squad car and took him to jail.

He sulked in his cell, fiddling with his hands. The guard walked in and opened the jail gate. He was a burly fellow, kind of like the Pillsbury Doughboy. As he opened the door, Jon just waited for him to say something.

"Some man paid your bail and cleared all your charges," said the guard.

"What man?"

"This man," said a voice from the distance.

He gazed upon the man, and his jaw dropped. The man was massive, probably six foot four inches. He had long flowing hair with a beard that made him resemble a lion and must have been around 40 years old if Jon had to guess.

"And who the hell are you?" asked Jon bluntly.

"The man who can save your life if you do your part for me."

"That's cute, but I need a name. Not going to go off with some random guy who looks like a deformed lion," said Jon.

The man chuckled. It perplexed him. "Was it something I said?"

"It is funny you mention a lion. Most people around this country call me the Lion. But you can call me Vladimir Ramirez."

Vladimir extended his hand for him to shake. He hesitated. Something about this man was familiar. But he would remember if he had met this man. This man, Vladimir, was a sight to behold.

A gigantic man with a look of a powerful lion was not something easy to forget. He did not shake his hand. Instead, he glared at Vladimir, hoping for a telling sign. He did not get any.

"Why did you bail me out? And apparently, erase my charges?"

"Because," Vladimir said. "A man with gifts is too talented to waste his life on meaningless bar fights and jail visits."

"Oh, you heard about that? That's nothing. You should see the other ones I have been in."

"I do and I have Jon Drake."

Jon's eyes narrowed. "How do you know my name?"

"Oh, come now, you have established a reputation for yourself around here. It is difficult to not know about you, Jon Drake, or should I say, White Warrior?"

He took this in, hearing his other nickname. He hated that nickname. "What do you want?"

"To offer you a chance at freedom in a philosophical sense," said Vladimir, who then looked around. "And literally."

"What is the catch?"

"My organization has been attempting to eliminate a man. An evil man. One that you know very well."

"I am not going back to São Paulo, after any cartel members."

He realized at that moment he probably should not have said that. But it was something he could not help. He waited for Vladimir to respond, but the lion-looking man did not give him that satisfaction.

"I know of your reputation with the cartel," said Vladimir. "But I assure you that the cartel is not who I am going after."

"Then who?"

Vladimir took out a newspaper and stretched it out. He held the paper out in front of him and he instantly recognized the picture in the front. It was an image of a well-dressed man taking a picture with a group of children to support some cause.

Dreadful memories came flushing back. Jon knew the actual truth. The man in the picture was evil. It would be difficult to not know who that man was. It was Alexander Caine! Jon shook his head vigorously.

"No, I'd rather fight 20 cartel members then deal with that shithead ever again."

Vladimir folded the newspaper back and placed it in his pocket.

"Jon, you are ideally situated to go after this man. He lives in your hometown and you hate evil as much as I do. As much as we do."

"We?"

"Yes, we. The Legion of Samurai. I assume you have heard of us," Vladimir's voice radiated with confidence.

He knew the Legion of Samurai. He had been on opposite sides of the spectrum with them. He also had worked with members of the Legion in the past. He knew who they were and what they were. The Legion of Samurai were self-proclaimed fighters of the good.

This violent group was like terrorist groups like ISIS and Al Qaeda, except they were better trained. They also did not cause violence in the name of God but acted on their own belief that they must save the Earth. The Legion of Samurai were extreme climate change advocates.

Whereas most climate change advocators posted about it online or randomly protested in front of city hall, these guys killed in the name. But somehow, he had never met Vladimir. This lion-looking man was unknown to him. How was that possible? Jon did not think about that at the moment.

"What exactly do you want me to do?" asked Jon.

"It's simple," said Vladimir. "I want you to go back to your hometown and kill Alexander Caine."

He took this in, considering it for a moment. Then he looked at Vladimir and could tell that the Brazilian man was not joking around.

"And if I refuse?" Jon asked.

"Then I change my mind and you stay in this jail to rot until corrupt officials try you for crimes they are aware of, and some they are not," said Vladimir.

Jon studied him but said nothing.

"Find a place to stay tonight and then consider my offer. I will be at my home in the mountains," said Vladimir, who then handed him a card. He looked at this. The card looked old-school with a number and address written in Old English. Vladimir had planned this. Jon considered his options.

The Next Day: Pico do Roncador.

He found his way toward the area written was on the card. He had to climb a mountain to get to the top of the summit. He knew this and took some hiking clothing he would need, along with the correct gear. He had hiked many mountains in Brazil over the years, mostly in situations of utter chaos. Often, he was usually running away from one guy trying to kill him. That is usually how it would end.

He climbed the summit and noticed how it was getting colder the higher he went. He did not mind the frigid weather, as it was something he got used to.

As he made his way up to the top of the mountain, he spotted a sizeable house on the top of the mountainside. He slowly trekked through the snowy ground and the mini blizzard that was occurring simultaneously. Approaching cautiously, he put his hand on the doorknob and twisted it open and entered slowly and cautiously, not knowing what the next step would be.

A man charged at him with a sword. Jon ducked, barely avoiding getting cut in half. The man kept coming at Jon with the sword.

He swung his sword and Jon caught it this time, deflecting it away. Jon used his right hand to deck the man in the face.

He quickly grabbed the sword up and held it against the now fallen man, while stepping on his chest. Jon heard clapping and turned to see Vladimir walking into the room.

"I see you have passed my test," said Vladimir.

"Test?" asked Jon, a little bewildered now.

"I wanted to see what you were capable of, and so I had my assistant, Manuel, attack you to see if you would survive," said Vladimir.

"He could have killed me!"

"Then you would not have been worthy," Vladimir shot back.

He increased his hold on Manny now, squeezing his boot into his upper chest, choking him.

"And what makes you think I won't kill your boy right now?" asked Jon.

Vladimir snapped his fingers. Several cloaked men with enormous swords appeared out of nowhere and surrounded them both.

"Because my men would kill you instantly."

Jon looked at the men, annoyed. He released his hold on Manny. The man scuffled himself off the floor, bowed to Vladimir, and exited.

"Come on, Jon," said Vladimir. "We have a lot to discuss."

They headed into another room. This was a training room, it seemed. There were plenty of swords, daggers, and other weapons that Jon was familiar with. He had a feeling that this would be the case when he agreed to come to see Vladimir.

"I want to see just how skilled you really are," said Vladimir. The long-haired man handed Jon a sword and took his own sword. Vladimir quickly swung his sword, and Jon, on instinct, blocked it with his sword. They exchanged shots with their sword, with neither man coming out on top.

"Impressive," said Vladimir.

"Not so bad yourself," replied Jon.

Vladimir tossed his sword. Jon did the same.

"Hand to hand," said Vladimir.

Vladimir struck Jon with a chop to the chest. His face fell when he realized it made no impact. He tried to chop him again, but Vladimir caught his hands, smiled, and backhanded him across the face.

Jon stumbled a little. He recovered and launched himself into Vladimir's stomach, taking the bigger man by surprise, causing him to fall to the ground.

Vladimir recovered and then looked at Jon and smiled. Before he could react, Vladimir leaped into the air and roundhouse kicked him in the stomach, sending him tumbling to the ground.

He groaned in pain, and Vladimir extended his hand to help him up. Vladimir pulled him to his feet.

"You are skilled, but very unpolished, Jon," said Vladimir.

"Not nearly as good as you."

"Patience," said Vladimir. "I could raise you to my level. But first, you need to share your pain with me."

He gave Vladimir a look. "What are you getting at?"

"Tell me about your father," said Vladimir.

There was a long, uncomfortable silence. He did not like the question and did not appreciate this man coming at him like this.

"Who are you and why do you want to know about my father?"

"As I have told you, we are the Legion of Samurai and we know all. I know about your legend, and I know how you came to Brazil ten years ago. You must not forget, this organization does not get along with the cartels," said Vladimir.

Now Jon was suspicious. He glared at Vladimir as if he was expecting a fight. Vladimir sensed this.

"If it makes you feel any better, I can share my pain with you," Vladimir suggested.

"What, you're going to show me your scars?"

Vladimir shook his head.

"Jon, the only way to heal a tortured soul is to learn how to embrace the pain and fight back against it." Jon contemplated this but said nothing. "I can help you."

"How?"

"Allow me to train your body and soul and you will return to your hometown and confront your demon. When you do that, you can finally overcome your fears."

He considered it. He did not trust Vladimir, but what he did not have much of a life now.

"What's in it for you?"

Vladimir smiled.

"When evil dies, then I prosper. I want to see the world balanced. I know who caused you significant pain, Jon. I have done my research on you."

He hesitated. "You creeping on my history?"

"I did not go to the trouble of releasing you from jail without doing research. We share the same enemy. The one called Caine."

"Yeah, you mentioned him. How do you know Caine?"

Vladimir brushed his hair back from his face. "Let's just say he has committed atrocities against some of my best interests. I have known of the man for a long time and realize what a terror he is, and what he has become. I know of your history with him and I would like to help.

"Caine is not just an American scum. His reach has extended here, as far as the Legion of Samurai's efforts. He makes deals with the cartels. The same cartels that my organization continues to hunt and destroy. We must stop him."

He took this in. He heard Vladimir and immediately thought he was insane. However, the offer intrigued him.

"Alexander Caine destroyed my life," He informed Vladimir. "He took my father away and ensured that I become an orphan. I have waited years for the chance to take my revenge."

"I don't completely trust you, but I feel like you and I have the same vision. The same end goals. I'll accept your help."

He extended his hand. Vladimir looked at him and then returned the handshake.

"It is good to have you aboard," Vladimir declared.

He stayed with Vladimir for about two weeks. The man called the Lion by many helped him hone some of his skills, while also teaching him some old Samurai ways. They had a verbal agreement, but he knew that he needed to be careful with this man.

He knew what he had to go. It was time to go home. He had a mission to do, and that was to destroy Alexander Caine.

Chapter 2: Jessica Hudson

January 20th, 2016

Jessica had gone to Alcoholics Anonymous meetings since she was 14 since her father was aware of her drinking and drug problem. It was something she had grown accustomed to. But now she was 22 years old. She did not even feel the need to inject crack into her system anymore. It was a lifetime ago. But her father felt that she needed it.

Jessica was a pretty girl, according to most people. Plenty of guys hit on her, and most of the time it annoyed her. She did not have time for douches that were trying to get into her pants, dress, or whatever the hell she wore.

She was a tall brunette who stopped growing at 17. But by then, she was taller than most girls. It did not hurt her most of the time; it just meant she got more attention than most. Some of it was good, and some of it was bad. Her skin was pale and too white for her taste. It caused her to get sunburned easily. She hated it. Her mother had been the same.

The room was small and uncomfortable. The walls were white and bland. If she ignored these losers, she would watch paint dry. It was an eyesore and not one that she could easily forget.

The ventilation in this joint needed fixing and she could smell the people near her. It was disgusting. She wanted to heave. They needed to make some social distancing rule for people in AA. The rule would state that you cannot sit within six feet of anyone. She needed her space and these fools were up in her business.

Jessica stared at the parasites in this room, and it made her sick. She hated speaking to any of them. They were all attention-seeking, worthless losers to her. One guy even tried to hit on her. Like, who does that?

He used some lame line about her hair looking nice. She knew her hair looked nice, even when she did not attempt to make it look nice; she did not need some creepy weirdo telling her that. A drug rehab meeting was the worst place to meet people. She was not about to fall in love with any of these people. No one had ever made her feel that way. Well, two people made her feel close.

When Jessica was younger, she felt a lot of affection for Jon Drake. But then someone killed his father, and he disappeared. She was heartbroken over that. She felt she was falling in love with Jon. But then, before she had any time to get over that, someone killed her mother.

She could not prove it, but she knew in her heart that someone intentionally killed her mother. She remembered her mother pushing her out of the way, and it all happened so fast. She also recalled seeing a hand poke itself out the window before hitting her. She saw blood on her mother's chest. It was in a spot that was too precise. It could not have been an accident.

But as Jessica sat there in a chair listening to these miserable losers drone on about their problems, she could not help but feel like she no longer belonged here. Her father made her go to these things. It did not deter her progress.

She could proudly say she had not taken a drink or shot her arm up with crack or any other drug in six years. There was a hazy three-year period where she shot up drugs with Rion Caine on an almost daily basis. But those days were over. She was a rebellious teenager, angry at the world for taking her mother away from her. Now, she was an angry young adult that was still angry at the world for taking her mother away.

Only no one cared anymore. Everyone else dusted off her mother's body and pretended everything was okay. Stupid adults even kept telling her that everything was okay. How could it all be okay? She watched someone kill her mother in front of her. Jessica was trying to tune these people out, but one idiot broke through.

"It was at that moment where I knew I had to take a drink. I had that urge and I couldn't hold it anymore," announced the idiot standing in front of the crowd. This was a new guy who had not been with the class before. He spoke with meek courage and also looked like he wanted to die. If Jessica had to listen to any more of his weak ass monologue, she might help him get there.

The idiot took his seat as the room gave a mild clap, some out of necessity, and some out of actual pride. Jessica was in the former, not the latter.

The head counselor stood up. She was a stern-looking woman. Her name was Shondra Williams. She was in good shape, as Jessica saw her running a couple of times. Shondra was a black woman in her late 30s with three kids. She had short black hair and wore a pink style of lipstick every time. Jessica had always wondered where she got the lipstick, and why she wore it. Shondra had invited her over to her house several times, but she declined, making an excuse each time.

"Anyone else like to share?" Shondra asked the class.

The room was silent. No one wanted to talk. It was like school, except for people who had drug and drinking problems. In this school, you were not learning anything. Instead, you were learning how to not do something by talking about it. Jessica found it weird, and a major waste of time. Shondra looked at Jessica, who did not notice it at first.

"Jessica, you haven't said anything all day. What's on your mind?"

Jessica rolled her eyes and looked around the room at all these losers. She was not one to talk; she felt she was a loser too. But she had an excuse. Someone killed her mother. These people had all descended into their issues with idiotic reasons, at least to Jessica. She stood up slowly, not wanting to appear too eager.

"My name is Jessica Hudson, and I am a member of Alcoholics Anonymous."

"Hi, Jessica," replied the room of idiots.

She waved awkwardly, really wishing for lightning to strike her at that very moment, or at least something to zap her anywhere else.

"I have been coming here for a few years now, um," Jessica began, not knowing where to go with this.

She cleared her throat. She glanced at the room and was not sure why she was nervous. Jessica could not give a damn what these people thought of her. She was just surprised, and a little irritated.

"I originally came here because I was addicted to Ecstasy and did some crack—crack cocaine, in case you're not sure what I'm talking about. Also, there was some drinking. Lots of excessive, amazing drinking."

The entire room was silent. Some of these losers were looking at Jessica like she had killed their puppy. She went on.

"Basically, I was addicted to two powerful drugs and I couldn't stop myself, so my father put me in here to try to fix me—and it clearly did not work. While I am no longer addicted to crack or alcohol, I am addicted to coffee, so…"

Jessica sat down before she could finish. Shondra's jaw dropped, knowing that she set herself up for that one. Jessica smiled for the first time in a while.

"Uh thank you, Jessica," Shondra began. "That was very uh—enlightening."

"It's what you wanted," Jessica snapped back.

"Anyone else like to share?"

"Can I just ask one question?"

"You had your moment, Jessica," replied Shondra.

"Why are we even here?"

"I beg your pardon?"

"Us, all of us," said Jessica as she pointed at the entire room. "Why are we all here? You haven't really solved any of our problems."

"My dear, you are not an addict anymore," said Shondra.

"Bullshit!" replied Jessica defiantly as she stood up.

"Jessica! You will sit down!"

"I am and always will be an addict," said Jessica. "You haven't solved my actual issue."

"And what would that be?" asked Shondra.

"My mother's killer is still out there, and no one gives a damn!"

"Jessica now is not the time or place for…"

"No, seriously," Jessica interrupted. "Talking about our feelings will not solve our issues. All you see are labels. You see each of us as a certain demographic and then try to talk us through our feelings."

Jessica pointed to the man next to her.

"He's a sex addict," she said. "In fact, he's probably thinking about having sex with me right now."

Before the man could react, Jessica pointed to the moderately attractive woman sitting to the other side of her.

"She's a crack whore," she said.

The attractive woman fumed. Jessica paid her no attention. Now, she pointed to the middle-aged man across from her.

"He's a drunk that lost his wife and kids," she said. "I don't mean that they died, I mean that they left his ass after they saw how much of a drunk loser he was."

The man's jaw dropped. Jessica pointed to the handicapped man sitting next to the middle-aged man.

"And he's addicted to opioids, and instead of helping him with that, you want to talk him to death, you self-absorbed hack," said Jessica.

"Jessica, that is enough! I will have to ask you to leave!" said Shondra.

"Fine! But I think I made my point," Jessica stood up and headed out.

It was not the first time they had kicked her out of AA meetings. It likely would not be the last. They kept allowing her back. The only reason Jessica went was to appease her father. It was ironic how she missed her mother, yet her one living relative was as far as one could be. She saw her father every day, but he had not been the same since their mother died.

She relaxed a little, listening to house music. She had been into that music since her teenage years. Back in the day, she used to sneak off and go to raves. Occasionally, she still did that, but she did not take Ecstasy like before. It might have helped her moods. There was a knock on the door, and Jessica cautiously walked over.

"Who is it?" she asked.

"Your father," replied the gruff voice.

Oh, great. Jessica figured she knew why her father was here. He probably wanted to check on his only child and see how AA went. Jessica allowed him the pleasure. She opened the door. He stood there, looking as grumpy as ever.

Frank Hudson had always been a big guy, but age and this city had taken a lot out of him. He was not an old man at 52 years old, but he was getting up there. Hudson stood there despondently as if the world had taken a lot out of him. He did not look pleased. Jessica stood her ground, staring at her father.

"What's up, Dad?" she asked with petty emotion.

"May I come in?" asked Hudson.

Jessica gestured for her father to come in, without realizing how rude she was acting. Hudson did not pick up on this. He walked in without looking at his daughter. She closed the door behind him. Hudson stared around the apartment, almost as if he was timid about what he would do and say. He waited for something to happen, and Jessica just looked at him.

"Well?" she asked.

"How did AA go?" asked Hudson.

Jessica scoffed.

"You already know how that went," she snapped. "Why do you insist I keep going there?"

"Because you need it," said Hudson.

"Newsflash, Dad! I haven't done any drugs nor taken a drink in years and have no intention of doing so."

"Then go for my well-being."

"Why don't we talk about the elephant in the room? The one thing you have never given me!"

"We are not going to talk about this, Jessica," Hudson said.

"Yes, we are!"

Jessica got in her father's face. She was as tall as her father now, if not a little shorter. She stood her ground, not showing the fear she once displayed.

"My mother, your wife, was killed 10 years ago and you still haven't brought anyone to justice."

"I already explained this to you, Jessica," Hudson began. "Things are a lot more complicated than you realize."

"Spare me the bullshit, Dad! Tell it to me straight! Tell me what I have to do to get around the complications."

Hudson hesitated. Jessica just glowered impatiently at him with a look that could kill.

"Caine," he said.

Jessica gave him a look. It was one of irritation. She had heard something like this before.

"Then let's go arrest him!"

"I tried once," Hudson contested.

Jessica looked at her father with surprise. This was something she did not know. Could she have been wrong? Did her father really put in the effort and fail?

"What are you talking about, Dad?"

"Like I said," her father started. "I brought him in and charged him. His hotshot lawyer got the charge dropped on insufficient evidence. Then he threatened your life."

"He what?" asked Jessica.

"Exactly like I said," said Hudson. "Why do you think I was so opposed to you spending time with his son and daughters so much?"

Jessica considered this. She had spent many nights with Rion and Amy Caine. She even hung out with the youngest one, Scotti. But she rarely ever saw Caine there. She saw their mother, Ivy, a lot.

"All this time, you knew Caine had involvement in my mother's death and you didn't tell me?"

"I had to protect you!" Hudson claimed.

"I don't need protection!" Jessica cried. "You taught me how to defend myself. You taught me how to use a gun and other weapons. Also, my gymnastics training is a help too. I can take care of myself, Dad!"

"Not against Caine and his thugs," said Hudson. "They're a unique breed of animal."

Jessica listened to Hudson's words but became disappointed. Her father gave up so easily. He was a coward in her eyes.

"If you will not help me find evidence against my mother's killer, then I will find someone else that will," said Jessica.

"You're in over your head, Jessie Bear," said Hudson.

"I don't care," said Jessica. "My mother was killed, and you gave up. You gave up because you got scared. You're a coward. Get out. The sight of you sickens me."

"Jessica…"

"Get out!" she said again, louder.

Hudson shook his head and walked out of the door, slamming it behind him. Jessica watched him go, and she was livid. She would get justice for her mother.

Jessica went to work at the Harbor House Diner, where she worked in Sunset Beach. The diner was tight and almost claustrophobic. The exterior was red all over, including the door. The inside had red stools at the counter where customers could eat and several booths inside. It also included a patio on the outside with a covering so customers could get a view of the ocean.

Her job was basically as a waitress until she could get her shit together. She passed the time drawing and also working out details for her new studio she hoped to build.

Jessica had two dreams. The first dream was to start a successful career as an electronic dance music disk jockey. If that dream did not come true, she had a second plan. Her second dream was to open a dance studio and teach young girls how to dance. She was saving up money so she could open up a studio and start that up. But between paying rent and all the other expenses she had, she was in a bit of a bind.

Her shift went by slowly, as they were not busy at all. Most of her clientele were older people, or they were just drunk, but the drunk people usually showed up at night. Thankfully, they gave her the decent shift tonight and she only worked until 11 o'clock.

Eventually, it was 11 p.m. Her shift was ending, and she made her way to the parking lot. It was a foggy night tonight. She could barely see anything. If she could, she would have noticed a shadowy figure lurking near her car. As Jessica made her way to her car, she stopped. She got a sickening feeling that something horrible was going on. Jessica scanned her car in front of her and shook her head. As she took another step, a man with a gun appeared between Jessica and her car. Despite the foggy night, she could see the gun, and for the first time, she felt fear.

"Well, hello there, sweetheart," said the thug.

The thug was a creepy looking white man in his 30s. He probably was homeless or a convict down on his luck. That was not relevant right now. Jessica had a gun pointed at her.

"What do you want?" asked Jessica.

"Usually money," said the thug who checked out Jessica, and licked his lips. He was a total creeper. "But tonight I think I will settle for you too."

Jessica stared at the creep. This was it. This thug would kill her, probably after raping her first. She had self-defense skills but froze. The terror of the gun threw her off. But she realized she had to snap out of it if she wanted any chance of surviving. Before she could do so, something happened.

"Let her go!" a loud voice boomed in the fog.

Jessica turned and saw a man standing there. She was not sure who this is, but he was ruggedly handsome. She could not help but feel a familiarity with this person. Jessica looked at the man and wondered who he was, but something inside her felt like she knew the answer.

The handsome man stood his ground as he stared at the creeper with the gun.

"You better leave, man, this is between me and the lady," said the thug.

"No, I will be the one between you and the lady," said the handsome man.

"Is that right? And who the hell are you?"

The handsome man smiled. "I will be the last thing you see before you die."

He flung a dagger toward the thug, knocking his gun away, causing him to shriek in pain. The thug staggered back, his hand in pain from the dagger. Jessica's new friend grabbed another dagger and hurled it toward the thug's chest, instantly drawing blood. The thug staggered toward the floor and succumbed to his wounds. The good-looking man watched him slowly wither over and did not change his expression.

Jessica stared at the thug lying dead on the ground. She looked up at this man who saved her life, but could easily be just as violent. She approached carefully. Jessica got a good look at the man, and they locked eyes. She stared into his soul and saw something troubled, but also saw something she had not seen in a long time.

The man stared back at Jessica. He looked at Jessica like he knew her. The man just gazed at her with a saddened face, and Jessica instantly knew who this was. She was no longer terrified, but now she was in shock. She knew who this was, and it confused and surprised her simultaneously.

"Jon?"

Chapter 3: Reunion

They just stared at each other for a moment. Jon had not seen Jessica in a decade. She probably thought he was dead. He had not thought about the range of emotions she must be feeling.

He was nervous. She stared at him as if she saw a ghost, but he also noticed how she observed him. It was a weird feeling. He never got nervous when going on a binge of excessive drinking.

"Is that really you, Jon?" she asked.

He nodded. There was no going back now. He had revealed himself to her, so he would have to give her something.

"Yeah Jess, it's me."

Without warning, Jessica rushed him and snuggled him. It was sudden and took Jon by surprise. Her arms wrapped around his neck and muffled him.

"I missed you so much. Every day I missed you," she whimpered in a smooth voice.

"I thought about you too."

She released her hold on him. They stood within inches from each other. There was an attraction there, but neither wanted to act on it. He looked at the dead body.

"Let me clear this up and we can talk," he told her.

Jessica looked at the dead thug and then back at him. "What are you going to do?"

"I'll explain later," His face tightened. "We'll meet at your place."

"My place? You know where I live?"

He ignored her and picked up the body and hauled it over his shoulder. The weight of the dead man held down against his shoulders, but he persevered. He drove a few miles and found an empty field and buried the body. He wore gloves the entire time to ensure his DNA did not spread across.

He met Jessica around the same time she arrived at her apartment. They entered it, and Jessica closed the door behind her. Jon scanned the place, studying it for a moment. He spotted a picture frame containing a picture of them from when they were younger.

"Sorry about the mess," she apologized.

"You got anything to drink?" asked Jon as he stared at the picture.

The question kind of took Jessica by surprise. Of all the things he could say to her, alcohol was the first thing on his mind?

"Um, no, I don't know if you know this…"

"Oh shit, sorry."

He just remembered that Jessica was a recovering drug addict. She would not have alcohol.

"Sorry for what?" she asked.

He just looked at her. He would not admit he had been keeping tabs on her. That would lead to too many unwanted questions.

"I have --- had," Jessica began. Jon just waited. "I had a drug problem in my teenage years. I did crack, molly, and various other drugs. So I don't have any alcohol, because I don't want to, you know --- fall back into old habits."

He understood and nodded. There was no point pushing forward. He also could not reveal what he knew either.

"I still can't believe you have this," he said, changing the subject.

"I kept all my old pictures," replied Jessica. "Especially the ones with you in them, hoping someday you might come back."

"Jessica, about what happened…"

"You mean how you killed a guy in front of me?"

"Yeah, that."

"I will not bitch at you so much over that aspect. You saved my life. That's all that counts. I've been having a really shitty week and you come back into my life out of nowhere."

He still did not know what to say. His nerves were creeping up again, and he was losing track of where he wanted this to go.

"Jessica I…"

"Where did you even go?"

It was a simple question. Jon pondered the best way to answer the question without giving away too many details. He also knew that Jessica was sharp as a tack and would not tolerate any made-up story.

"I was kidnapped and sold into the child trafficking trade," Jon told her.

Jessica's jaw dropped. "How? When?"

"Not long after my father died," he replied. "I was able to escape them once I got there."

"What have you been doing all these years?" she asked.

"Surviving."

He did not like the questions. He had not even intended to run into Jessica, so he figured giving her part of the truth was enough.

"Why are you back?" she asked.

He glanced at her, not expecting this question. He should have expected the question.

"I have a business deal to attend to," he replied.

She did not buy it. "Why do I feel you are bullshitting me?"

"Now why would I do that?" he asked, defending himself.

"I don't know," she said. "But I have never cared for bullshit. If you're going to be in my life, I won't take that."

"That's the thing, I'm not here for long."

Jessica gazed at him for a moment before responding. "Where are you are staying?"

"At this place I found," he informed her. "It's short term. I have a life in Brazil now, I can't leave it."

That was a partial lie. He had a life in Brazil. It was a life of looking over his shoulders, making sure no one would kill him.

"I have to go," he said.

"Am I going to see you again?" she asked.

He headed toward the door, turned the doorknob, and looked back at Jessica.

"I'm glad you're okay."

He opened the door and left before she could say another word. If he had taken another look, he would have seen Jessica throw herself on the couch in frustration.

January 21st, 2016

He appeared before Ulisez without even entering the front door. Two enormous dogs barked at him as he stood there, and Ulisez sat up from the couch he was on.

"Can you tell your dogs to stop barking? It's giving me a damn headache!" he complained as he walked out into full view.

Ulisez's dogs, Chase and Lex, kept their growls on as Jon cautiously walked up to Ulisez, who just smiled shyly.

"It's okay boys, don't eat him yet," said Ulisez.

Ulisez softly petted Chase and Lex and it calmed them down and they returned to slumping on the couch and watching television. Jon came closer and stood in front of Ulisez, who just looked at him.

"I'm surprised you're still alive," said Ulisez.

"Is that any way to treat an old friend?" asked Jon.

"You broke into my house!" said Ulisez.

"I wanted to surprise you."

"My dogs were about to surprise you by chopping you to death."

"If your dogs had touched me, I would have flung them across the wall," said Jon to Ulisez. He turned toward the dogs. "No offense boys. I still love you."

"Why are you back?" asked Ulisez.

"It's like that, huh?" asked Jon, partly hurt.

"We both know you are long past the days of caring only about who had the better football team. By the way, the 49ers still suck."

Jon flipped him off with two fingers.

"I already know what you are, but others might not be so kind," said Ulisez.

"I'm just here to see an old friend," said Jon.

"Uh, huh."

"Really."

"How do you know where I lived?"

"I make it my business to know such things."

"Uh-huh."

"What's with all the questions? You're supposed to be my buddy?"

"Why are you back?"

"You already asked me that," replied Jon. "Do you have any alcohol? Please, I need something."

Ulisez looked at him irritably. He trudged to the liquor cabinet and pulled out some whiskey and two shot glasses. Jon eyed the whiskey with joy. Ulisez poured a shot into each glass and handed one to Jon.

"Just like old times, Jonny," said Ulisez.

"I told you to never call me that!"

"Drink up," said Ulisez.

They both took a shot of whiskey at the same time. Jon felt the whiskey flow through his mouth. The contents of the alcohol did its magic and gave him a jolt. He felt the alcohol rush through his blood with an incredible sensation.

Anyone who knew Jon would assume he was an alcoholic. Jon corrected them. He was not a pathetic alcoholic loser. Jon was a high functioning alcoholic. He could out-drink anyone and then kick their ass. It was his way.

"Another," he told Ulisez.

Ulisez did as commanded and gave Jon a shot, and both of them downed their shots. Jon did his in three seconds. He slammed the glass down and let out an excited yelp. Jon had never felt so alive. Ulisez just laughed at this right now.

"So did you go see Jessica?"

Jon nodded.

"I actually saved her life by killing a dude."

Ulisez gave him a look. He shook his head. "You realize I am a cop, right?"

"Still?"

"Yeah, still," said Ulisez.

"Go ahead you little bitch, arrest me," said Jon mockingly putting his hands out in front of him and Ulisez just shook his head and turned away.

"What did Jessica say when she saw you?" asked Ulisez.

"She had all these questions. Where was I? How was I still alive? When are we going to bang?"

"She did not say that last part," said Ulisez.

"She might as well have said that," said Jon.

"I'm assuming you know about her, right?"

"The drug addiction thing? Yeah, I know. I have known for a while," said Jon.

"Just what else do you know about all of us?"

Jon smiled. "Wouldn't you like to know?"

"I would actually," said Ulisez.

"I know that you stupidly got married three years ago and didn't invite me," said Jon. "Thanks for that."

"Then you know that I'm…"

"Divorced? Yeah, I know. What happened? You beat her like Ray Rice?"

"What? No. Of course not! She just stopped wanting to be married suddenly. I don't know. It sucked. I tried my best and…" Ulisez stopped himself. "Never mind, you still haven't answered my question."

He sighed. He supposed it could not hurt that much to tell Ulisez the truth, or at least parts of it.

"I'm here to destroy the man that destroyed my life," Jon informed his friend.

"What do you? You mean Caine?"

He nodded. "He killed my father. Now he will pay."

"What do you mean by that?" asked Ulisez.

Jon smiled. "I got to go." He knelt beside Chase and Lex and petted them both. The dogs showed their appreciation by licking Jon all over the place. After getting a licking, he stood up.

"Where are you going?" asked Ulisez.

"To see Frank," he went out the door this time.

Jon drove to Hudson's house. The house was the same as it once was. It was a white house with a red roof that was aging just like the owner. He never used front doors, and this was no exception. Jon found an unlocked window, and it surprised him that Hudson was so lazy about it. He purposely allowed Hudson to hear him.

"Who's there?"

Jon heard a click and as he emerged out of the shadows realized the older man had a gun drawn on him. Hudson stared at him curiously, apparently, he had not yet recognized him.

"You would think after ten years, you would have changed the locks, especially on the window," said Jon.

Hudson glanced at him, analyzing this bearded man with curiosity. He took a few seconds to determine what he was looking at until he realized who this was.

"Jon?"

Jon nodded. He walked over to Hudson and embraced his former caretaker. There was some slight sobbing and the older man was a little emotional.

"I can't believe how long it's been," Hudson exclaimed.

"I know," Jon replied.

"I wasn't sure you were even alive, or worse…"

"I'm so sorry for everything. I am so sorry…"

Hudson peeled Jon off of him. He inspected this man, and Jon could tell the older man felt a little uneasy.

"Where did you go? I did everything I could to make you feel at home. I know I could never replace your father, nor did I try, but.."

"It was not you at all, Frank. You were an amazing man."

"What happened to you? God, it's been ten years."

"That doesn't matter anymore."

There was a moment of silence. Hudson kept staring at him like he was some homeless man.

"What happened to you?" asked Hudson.

"A lot."

He waited on Hudson to say something else. He did not want to reveal too much to Hudson, but figured coming to him personally would be easier than allowing him to find out from others. Hudson was too smart to not figure it out, eventually.

"Do you need a place to stay?" asked Hudson.

"I appreciate it, but I have a place to crash," replied Jon.

"Do you want anything to drink?"

Jon shook his head. "I'm not staying long."

"Is there anything I can do to help you? Do you need a job or anything else?"

He could not believe how much Hudson cared. He had not been sure how the man would react to his return. There had been an underlying fear of this reunion.

"I really wish I could have done more for you, Jon."

He placed his arm on Hudson's shoulder. "There wasn't anything you could do for me, that anyone could."

He released his grip and looked at Hudson and then nodded.

"Jon, if you ever need anything. I am here for you."

He motioned with approval and thanks as he left. He did not realize how much of a support system he had until the last couple of days. He honestly believed it would be easy to come back to Orange Grove and just complete his assignment. But now, things were more complicated than ever.

Chapter 4: The Pain That Endures

January 22nd, 2016

Caine Enterprises was the most industrially successful business in the small Orange Grove town. It also was one of the top businesses, according to the Orange County Business Journal. The building was majestic, with several stories and 50 floors. The company specialized in several brands, including aviation, robotics, computer hardware, weapons manufacturing, and oil.

He wanted Caine to know he was here. It might have been stupid or even selfish, but Caine had to know Jon was here.

There were two large burly security guards at the front, and Jon secured a visitor's pass from a guy on the street. The guards allowed him to pass without a second look. Jon wore a hat to conceal part of his head and black clothing.

He headed up for the top floor. There were nerves running through his veins. What was he going to say? This was the man that ordered the death of his father? What could he say? The elevator to the top floor opened, and Jon stepped out. Caine's office was all alone on the top floor. He walked up to the front desk receptionist. She was a bubbly, ditzy receptionist with blonde hair and blue eyes. He walked up to her.

"I'm here to see Mr. Caine," he declared.

The receptionist looked up at Jon and smiled. She touched her mouth with her fingertip while gazing at Jon.

"Can I get a name handsome?"

He smiled. "A.J. Walker."

He gave a name that was not quite a made up fake name, but one that Caine would recognize. The receptionist got on the phone and Jon saw her mutter something pleasantly. He waited in anticipation. She turned back toward him and beamed.

"He'll see you right away."

"Excellent."

He walked past the receptionist and toward the enormous marble doors. He pressed on the doorknob and entered the room. As he entered, he spotted a man in the distance behind a desk. This was his enemy, the man who ordered his father's death.

Caine was a tall bald man, with a small goatee. He had large broad arms, and a muscular build, showing that he kept himself in shape. He wore a power Armani suit that showed off his wealth, almost flaunting it in front of anyone that appeared in front of him. Caine looked up, saw him, and his eyebrows rose. Jon walked toward his desk and stood in front of him, displaying his form.

"You're not Deathstalker," Caine hissed, standing up abruptly. "Who the hell are you?"

"Alexander Caine," Jon remarked, confusing Caine. "I expected a lot more."

"That's rich. But you still haven't answered my question. Who the hell are you?" Caine demanded.

He stared at Caine's blank eyes for a moment, attempting to see if something was there. This was a moment that he had expected for a long time.

"I'm surprised you don't recognize me," said Jon.

"Wait a minute," Caine realized as he walked over in front of his desk and stood face to face with him. They were about the same height, with Jon having a half-inch on Caine. "Jon Drake?"

He nodded, relieved that Caine recognized him somewhat. "Took you long enough."

Without warning, he grabbed Caine by the throat and strangled him. He pressed Caine on the desk, and the older man gagged. He moved his arms around like one of those mascots you see in front of those car dealerships, trying to escape. He held his grip strongly. This moment, he had pictured it for a long time. He heard a click and felt a gun to his head. He turned slightly to the left and spotted him.

It was Freddy Hunter. The handgun was a .38 Special, and Jon had seen many of those over his lifetime. Freddy had short cropped off brown hair and no facial hair. He was fit but leaner than Jon, not as strong. His blue eyes were as vacant as his expressionless face.

"Let Mr. Caine go," he ordered.

"Freddy Hunter," Jon replied with some weird twist of joy. "I was hoping to run into you."

"Let Mr. Caine go or there will be two bullets through your head," Freddy demanded again.

Jon did as asked, releasing his grip on Caine's throat. The businessman gasped for air and held his throat with his right hand, caressing it in pain. Freddy had his eyes locked on Jon and forced him a few feet back, and then quickly checked on Caine, while still holding Jon at gunpoint.

"You okay, boss?"

Caine nodded slowly. "I'll live."

Freddy kept his gaze on Jon, who did not move. He had done his homework on Freddy. He was once a small-time hoodlum until his many crimes as a degenerate teenager landed him in juvenile hall. Caine saved him from the gutter and helped get his head on straight. Freddy enlisted in the army and did some training with them, and Caine pulled him out and enlisted him as a bodyguard.

Freddy moved in front of Caine to protect him, with his gun still aimed at Jon.

"Who is this loser boss?" he asked.

Jon scoffed. Freddy had not heard Caine say his name. This would be fun.

"This is—"

"The guy who will pay back the dick who killed my father," Jon cut him off. "You're still a little bitch Freddy."

"—Jon Drake. Apparently, he has come back for revenge," Caine roared as if there was a joke and it amused him.

Jon and Freddy glared at one another. He could tell the hitman was analyzing the situation carefully, and he savored every second.

"Jon Drake," Freddy looked like he had seen a ghost. He attempted to compose himself, but Jon could see the fear in his eyes.

"I see your boy still covers your ass Caine," Jon said to Caine. Freddy's eyebrows furrowed. He doubled down on aiming his gun at Jon.

"You made a mistake coming back, Drake," Freddy insisted, cocking the revolver.

"No," Jon chuckled. "You made a mistake not killing me."

Without warning, and with a quickness unheard of, Jon grabbed the gun and elbowed Freddy in the face. He emptied the bullets from the gun. Caine and Freddy stared at him in shock.

Freddy's face wrinkled up in anger, and he reared his right fist back to punch Jon. He caught Freddy's arm with his own right hand and then unloaded with a left hook to his nose.

He charged toward Freddy, grabbed the gun, and pistol-whipped him across the face. Freddy recoiled from the pain. Jon turned and faced Caine.

"You have anything else you want to throw at me, Caine?"

"You have grown, Jon," Caine marveled, amazed at this man standing in front of him.

"I'm back to show you that not everyone is afraid of you, Caine."

Caine laughed, which threw Jon off. He simmered down after a few seconds. "You remind me of myself when I was younger. I admire your ferociousness, your vigor, your balls."

"I am what you made me into," snapped Jon.

Caine glanced at Freddy, who still winced from the pain. He turned back to Jon. "Where have you been all these years, Jon?"

"Now why would I tell you that?" Jon replied.

"I am just astounded by the abilities you have shown me. You and I could work wonders together."

Jon looked at Caine curiously. This was unexpected. He expected anger or even fear. But Caine was looking at Jon like he was the most interesting man in the world. Caine walked around Jon, studying him and analyzing him for a moment.

"Yes," he intoned. "You could make an excellent ally."

Jon laughed. Was Caine serious? Did he understand that Jon hated him? This was nuts!

"I hate your guts," Jon spewed. "I would never work for you."

"Then why the hell are you back?" Caine sneered, his voice rising from calm to anger in a split second.

Jon leaned in, inches away from Caine, so close he could smell his bad breath. "I am back to destroy you," he hissed. "And I won't stop until I burn you and your entire company to the ground."

Caine smiled. "Good luck."

Jon grinned back at him. He turned around and walked off. Freddy stood up and tried to attack Jon from behind. He telegraphed this and turned around and elbowed Freddy across the face, sending him tumbling to the ground. Jon stared down at Freddy, who clutched his stomach. He looked at Caine, who was no longer smiling.

"This is the beginning of the end for you," he told him.

Then, he headed toward the door, opened it, and headed out the way he came, leaving Caine and Freddy stunned.

He made his way to the Orange Grove Bar and Grill, a sports bar on the outskirts of town. He had always enjoyed these little places because they were where he felt most comfortable. A dive bar or a sports bar was the perfect place to get hammered and then unload. He trudged on somberly. His confrontation with Caine had not been what he had expected. Though he revealed himself, Jon did not fear any consequences from his action. Caine had to know that he was coming for him, so he could see his ending coming.

Jon slid into the bar and sat at the barstool. He placed his elbow on the bar and placed it there for a moment. The bartender approached him to take his order. She was a pretty girl, with black raven like hair, an affable smile, and a small round face. Jon felt like he knew her from somewhere, but he could not place where. She smiled pleasantly.

"What can I get you?" she asked sweetly.

"Snakebite," was all Jon said. The bartender went back to make the drink, and Jon realized he wanted something else. "Um—bartender—also give me a whiskey on water."

The bartender turned around, a bit surprised. "The name is Scotti."

"I don't care if your name is Wonder Woman, get me a damn whiskey with that snakebite."

Scotti scoffed at Jon. She went to make his drinks, both of them. She prepped the whiskey and the Snakebite and returned. She gave him the drinks.

"That will be 20 dollars," she announced, not as pleasant this time.

He pulled out a crumpled 20 and then handed it to her. Then, he pulled out a five-dollar bill and gave it to her as a tip.

"I'm not a complete asshole."

"Glad you admit you are one," she shot back.

He handed her the bill. Scotti took it in a snap. She turned around to place the cash in the register. He took the whiskey and swigged it with ease. Then he took the Snakebite and swigged that quickly.

He looked at Scotti for a moment, trying to figure out where he knew her from. It hit him like a ton of bricks.

"Scotti Caine," Jon spat out, almost as if realizing.

She turned around, a little intrigued, and a little shocked. "How do you know my last name?"

Jon smiled. "I used to play with your sister when we were kids."

Scotti's face lit up, realizing. "Jon Drake?" She exited the bar area and then came around the counter and rushed him and engulfed him in a hug before he could do anything. "I thought you died."

"No," he replied, peeling Scotti off him. "I'm not that lucky."

"What are—" Scotti searched for the words, observing Jon for a moment. "—what are you doing here?"

"I'm back in town."

"For how long?"

"As long as it takes."

"What the hell does that even mean?"

"How is Amy?" he asked, changing the subject.

"She's okay."

"Tell her I said hi," he abruptly stood up and walked off.

"Where are you going?"

But he was out the door. As he made his way out, he felt something strange. It was a feeling of familiarity, and one he did not particularly appreciate. The wind was calm that night, so he could scan the surrounding environment. He looked around for signs of trouble, not sure where it was coming from.

He moved cautiously. He was sure it was not Caine or any of his forces. It had to be somebody else. This felt oddly familiar. Jon closed his eyes for a moment and stood still, attempting to locate the source. All of his senses became stronger at once, as he tried to feel everything around him. Armando Escobar not only trained him how to use weapons and how to fight but also how to sense the danger. He heard steps and immediately opened his eyes and saw a man running toward him.

He ducked the man's attempt at punching him. He kicked the man in the stomach, sending him staggering, but not on the ground. The man huffed heavily.

"You should have never come back, White Warrior," huffed the black man standing in front of him. Jon stared at him, attempting to find out what to do next.

Chapter 5: Old Scars

Jon looked at the man, attempting to gauge who this was. The man looked very familiar, but he could not place where.

"Who are you? And how do you know about that name?" he asked the man.

The man smiled. "The name is Martin. Thomas Martin. I know all about you, Drake. You are trouble. I know about all the stuff you have done."

He examined the man standing in front of him, making these accusations. He was a large black man with curly black hair. His cheekbones were high and wide, and his shoulders were broad and lean. Thomas was about the same height as Jon, if not slightly taller. One thing was for sure; he did not like Jon.

"I should beat your ass for attacking me," Jon suggested.

Thomas took something out, and Jon expected it to be a gun. Instead, it was a police badge.

"You do that and I'll be forced to arrest your ass."

"That's not where I know you from. Where have I seen you from?"

Thomas chuckled. "I've probably beaten your ass in the past and you don't remember because the beating was so damn good."

"You wish."

"I know."

He and Thomas just stood there for a moment, sizing each other up, each trying to determine what the other would do. "What do you want Martin?"

"For you to leave town, Drake."

"Why would I leave when I just came back? Unless there is something you are hiding from me."

"You don't know what you're getting into Drake."

He laughed. Thomas chuckled. They immediately stopped laughing at once.

"You work with Ulisez?" asked Jon, though he already knew the answer.

"You know that bitch? Figures you would."

"Hey! Only I may call him a bitch."

"Would never figure the great Jon Drake to have any friends."

"I don't have the luxury of many friends."

"Because you are a bitch."

Thomas got in his face. They were inches apart now, as they were in a game of intimidation now.

"Get out of my face, Martin."

"You better heed my warning, boy," he said. "You better not cause any trouble or I will be on your ass like glue."

"Because that's what I want, your ass stuck to me. I don't flow that way, Martin."

Thomas chuckled. "You're funny, Drake. You won't be laughing when I am done with you."

Without another word, Thomas backed off and he watched him go, not taking his eyes off of the man for a second.

January 23rd, 2016

He trudged into Woody's Coffee Shop in Sunset Beach the next morning. The coffee shop was small and cozy and dedicated to surf culture. There were red booths and stools throughout the diner, and pictures of celebrities sprawled all over the wall.

He no longer got hangovers, as his body had become immune to it. But he loved his coffee, black with no sugar or any of that other crap. He took his seat into a booth and just slouched there, groaning as he took his seat. The waitress took his order and he just muttered the word 'coffee' and then stared into space.

A woman walked into the coffee shop. She walked toward his booth, but he was too tired to notice or care. Finally, she stood in front of him. He looked up at her.

"Scotti told me you were back," the woman said as she stood in front of him. She took a seat in the booth across from him. Jon looked at her, realizing.

"Amy?"

Amy smiled. "You remember me. Good."

Amy Caine was a beautiful woman. She had long ebony hair that ended just below her shoulders. Her face was round, and her dimples came out when she smiled. She wore a flowery dress that exhibited her colorful personality. She always stood out in a room, not just because of her beauty, but because of her confidence. Amy was Alexander Caine's second child and his oldest daughter. She was also tall, almost as tall as him. Amy and Scotti looked alike, with the exception that Scotti was short, and Amy was not. Amy was sharp, and a lot calmer than Scotti.

"How d'you know I would be here?" he asked her, genuinely curious.

Amy beamed. "I am a Caine. I can find out where people are when I need to."

The waitress came over and inquired about Amy's order. He watched as she murmured 'coffee, some cream' and then politely thanked the waitress as a way of telling her to leave. He sipped his coffee. It tasted like nothing in particular. When he drank black coffee, he did not taste anything. It was strong. But he believed that all coffee tasted the same. Like with the hangover, Jon was likely immune to coffee taste differentials.

"So what, you wanted to come to see your childhood friend alive and well or something like that?" he inquired. The waitress returned with Amy's coffee, and she sipped it slowly, taking in the flavor.

"From what Scotti told me, you apparently can drink anything within seconds," Amy teased.

"I developed a high tolerance for alcohol since I been gone."

"Where did you go, Jon? We all thought you died."

"I'm sure your father would have liked that."

"My father? What does he have to do with anything?"

"You realize he ordered my father's death right?"

"And you're what, back for vengeance?"

"He deserves everything he gets."

Amy sipped her coffee. This was the most awkward conversation for her. Jon and Amy were childhood friends, but he hated her father. There would always be a tension between them because of that.

"You realize—" she began. "—you realize if any harm comes to my father, it will force me to come after you legally, right?"

"Do you honestly think I'm afraid of you, Amy?"

"No," she replied. "But you should be afraid of destroying my family. I don't approve of my father's actions, but an eye for an eye is never the answer."

"Who do you think you're talking to Amy? Some scared little boy who you used to play hide and seek with? I changed and a lot of that was because of your dad."

"That may be so," Amy countered. "But killing my father won't bring yours back."

It impressed him at how quickly Amy picked up on his intentions. Jessica did not suspect a thing, and neither did Hudson. Ulisez sort of did but did not show it. Scotti was none the wiser, but Amy, she knew exactly why he was back, and it could be a problem.

"Why are you here Amy?" he was very direct, because he felt Amy was someone that did not beat around the bush, and probably respected the direct approach.

"I am here to welcome you back to town, and to see if the boy I played with is still there."

"Is he?"

Amy shook her head. "I don't see him. I just see a sad little man who is still crying over his daddy and badly needs a therapist."

"You would too if someone killed your dad and then didn't suffer for it."

Amy just stared at Jon blankly. She took out some cash and slammed it on the table and stood up.

"Here, it's on me."

He did not object. He watched her leave. The coffee was bitter now. He got up to leave and walked over to the park bench. He sat down for a moment, just taking things in now. There was a slight worry now in his mind about how things would pan out. The goal originally was to discreetly come back to town and systematically destroy Caine and everything he built. But that was too late now. Once Jessica recognized him, he knew he had to alter his strategy. But his arrogance and stupidity caused him to reveal himself to Caine. Looking back on it, that was a terrible strategy and he had to be even more careful. Now he had Amy Caine keeping her eye on him. Under any other circumstances, he might have potentially ended up with Amy. He played with her almost as much as he did with Jessica. But in the end, they came from two different worlds.

He sat on the park bench watching the birds. Despite all the darkness in his life, and the drinking, he oddly found peace with nature. It calmed him down for some strange reason. For years, he had pinned for any happiness following the death of his father. Being in nature gave him a reprieve. He closed his eyes and felt the wind pass through his veins. Jon did this for a few seconds and then reopened his eyes. There was work to do.

He walked back to his apartment. It was not a pleasant apartment, but it was good enough. He had found the place on the outskirts of town, on the border of Orange Grove and Irvine. Jon had bribed the landlord double the rent to get the place with no interruption or debate. At first, the landlord fought against it, but then Jon's cash changed his mind.

It was a small apartment studio. There was a bed, a small couch, and a desk. A small kitchen also laid next to the small living room that also doubled as a bedroom. The kitchen had a small fridge, a stove, and a microwave he brought himself. Jon stocked the fridge with eggs, chicken, and beer. That was all he needed. He knew how to cook, as Escobar had taught him when he was a child. Jon could say that a dangerous cartel leader taught him cooking skills, as that was unusual.

He also had a laptop he connected to several security feeds that he could hack. He still did not have the cyber skills that he wished he had; there was a plan to hire someone like that down the line. Since Jon did not get past the fifth grade, he taught himself basic computer skills, and other skills needed to survive in the world.

He grabbed a few maps and took out a pen. He began scribbling information on the map. The map summarized Orange County, including the only nightclub in Orange Grove. Caine's picture was there, and Jon knew he would be there. There were also pictures of other drug lords and several gangsters.

He scribbled some details on the map, showing the address and the information he needed. He pulled out another map. This map featured footage only of the Orange Grove Lounge. That is where the drug deal would take place. The map included security photographs of all three levels of the lounge, including every single entrance. He always prepared before he undertook a mission. He searched for the perfect entrance to make his way into the club. A spot on the map intrigued him, and he circled the spot.

He rolled up the map neatly and folded it perfectly, then placed the map inside a small container for use later. He knew what he had to do, and where he had to go. There was a plan, and he would execute it to perfection.

He placed his pens in the drawer neatly and then tucked them away. He had a couple of days before he had to overtake this mission, so there was time to plan out. He walked over to his bed and laid down on it, thinking about everything that needed to happen. On Friday, he would make his move.

Chapter 6: The Day Love Died

Orange Grove, California December 22nd, 2005

    A 12-year-old Jon Drake walked along a hallway with a large man. This man was tall, lean, and stout. He had brown hair, similar to Jon Drake of the current day. He was not nearly as big as Jon in his current day, and he had a mustache. He was 40 years old. This was his father, Robert Drake.

    "I'm so glad I got to come with you to work dad," said Jon. "Sure beats going to school."

    "Hey, I gave you the option to go to school and party with your friends, kid," his father teased him. "For some reason, you wanted to hang with your old man."

    They walked along the hallway. Before they could make it to the end, a man intercepted them. This man was 20 years old with no facial hair and a buzz cut. His face looked mean and angry. When he approached them, his expression changed, if just for a moment.

    "Mr. Drake. Mr. Caine needs to see you really quick," said the man.

    "Can't it wait, Freddy?" asked Robert.

    "He says it's urgent," replied Freddy.

    "Very well," said Robert. He turns to Jon. "I'll be just a moment."

    Robert turned back to Freddy. "Do you mind watching my son for a moment?"

    Jon looked up at his father with confusion.

    "Yeah, no problem," said Freddy.

    Robert headed into Caine's office, leaving Jon with Freddy. He panicked silently, wondering why his father would randomly trust this man. There was an uncomfortable silence as Jon stared at the older man, who just smirked at him, unintentionally creepily.

    "What's up, kid?" asked Freddy.

    He said nothing in response to the guy's question. He stared at this man and into his vacant eyes. Freddy terrified him. Just the way his body language reverberated. He was a little afraid of what this man would do. There was a bad vibe reverberating from this man, and he could feel it even back then. He stood there silently and waited for his father to finish, hoping his dad would not take too long.

Later

He was in his father's car. They drove home from whatever meeting Robert had to take with his boss, Alexander Caine.

He looked at his dad, noticing that he was a little on edge. He touched his father gently on the arm, hoping it would get a reaction.

"Dad, are you okay?" he asked his father.

"Yeah, I'm okay, just tired," replied Robert.

As Robert said this, a car sped up behind them. Before Robert could react, the car rammed into his car with authority.

"Hey!" Robert screamed.

The car again rammed into theirs, this time sending their vehicle careening off the road. Robert barely adjusted his car to hit the side of the road ditch. His father checked on him to make sure he was all right. Jon groaned.

"Jon! You okay?"

"I'm fine dad, what just happened"

Before they could say anything else, a shadow walked up to their car. He recognized the shadow instantly and saw that it was Freddy. Robert turned to the man.

"Freddy?"

"A gift from the old man," said Freddy as he aimed his gun at Robert and unloaded several gunshots into Robert. He cried out in horror as the smell of the gunpowder penetrated his nostrils and the noise of the gunfire exploded in a matter of seconds. Freddy smiled the entire time and then aimed his gun at Jon.

"Your turn, kid," said Freddy.

Before he could pull the trigger, a passing motorist yelled at him.

"Hey! You!" the Good Samaritan yelled.

Freddy panicked. He saw the Good Samaritan and turned his attention to him and aimed the gun, but did not fire. Instead, he ran off in the other direction. He got into his car and sped off. The Good Samaritan ran toward Robert Drake's car and saw the dead body and Jon beside him.

"Are you okay, kid?" he asked.

Jon shivered, panicked, and horrified at the events that transpired. He was unsure of what to do or say. He could not bear to look at the dead body of his father next to him.

"My dad! He shot my dad! He… he…. he…"

He could not get the words out. The Good Samaritan went over toward his door and opened it and slowly helped him out and after a few seconds passed, he broke down, crying in this stranger's arms. The Good Samaritan did not know what to do. He just hugged Jon.

"It will be okay," he said with little confidence.

Jon continued to bawl his eyes out as other cars stopped at the scene. Within minutes, police cars arrived and entered the scene.

A police officer walked up to him as he seemed to know him. This man was Frank Hudson. He was about the same age as his father. He had graying black hair that is curly and a beard. He had large broad shoulders and looked like he could win a fight with a man half his age. He was the lieutenant of the Orange Grove Police Department. They sent him on this beat when he got the call that there had been a shooting and an accident. He walked over.

"Jon? What happened?" asked Hudson.

"Mr. Hudson, the man, he killed my father," he held back tears as he spoke.

Hudson looked at him and consoled him. They embraced, realizing that nothing else would be the same ever again.

December 29th, 2005: The Funeral.

The funeral took place a week later. He was in the front row and had Hudson sitting next to him. There were also two other kids his age sitting next to him. One was a Hispanic kid, with curly black hair and sprouting facial hair. This was his best friend in the world, Ulisez Saucedo.

The kid on the other side of him was a young girl. This was Jessica Hudson, Frank's daughter. She was his other best friend in the entire world. She was emerging into a beautiful young woman, and she had a magnificent smile. On this day, she did not smile. She sat closer to him than Ulisez did.

He held back tears and felt something touching his arm and glanced over and realized Jessica holding his hand.

But he was in his own world. He looked straight ahead as the funeral mass continued and tried to keep a straight face and not show emotion. He was an orphan now. He had already gone through the death of his mother, and now he lost his father. Nothing his friends did could salvage that.

The funeral went for an hour. Jon could not stomach it at all. He ran out of the church after toward the end of the mass.

As he exited the church, he heard footsteps behind him. He turned and saw Hudson standing there.

"I know I could never replace your father," he began. "But I want you to know that I will always be there for you, Jon."

He just looked at him, his emotions dead. "Why'd they kill him, Mr. Hudson? Why?"

Hudson hesitated. He was not sure how to answer the question. Hudson took his time and contemplated his answer.

"I cannot explain the motives of a psychopath. All I can do is promise I will do everything in my power to catch who did this."

"It was Mr. Caine," he claimed. "It had to be. I saw his assistant, what's his name, Freddy. I saw him pull the trigger!"

Hudson hesitated. Jon noticed it and stared at the older man, waiting for a response.

"Some matters are more complicated than others," said Hudson sadly.

He looked at Hudson, perplexed. "What do you mean, Mr. Hudson?"

He saw Hudson visibly shake. He had never seen an adult look nervous or even scared ever. But when he looked at Hudson, there was fear, and it was not of him.

"There are a lot of bad people in this world who know how to skirt the law," said Hudson.

He suddenly realized what Hudson was telling him. He got angry.

"Are you telling me you want me to drop this?"

"No, of course not," said Hudson. "I just don't want you involved because I don't want anything happening to you."

"He killed my father!"

"I know, Jon," said Hudson. "I'm so sorry."

"My dad was all I had," he replied. "I'm all alone now."

Before Hudson could react, he walked away.

February 8th, 2006, Orange Grove, CA

He had lived with the Hudson family for the last month. It had been difficult for him and not something easy for him or their family. Despite liking Jessica, even to where she could be his first crush, he felt nothing. It broke his heart. Watching his father die had been difficult and he was an orphan now with no one to support him.

He rode his bike. It rained uncontrollably, which was not normal for Orange County. He tried to make it back to the Hudson home before the rain soaked him.

His bike sputtered as he rode it. His mind raced with many thoughts and tears flowed down his face. He thought of his father, and he flashed back to when the evil man shot him. He could not get the image out of his mind and it destroyed him.

He hit something and his bike faltered and he went down hard. His knee bled a little as he had scrapped it badly. He held onto his injured knee and his bruise distracted him, or else he would have noticed a black van in the distance. If he focused on the van, he would realize that danger was imminent. He paid no attention to the van.

His hand clutched his knee and he held back tears. He dragged himself. Had he been aware of his surroundings, he would have heard the emerging footsteps.

As he turned around, it was too little too late. Two large men emerged out of nowhere and grabbed him. He cried loudly as these men rushed him without saying much of anything. They roughly held onto him and lifted him into the air. One of them punched him in the side and he felt the blow with a sickening thud. They put a mask over his head and he could not see a thing.

They walked a few blocks and then he heard them open a van. They threw him into the van without caution. His body landed roughly and he groaned in pain. He felt one of them grab his hands violently and then zip tie his hands so he could not use them. One of them punched him in the stomach, and it felt like someone put a hole in it. He gasped for air as this occurred and wondered at that moment whether he was about to die.

The kidnappers slammed the van doors shut and he heard them yell out something, but could not place exactly what it was.

He heard them start the van and drive off. He stayed conscious throughout this ordeal and the van drove cautiously, but not cautious enough to avoid speed bumps. They drove a few miles and he moaned silently. After a while, the van stopped and he tried to pick his head up, but he was in too much pain.

They opened the van doors and he felt two men grab him again. He attempted to listen carefully and realized he was at an airport. Airplanes flew overhead and zoomed loudly in the distance. How could this be happening?

He cried silently as the men roughly hauled him and then they threw him onto another vessel. The vessel was loud, and he realized he was on an airplane. The doors shut and he heard the men shout out orders in Spanish or Portuguese or some other language he was not sure of. As he laid there helplessly, the plane ascended and then before long, he was in the air, off to begin a horrible journey.

February 10th, 2006, São Paulo, Brazil.

He was frightened, and they had tied his hands with zip ties. There were several men with guns who stood up in front of Jon and many other children. A van approaches and a large man exits. This man had a full-fledged goatee and curly brownish-black hair. He was a little chubby, but still strong where it counts. As the man exited the van, the other men suddenly cowered with fear. This man is Armando Escobar, the leader of one of the three major cartels in Brazil. His cartel was the Command of the Nation, and he led it through fear and terror. Escobar exited the van, and he did not look happy as he slowly, methodically approached the man.

"Mr. Escobar? What are you doing here?" asked the leader in Portuguese.

"You realize where you are right?" asked Escobar in the same language.

"With all due respect sir, we are passing by, we will be out of your territory soon," replied the leader.

Escobar walked right up to the leader and got in his face. The man was nervous now as Escobar glared a hole through him.

"What did you say to me?" asked Escobar.

"We are passing through," the leader said nervously. "Let us pass."

"With children!"

"This is our operation," said the leader. Armed men arrived behind him, giving him more confidence stupidly. "Let us pass or face the consequences."

"Is that right?" Escobar asked.

Without warning, there was gunfire. The armed men got hit, and Escobar's backup arrived. Jon to his horror saw the other kids get hit by stray bullets and took cover behind a rock. The leader was still standing, but cowering. In an act of desperation, he pulled a gun on Escobar, who grabbed it, disarming him quickly. Escobar pulled out his gun and fired the trigger, killing the leader instantly.

The shooting stopped after a while. Escobar and a few of his men were the only ones left standing. Jon looked to his horror as he realized he was the only kid still alive. He saw bodies around him. He cowered his head and shivered.

Jon heard footsteps, and he still kept his head down, fearful for his life. Escobar stood above him. The man put his gun away. He looked right at Jon and waited for the young man to say anything. Jon would not budge.

"Boy, you are safe now," said Escobar in near-perfect English.

Jon said nothing. Escobar realized he needed to say something else.

"My name is Armando Escobar. What's yours?"

Jon hesitated. Then he looked up. He looked at Escobar's face and it did not seem as frightening as it was before. Escobar stood there unassuming.

"Jon," he muttered.

Escobar pulled Jon's hand and raised him.

"You are the only survivor here," Escobar began. "And I will ensure that you continue to survive."

Later

He rode in the van with Escobar and his armed men. He stayed silent, not daring to upset the man. He saw firsthand what Escobar could do.

Escobar led the way, and Jon followed him into the house. He looked at the armed guards around him as he walked and felt slightly frightened. But there was something inside him that told him to keep marching, and to not mind the gunmen. He entered the house behind Escobar, and he closed the door behind him. Escobar turned toward him.

"Today, your new life begins," said Escobar.

Escobar grabbed a sword off the wall and handed it to Jon, who looked at it with astonishment.

"Feel the power as you touch it," said Escobar.

Jon was not sure what to do, but at that moment he felt something he never had felt before. He gripped the sword and clenched it. Escobar motioned for Jon, who handed it back to him.

"I will teach you to use many weapons," said Escobar.

He could not even say anything. He should have said something. A rational person would have told Escobar that they did not want to learn how to use any weapons. They would protest and *show that they did not wish to use killing machines. But Jon, aged 12 with no living parents, was no longer rational. This was his life. He embraced it.*

"You need to learn how to fight," said Escobar.

A moment passed. Escobar chuckled.

"Come on, hit me," said Escobar.

He just glanced at him, not knowing if it was the right idea. Escobar motioned him to cooperate.

"It's okay," said Escobar. "Do it."

He complied, and he punched Escobar as hard as he could. He saw his fist connect with Escobar's stomach, but nothing happened. Escobar grabbed his arm and flipped him over, causing him to land with a thud. Jon groaned. Escobar chuckled. Escobar helped him up.

"Lesson number one," Escobar said as he helped Jon up. "Never underestimate your opponent. You probably assumed because I was a slightly bigger man that I would tumble. Well, you were wrong."

He looked at Escobar, annoyed. Then he laughed. It surprised him, and he laughed for a few seconds as Escobar watched. It was the first time he had laughed since before his parents died. Escobar smiled. He extended his hand and Jon took it and rose from the ground. This was his home now.

Chapter 7: The Club

January 25th, 2016

Jessica hated going out. She did not enjoy going to anything but raves. Going to raves like EDC was the only thing Jessica liked to socialize in.

She blow-dried her hair and made it all poof. The door opened and Amy walked right in.

"Still not ready yet?" asked Amy.

"No," replied Jessica.

Jessica and Amy had been friends for a long time. Despite their families being opposites, there had been a spark in early childhood. She established a friendship with Amy before all the bad times. She could sense, even at a young age, that Amy was not like her family.

She finished blow-drying her hair and then put on a black dress with reluctance. She put on her black dress. It seemed appropriate. The dress resembled her personality and her feelings. She could not have felt any bleaker than she did now. Now she wore a dress and was about to go to a club. But she did it anyway. She enjoyed hanging out with Amy, despite some of their differences.

She grabbed some black stiletto heels and forced them onto her foot, straightened out her dress to fix any cleavage sticking out, and turned to Amy and grinned.

"Ready?" asked Amy

Jessica nodded. "Let's do this."

They stepped into the Orange Grove Lounge and scanned the environment. They just wanted to dance and drink, but there was the inevitability that some creeps would hit on them. It was just the way it was.

They walked over to the bar and stood there patiently. The bartender almost immediately greeted them.

"What can I get for you ladies?" he asked warmly.

"Vodka tonic," Amy ordered. She pointed at Jessica. "She'll have water."

"Glad you remembered," Jessica teased.

The bartender walked back and made the drink for Amy, and the water for Jessica. He returned with their beverages. Amy held her drink and Jessica held hers, and they toasted to nothing in particular. Jessica took her drink with no hesitation because it was only water. She spotted people on the dance floor just shaking their ass all over the place. Amy took her drink quickly, absorbing the full effect of the alcohol.

Amy grabbed Jessica by the wrist and led her to the dance floor. They danced together for a good few five minutes, embracing the song. She watched Amy vibe to the music and found it sort of arousing for a moment. While Jessica had only been with one guy, she had some attraction to women. Despite that, she never really acted on these urges. Jessica would never attempt to do so with Amy. If she ever tried to get with another woman, it would likely be someone new. It definitely would not be her ex-boyfriend's sister. That would be weird.

Jessica and Amy danced through several songs, and she noticed out of the corner of her eye some dudes checking out her ass. This was typical. It was always the first place guys looked when they looked at women like fresh meat. Jessica ignored them for as long as she could.

When the song ended, two guys walked over. Jessica and Amy did not immediately notice. As the guys approached, Amy turned and realized they had company. She gave Jessica a glance that said 'oh shit, here we go'. Before they could say a word, what sounded like gunshots rang out. Everyone in the club immediately panicked. They ran in all directions in sheer panic.

Jessica and Amy struggled to avoid being stomped to death while trying to find an opening. A ball hit the ground and tear gas started spreading.

She wondered what was happening and ducked her head under the table and covered her nose to avoid being knocked out and realized that Amy did the same.

She looked up and saw Jon walk through the tear gas with a mask on. She squinted her eyes to make sure it was Jon. He knelt beside her, and Amy, who now realized Jon was here.

"Are you okay?" he asked Jessica and Amy.

"Jon, what the hell are you doing here?" asked Jessica.

"Saving your ass," he replied.

Jon grabbed Amy and held onto her and before she could react, shot the grapple gun toward the third level and flung toward it, leaving Jessica sitting there. It was about a minute or two before Jon came back.

"Jon, what are you doing? You…"

Jon grabbed her and Amy before she could finish her sentence and swung into action. They landed on the third level with a thud and Jon released her. Jessica quickly recovered and saw Amy sitting down, accessing the chaos. She looked at Jon, who had landed on his feet from their brief grappling adventure.

"Jon, what the hell was that? Someone got shot!"

"Not someone," replied Jon. "A drug dealer named Blood. Caine's hitman Freddy shot him and his associate multiple times when Blood would not take their deal."

"What about the gunshots that happened after?" asked Amy, who was interested and alert now.

Jon smiled. "That was me, sending off warning shots to Caine,"

Amy got in Jon's face. "You shot at my father?"

"He shot two drug dealers in cold blood," Jon snapped. "Don't come at me with your preaching if you don't want to acknowledge what your father is."

"And what are you, Jon?" asked Jessica, interjecting herself back in.

He just looked at Jessica and scoffed.

"I'm trying to make things right," said Jon.

"Is that what you call walking back into my life after ten years of God knows what the hell you were doing and killing a man in front of me?" asked Jessica.

"Wait, what?" asked Amy, interjecting.

Jessica turned to Amy. "Long story," she said, then focused back on Jon. "You never told me why you were here tonight Jon."

Jon turned the tables on her. "Why are you here?"

"I came here to escape the shittiness of my life and you just followed me here." snapped Jessica.

"Were you trying to kill my father?" Amy interjected.

Jon glared at Amy, annoyed. Jessica could tell that they had shared a conversation, and this was the head. She waited for an answer, but Jon gave none. He just glared at Amy, then back at Jessica.

"We're wasting time," Jon proclaimed.

"Answer the question," Amy demanded.

"You already know the answer!"

Amy slapped him across the face. Jessica watched in shock, all this taking place in a matter of seconds. Her friend was angry.

"I warned you not to go after him," she reminded him.

"He killed two drug dealers in a public nightclub," he replied.

"And that gives you a reason to shoot him?" Amy shot back.

"I didn't shoot him, you crazy spoiled bitch!"

Amy got in Jon's face and they were close to enough to either kiss each other or bite one another's head off. Jessica got in between them, hoping to establish the peace.

"Guys, this isn't solving a thing," she insisted.

Jon looked at Jessica, his face calming down. Amy also looked at her, and she appeared to come down from her anger.

"I'm sorry, Jess," she apologized.

"Same Jess," Jon added.

The three of them just stood there for a moment. The lower levels had dispersed and they could hear sirens in the distance.

"Listen," Jon began. "I'm glad you're okay."

"I still want an explanation, Jon," Amy chirped in.

"I don't owe you a damn thing," said Jon to Amy as he picked up his rifle. He scanned the chaos below as Jessica and Amy stood next to him. He glanced back at them.

"You should be safe here," said Jon.

Jon moved a little, and Jessica grabbed him by the shoulder. She held firm, trying to prevent Jon from going anywhere.

"So what, you will disappear again?" she asked.

Jon just grabbed a pen and paper. He wrote his number on it and handed it to Jessica.

"You text me anytime you want to talk, I will tell you everything," he said.

Then, as Jessica held onto it, she looked up and Jon had vanished. Amy was astonished as this happened.

"Seriously?" she asked.

Jessica practiced by herself at a dance hall. She liked to do this from time to time to clear her head. She had a lot on her mind. The last week had been hectic. Life was a hot mess.

But she persevered and knew that she had to do to survive. There was a time in her life when she did nothing but dance. It was her favorite thing to do as a child. The therapist recommended getting back into it to help her cope with life. Even her psychiatrist agreed. It was harmless, and something she treasured.

Most of the time, Jessica did ballet dancing. Sometimes, she square danced and line danced, but then she learned that she hated people. Instead, Jessica paid the owner of this dance building in Orange Grove to allow her to use the studio for an hour or two once a week. She needed it after the chaos of last night. Jessica just wanted the world to stop bothering her for a few hours while she worked on some therapeutic dancing. She moved in a fluid motion, displaying the skills she gained over the years. Every motion she did, she did carefully.

The door opened in the background. She did not mind it. She kept doing her routine as the person who opened it walked in and watched for a moment.

"What, you following me now?" asked Jessica without looking.

"Not yet," replied Jon shyly as he stood there staring at Jessica in her leggings and dance outfit. She did not look at Jon right away, maintaining her focus. Finally, she ended her routine and turned to face Jon, and he handed her a towel.

"What are you doing here, anyway? And how did you know I would be here?"

"I always remembered that you enjoyed dancing," said Jon. "And I saw the studio opened and figured it would be you."

"Oh, I see."

"You have been through some shit over the last week," said Jon.

"Yeah, you come back to town and I almost get killed twice," she replied.

"I'm sorry about that."

"I never thanked you for saving my life, twice."

"Don't mention it."

She glanced around the room, then at Jon. She threw the towel on the ground and grabbed Jon, which took him by surprise.

"What are you doing?"

"Dance with me," she insisted.

"Jess, I don't dance."

"Dance with me."

"Come on, this is ridiculous.."

Jessica was not having it. She forced Jon's right hand around her waist, and he reacted by clinging. Then Jessica moved right and Jon moved with her fluidly. Jessica directed the action, going left and right and back. Jon kept up with everything she did. He held onto her tightly and Jessica could feel the attraction there. She would admit that she found Jon very attractive.

Looking at him now, she realized how much of a good-looking man he was, despite the rugged look and the attitude. She was not sure why he was attractive to her. She saw him kill a man. Maybe she liked him because they both had something in common. They both had an element of tragedy in their history, and that sadly brought them together. Unlike Jon, she would catch her mother's murderer and do it by the book.

They danced in a room with no music. They stopped after a few moments. Jon and Jessica were inches apart, staring at each other in the face. There was a small tension between them, and for an infinitesimal moment, they both felt complete. Jon looked straight into her eyes. He leaned in to kiss her, and she also leaned in. Before their lips touched, his phone buzzed. That killed the moment completely. He looked at his phone and frowned.

"Are you okay?"

"I have to go Jess."

"What's wrong?"

"Nothing, I will see you around."

Jon left Jessica standing there by herself. She wondered what the hell just happened in that room and if she should pursue anything about it.

Chapter 8: The Lost Mother

Pacific Coast Highway February 14th, 2006

Jessica was 12 years old. Jon had been missing for a week now. No one knew where he went. Her father worried that someone might have harmed him. He shielded his suspicions from Jessica, but she knew the truth, even back then. Jessica knew that something had happened to Jon and that she might never see her best friend again. It felt like tragedy after tragedy.

Rachel Hudson was a stunning woman. She had brown, auburn hair, like her daughter. Only her hair was a little redder. She had a vibrant personality and a free spirit, which Jessica admired. Her father, even back then, had been gruff and no-nonsense. It amazed Jessica that these two had found each other. They were opposites.

On this day, Rachel and Jessica had just spent the day hanging out on Newport Beach. Jessica had asked her mom to take her to Fashion Island. But first, Rachel wanted to stop at some small businesses in Newport Beach. Jessica could not have cared less for any of this. Had she known it would be her last few hours with her mother, her attitude might have changed. At 12 years old, all she cared about was her stuff. She loved her gymnastics. She loved to fly and leap off anything. Her mother had always taken her to gymnastics class. On this day, they would buy new clothes for that.

It also was a confusing time for Jessica. She had grown into womanhood, that is what they called it. Jessica had her period. It was uncomfortable; it was disgusting, and it was embarrassing. She hated it when it came on days in which she wanted to go swimming, but magically could not. She did not feel like bleeding all over the place because it was 'that time of the month'. Jessica resented people who spoke to her that way, even back then. She had her mother's free spirit and her father's anger, and everyone knew it.

They were in front of the New Port Theatre. Rachel Hudson loved these old places. To Jessica, it was just an old movie theatre that needed to die.

As they walked next to the theatre, they approached a crosswalk that intersected PCH and Heliotrope Avenue. The crossing light showed that they could. As Rachel and Jessica started walking, a car was coming in hot. Jessica did not notice, but Rachel did. Her mother grabbed Jessica with the force of all her weight and threw her back toward the sidewalk, out of harm's way. Jessica's body collided with the sidewalk, and she felt some pain. The next thing she saw was her mother being hit by this car going 60 miles per hour in a 35 zone. Jessica screamed in horror. That moment flashed for what seemed like an eternity. For one brief second, Jessica remembered seeing her mother clutch her stomach a few moments before the impact.

The car took off before anyone could understand what was happening. Her mother fell to the ground with a sickening thud. Jessica saw her mother fall. She quickly recovered from her issues and rushed to Rachel's side.

"Mommy! Mom! Mom! Wake up! Please God, wake up mom!" Jessica cried out as people surrounded her.

Traffic came to a full stop, and it appeared as the entire world had stopped. Jessica's mother lay lifeless on the pavement, and her stomach was bleeding all over. This led Jessica to believe it was not an accident.

Her father showed up shortly and Jessica ran into her father's arms crying. Hudson just stood there as he held his daughter while looking at his dead wife on the ground.

"Daddy, they killed her, they killed her!" cried Jessica.

Hudson looked down at Jessica. "Who did this?" he asked calmly.

"Mommy pushed me out of the way," she started through the tears. "But mommy flinched and got hit by something else before the car hit her. Someone did something to her on purpose."

Hudson did not react. It unnerved her that her father did not react. He kind of just looked at her and held her a little longer. That bothered Jessica a lot. He did not immediately react. It was as if there were some external force preventing him from doing so.

"Everything will be all right, sweetie," said Hudson.

That was the day Jessica knew she could no longer trust her father completely. He was not a bad guy or anything like that, but he did not help her find closure. Jessica just took it and continued to cry her eyes out.

Chapter 9: The Compound

January 26th, 2016

    The Caine Compound was massive. The building was a giant warehouse being protected by multiple armed guards. A gate stood in front of the entrance, with a small security checkpoint before entering fraught with a loading dock.

    Jon took a vantage point and watched and waited as Caine's men started appearing. Jon believed he had the advantage. He was wrong. A van barreled into him. He had about three seconds to prepare for the impact, and he quickly ducked to his right side to avoid being crushed. His sedan spun out of control until it finally came to a stop. The van locked on his sedan, blocking the path.

    Two men in terrible masks exited the van. They had semiautomatic guns locked on him. Then one of the men grabbed him, yanking him out of the sedan. The impact had weakened him. He could not defend himself. They placed a hood over Jon's head. He could see nothing as the darkness overtook him. He heard footsteps and some distant yelling, then the next thing he heard was machine gunfire. These bastards had killed someone, someone who had been trying to help him.

    They moved him, and he went along with it for now. He wanted to see where they took him first, and if they were stupid enough to take him into the compound. Within moments, despite the hood, his intuition was correct. They were stupid enough. He heard voices and figured he was about to meet their leader. They yanked his hood off and he now found himself tied to a chair. He looked up and saw a burly guy, one who probably could be in a motorcycle gang. He had large forearms and tattoos all over, along with grungy brown hair and a brown beard. He was slightly overweight, which could give Jon an advantage later. He briefly glanced around the room and spotted a few other men. They were all smaller men, and they were all carrying semiautomatic weapons. He made a mental note of each person and each weapon. By his count, there were about five of them, including the grungy guy. The leader's name was Tank, who glanced at him and gave an unimpressed scoff. Jon gazed at him, returning a smile, almost sarcastically.

    "Now, what were you doing snooping around here?" asked Tank.

He did not answer him right away as he wanted to be sure of his surroundings. He counted the men again, then he looked around the room for anything he would use to his advantage.

"I asked you a question, dipshit, what are you doing here?"

Jon remained calm throughout. Tank took out a hunting knife and brandished it. Then he poked Jon with it, who grimaced, but otherwise did not make a sound. The impact of the knife drew some blood. It impressed Tank.

"Being quiet? Who are you and why are you here?"

Tank waited and again Jon did not respond, so the grungy guy did something else. He moved the knife against Jon's neck but did not stab him.

"It doesn't matter," Jon told him.

Tank looked at him with confusion but was astonished and relieved that the man he had tied up finally said something. He saw Jon smile, which threw him off. Tank pressed on.

"And why is that?"

He looked at Tank and instantly stopped smiling. "Because I am going to kill you."

Tank burst into laughter and his other gunmen joined him.

"That gun will be in your hands for a few seconds," he went on. "For being a smartass, I will give you the pleasure of dying first."

The laughter died. Now the gunmen were a little irritated. Tank leaned in toward him, still confident as ever. His words did not worry Tank. The grungy man had a gun, along with help from four other gunmen, and they tied Jon up.

"You're crazy, you're tied up…"

Jon dislocated his thumb. He took apart his zip ties. "Not anymore."

He sprung to his feet and flung Tank's knife away from him. The four other gunmen stared in shock, and they all pulled their guns.

He lifted the chair high and took a step. With accuracy, he brought the chair crashing down on top of two gunmen. The heavy blow struck them on the side of their heads, knocking them out. The other two gunmen started spraying bullets, and Jon evaded all of their gunfire with precision. The years of training, and practice, had made him ready for such an occasion.

Tank got up with his gun and Jon jumped on him, pressed his gun to the ground, and shot the grungy guy in the foot causing him to yell in pain. He grabbed Tank's gun and shot the two gunmen who fired at him, killing them instantly. His accuracy was deadly and perfect.

Jon scanned his damage and saw Tank on the ground with a bleeding foot. Two gunmen were unconscious and the other two were dead. Tank no longer was arrogant, and now instead was fearful and terrified. He stared at his bleeding foot and whimpered in pain.

He glared at Tank. It was funny how when someone had a gun; they had so much confidence. Jon saw it as arrogance, and he loved seeing it change. He had only intended to destroy the compound, not kill anyone tonight. But he could claim self-defense if he had to. He knelt beside Tank, who was still whimpering.

"Now, before I destroy this entire compound, tell me about Caine's next job."

"I can't," said Tank. "He'll kill me!"

"Death is death, does it really matter who administers it?"

He pressed his knuckles together and slammed his hand on Tank's foot. The grungy man screamed as the blood in his foot continued to pour out. He knew Jon meant business.

"Wait! Wait! Please, for the love of God!"

He smirked. This was the begging of a coward. He enjoyed how criminals could easily change attitudes when confronted with death or a simple pounding.

"He will be at the docks in Newport Beach in about a week! I swear that's all I know! Please… you don't have to do this."

"I don't," he shot back. "But I will."

He grabbed Tank's neck and snapped it in two, breaking it instantly. Four more gunmen appeared through the door.

Jon had expected this, as these were probably the guys guarding the exterior of the compound. He took out something from his pocket and threw it in their direction. He took cover.

Before they could react, a massive explosion resonated through the complex. The explosion caused a trickle effect, and now the compound was on fire.

He quickly left and headed toward his sedan. He got in and drove the broken down sedan away from the compound as it exploded in the background. Jon looked in the mirror, assessing the damage he caused, and shook his head. While these were criminals who worked for Caine, he did not want to kill them. But he had no choice.

He made his way to the Orange Grove Bar and Grill. He planked down at the bar and sat there accessing what to drink. Scotti walked over and smiled. He barely glanced at her. She stood there and stared at him for a moment. He paid her no attention, just looking at the drink menu.

"Is that what you've become? Just another drunk?" asked Scotti.

"I am a spectacular drunk."

"A spectacular asshole is more like it."

"I need a shot," he replied, ignoring her remark.

Scotti did as told. She got him a shot of whiskey and handed it to Jon, and he downed it quickly. He beckoned with his finger.

"Another."

She again did as requested and handed him another glass and he downed this one, just as quick.

"You better slow down," she suggested.

"Alcohol barely affects me anymore, anyway."

"What's got you down, anyway?"

"People are constantly trying to kill me, that's what's got me down," Jon snapped.

"Damn, calm your ass down," said Scotti.

"Please bar lady, I didn't come here to be lectured, may I have another shot?"

"First, my name is Scotti, not bar lady, and second, I am not lecturing you."

"I know your name," Jon shot back. "I just don't give a shit in my current state of mind."

"Dick."

"So," he ignored her remark. "Why the hell are you a bartender?"

"I wanted to do something separate from my family name," she said.

He could tell that she realized how stupid that sounded when it came out of her mouth. Instead of pressing further, he asked for another shot.

"You probably need to stop," she said.

She grabbed his hand and he grabbed hers. He stared at Scotti for a moment.

"Listen, Shooty," said Jon.

"It's Scotti!"

"When I lived in Argentina or Brazil," he thought about it for a moment. "Or wherever the hell I was, I drank so many dudes under the table."

"Oh really? You sure you're not just saying that to impress me?"

He scoffed at her. "I mean you're a cute button and all, but I am not here trying to bang you. I just want shots."

"You think I'm a cute button?"

"I mean, well, not now. Right now you're just annoying. Come on, Shetty, give me more drinks!"

"The name is Scotti, you piece of shit!"

"Shetty, Betty, Dotty, who really cares?"

He got up. Scotti looked after him.

"You're leaving?"

"Got to get this alcohol out of my system. Got people to kick the shit out of."

He stumbled out of the bar and headed for his apartment. It sprinkled a little, almost misting. He covered his head with his hands, trying to stupidly protect his head from moisture, and stumbled down the sidewalk, keeping his balance.

He finally made it to his apartment and fumbled with his keys. The keys went into the keyhole, and the door opened. He slammed the door behind him and stumbled into the apartment and plopped himself on the mini couch.

As soon as he did this, there was a knock on the door. He looked at the door suspiciously. Who the hell was here this late at night? Better yet, who the hell knew where he lived? He cautiously stood up and snuck toward the door.

"Who is it?" he called out.

"Ulisez," the voice replied.

What the hell, Jon thought. He opened the door to reveal Ulisez standing in the hallway. Ulisez walked into the apartment without an invitation.

"Come on in," his voice radiated with sarcasm.

Ulisez stormed in and then turned around. He shut the door and before he could do anything, Ulisez grabbed him by the chest and pressed him toward the door. Jon's face crumpled up.

"Hey what the—"

"I know it was you that destroyed the Caine Compound," Ulisez cut him off.

"I don't know what you're talki—"

"Don't lie to me, Jon!"

They stood silently for a moment, with Ulisez still holding him against the door. If it were anyone else, he would have instantly plucked them off of him. But he understood Ulisez's anger and gave him the benefit of the doubt.

"Okay," he began. "Let's say hypothetically that I was the one that destroyed the compound. What are you going to do about it?"

He still allowed Ulisez to hold him against the door. He wanted to see if Ulisez would fold or if he would react. Their friendship had a lot of history, and Ulisez was one of the few people he could trust. That is why he did not fight back, at least not yet.

"Do you realize what type of position you put me in?"

"That's you," Jon retorted. "I got to do me, man."

Ulisez released his hold on him, dropping him from the door. He turned around and headed toward the fridge. He opened it and took a beer out and uncorked the top and drank. He observed this with confusion but said nothing.

"I don't want to be forced to bring you in," Ulisez lamented as he held his beer.

Jon approached him and placed his hand on his shoulder. "You won't have to."

Ulisez turned around and looked at Jon. He brushed Jon's hand off his shoulder.

"You have to stop this buddy. We both know what you're capable of. I remember—I remember all you did when I went to South America."

"You know what happened to my father," Jon recalled. "I can't let that stand."

Ulisez eyeballed him with suspicion. He sipped some beer and pondered what he wanted to say for a moment. Jon could sense that something else bothered him, but stayed quiet.

"Why did you come back now, Jon?"

"What do you mean?"

"You could have come back anytime. You could have come back when we crossed paths four years ago. Why did you come back now?"

He considered the question. "I was given motivation."

"Who are you working for?" Ulisez asked.

"Who am I working for? What are you—"

"You said someone motivated you. Who are you working for?"

"No one," he relented.

"Bullshit," Ulisez countered. "I know you better than anyone else. Tell me who his name is."

He smiled. "You think you know me. You don't know—"

"No, I do. Trust me, I do. Stop bullshitting me and tell me the name."

"Why? Are you going to arrest me?"

He dared Ulisez to answer. He could see the internal struggle within his friend, as Ulisez debated the question. His friend sipped more beer, embracing the taste and the flavor.

"Even if I wanted to, I couldn't. But I need to know what you know so I can protect you," Ulisez admitted.

"Because I'd kick your ass," Jon joked.

"No," Ulisez shot back. "Because of our friendship, Jonny."

"Don't call me that!"

"Jonny shut up. Just shut up."

Neither knew what to say. Jon broke the silence.

"I really appreciate you, buddy. Everything you do for me."

"Just try to *not* break the law."

"I will promise to break the law."

"I said not break the law."

"I can't hear you," Jon placed his hands on his ears to mock not being able to hear anything. Ulisez slugged him in the shoulder. Jon touched his shoulder gingerly. "That hurt man."

"That's what you deserve."

He walked over to the fridge and grabbed two beers. He handed one to Ulisez.

"Here," Jon said. "Have another. Calm your bitch ass down."

"Why are you the way you are?"

"I blame the drug lords," Jon rebuked.

"Just shut up, Jon."

They both smiled and drank their beer.

Chapter 10: The Wildcard

That Same Night

It was about 11 o'clock now. It was time to call it a day. Jessica put her jacket on, turned off the lights, and exited the studio.

She cautiously made her way toward her car and entered her car while observing her surroundings. She entered the car and almost hit her head because of her paranoia. As she started the engine, she drove slowly at first, then making her way onto the city street.

As Jessica drove home, she noticed something in the distance. She ignored it at first. Then the car sped up behind her. Jessica knew something was wrong. The car rammed into her, causing a jolt. She lost control of her car and went spiraling toward the right side of the road and into a ditch.

She shook off the impact and checked herself to discover if she bled. Once she realized that she was fine, she tried to open the door. She did not know what had forced her off the side of the road and was in no mood to find out. All she knew that was she had to get out of the car now and survive.

Jessica finally got the door open. She heard footsteps and panic crept in. She looked everywhere and ran as fast as she could. But then the footsteps got closer.

"Stay where you are and you won't be harmed!" a voice shouted as Jessica grew more alarmed than ever.

She looked everywhere for the voice. Half of her was expecting Jon Drake to appear out of nowhere again. But this was not Jon. Nope, this was someone else. A young man appeared. He was about early 30s and Caucasian.

"Besides," said the man as he emerged. "Boss wants you alive, anyway."

Jessica's face grew with horror as the man advanced on her and grabbed her by force. She struggled and started hitting him, and something fell out of his pocket. Her feet kicked back and forth, laying the dirt everywhere. Finally, he elbowed her in the face. He then placed a cloth over her face, and she started to slowly fade. Her vision blurred and the darkness overcame her after a momentary struggle. Within a few seconds, she lost consciousness.

Her eyes flickered and she groaned. Finally, her eyelids were fully open and she scanned her environment.

Jessica found herself tied inside a room. She was not sure where she was or why she was here, but the last thing she remembered was some creepy dude chloroforming her. That was annoying. She did not spend her night cleansing her mind just so some random dude could kidnap her.

She heard footsteps and waited patiently. Usually, when people kidnapped women, they raped and murdered them. Jessica believed that they had not touched her. So, something else was afoot. There was another reason she was here, and she wanted to know why.

The door opened and Jessica looked up. Alexander Caine stood in front of her. She recognized him because his face had been a popular one around town. He built a majority of this town. She remembered hearing a lot of rumors, many of them unsavory, about Caine. He had a reputation for being underhanded and ruthless. Jessica was friends with his children. She had dated Rion, slept with him, was more like it. They were stupid kids that were getting high together. Drugs mixed with teenage hormones were not a delightful combination.

She rarely remembered seeing Caine around the house. He was always out. Jessica often remembered seeing either the hired help or Ivy Caine, their mother. Here he was, and he had ordered her kidnapping.

Jessica said nothing at first. Caine had someone with him, and after a second or two, Jessica recognized him as the man that kidnapped her.

"Where am I?" she asked.

"Not anywhere nice and sweet, I'll tell you that." The creepy abductor grinned.

"Who are you? Why did you take me?" asked Jessica. She looked up at Caine. "Mr. Caine, why am I here?"

"Someone is going to cap you if you don't keep asking questions," Caine's lackey threatened her.

"Now Frederick, is that any way to speak to our guest?" asked Caine.

"She talks too much."

"It's very nice to see you again, Jessica. Amy always spoke highly of you," said Caine.

"Why did you kidnap me?" asked Jessica.

Jessica got right to the point, and she could tell that Caine respected it. He gave an expression that her moxie impressed him.

"Jon Drake," Caine exhaled as if confessing some terrible secret. "He came back to town, threatened me in my office, and then blew up one of my compounds."

She stared at him blankly. He noticed.

"That doesn't surprise you for some reason."

"I know that Jon hates you," Jessica retorted.

"You also know about the Orange Grove Lounge incident?"

"Jon told me he saw you kill a gangster in cold blood," Jessica remarked coldly.

Caine smiled. Jessica could see the bemused look he probably gave to many people, as a way of attempting to intimidate others. She could see that he was processing her words, being careful about what to say. Despite the circumstances at the moment, Jessica felt no fear.

"That scoundrel dared challenge me," Caine muttered, trying to get the point across that he was bigger than life itself. "He keeps pressing and he will soon find out that you should never mess with Alexander Caine."

"God, you're so nauseating," Jessica bemoaned.

"So you know why you're here?" asked Caine, ignoring her insult.

"Because you have a sick obsession with kidnapping women who are your daughter's age?"

"No," Caine said curtly. "You, my dear, are bait."

Jessica rolled her eyes. "What are you some B-Movie villain?"

Caine chuckled. "That is very cute."

He motioned to the man called Freddy, who walked over to Jessica and grabbed her.

"Get your creepy hands off me!" cried Jessica and Freddy ignored her. He held onto her arm tight and she struggled to get her off. Caine leaned in as Jessica continued to fight.

"I don't give a shit if you are friends with my daughter," Caine proclaimed.

"You can't keep me here! People know I'm missing," said Jessica.

Caine said nothing. He stood over her while Freddy held her in place, restraining her and holding her down while she struggled. She shook violently to show her rebelliousness. Freddy reared his right hand back and backhanded her across the face.

Freddy's full hand slammed into Jessica's face full force. Her head snapped back. She went flying backward, her arms wailing in the air.

Freddy leaned in, angry, as he sneered at her. She glared at him, hating every fiber of his being. Caine stood by and watched this happen, and Jessica knew enjoyed this. She turned her head amid the pain and gazed at him for a moment and noticed he had no expression on his face. This man, this piece of shit dressed in an Armani suit, looked on. Freddy grinned like the cat that ate the canary. Jessica gave him the look of death.

"Now," Caine began. "Are we going to behave? Or is Freddy going to hit you again?"

"This how you get your rocks hard, Caine? Hitting women?" Jessica hissed.

"I am an equal opportunity entertainer," Caine shot back.

Jessica scowled at Caine. This was not how she wanted to end her night or start her day, or whatever the day was now. She had always stayed neutral with Caine, but now she realized he might be a bigger threat than she had expected. Jessica did not fear for her life at the moment. She knew how much her father hated Caine. He would also go Rambo on him if Caine harmed her because he would have nothing left to lose.

"What's your plan, Caine? What are you really after?" Jessica inquired.

Caine leaned in, almost uncomfortably, and pressed his face inches away from hers.

"I want Jon Drake to stop harassing me. I will give him a chance to make amends and that starts with you."

"Why me? I have done nothing to you."

"But you are valuable. You know my daughters and I know what happened between you and my son."

Jessica paused for a moment, thinking about it. Few people knew about her history with Rion Caine, except maybe Ivy Caine and her father. Even Amy and Scotti were in the dark about just how involved she was with Rion.

"You don't know shit," she jabbed.

"Oh?" Caine rebuked. "I know that my son, while he was a bit of a rebellious one, didn't turn into a drug addict until he met you."

Jessica did not answer. She just glanced at Caine blankly.

"I know all about that. My darling wife told me everything I needed to know about that great time in your life. Boy, does she hate you.

"You ruined her baby boy, and you became friends with her daughters. I heard you go to AA meetings, and that you routinely disrespect your counselors."

"That was a lifetime ago," Jessica insisted.

Caine shook his head.

"Everything is relative with the Caine family. Tell me, Jessica, do you even know where Rion is?"

Jessica did not answer.

"He is in a recovery center somewhere across the world," Caine answered emphatically and then pointed at her. "And you put him there."

"He took those drugs willingly with me," Jessica replied.

Caine laughed. "A red-blooded man would do anything for a pretty girl." He leaned in and caressed her hair. She turned her head away to avoid him. "And you are a pretty girl."

"Get your slimy hands off me," she roared.

Caine smiled. As he was about to do something else, something caught his attention. Jessica tried to see what they were looking at. Caine motioned to Freddy.

"When he makes his way inside, take care of him once and for all," he ordered Freddy.

Jessica knew exactly who 'him' was. Jon had come for her.

Chapter 11: The Power That Holds

Jon sat in a building across from Caine Enterprises. He could see in the distance exactly what he would have to deal with. He saw two of Caine's men perched in front of the security checkpoint. Both had guns, and they both seemed to mean business. Jon realized that the only way to find Jessica would be to do it the smart way.

He had discovered that Jessica went missing when she did not check back into her place. After that, he did some investigating and discovered her car by the side of the road. From that point, he knew something was wrong. He did some detective work and discovered a clue. Freddy was sloppy. The idiot left something that Jon identified as an item only he had: an e-cigarette that he usually smoked. Not only that, but he also left his name on it. Jon deducted that they took Jessica as some weird attempt to get at him. He would not let them harm a hair on her head.

He looked for angles in the building that he could exploit. It was about being discreet. He had studied the Caine Enterprises building and understood the mechanisms about the building. He also knew that Caine had a few secret corridors in the home. Jon had discovered this through his tactical discussions with Vladimir. This would be his first time breaking into Caine Enterprises.

He waited for security to check some people in. He studied the security guards and monitored their patterns. Every colossal idiot had a pattern. He realized that the two at the front were the priority first and put on his disguise and had a keycard ready. He approached the security checkpoint at the front of the building. There were two guards there, both as huge as ever. Jon looked at one of them as they looked at the card. The guard looked at Jon and then scanned him in.

He was in, at least on the first level. He still had to get to the part of Caine Enterprises where the secret corridors laid. While everyone was going about their business, Jon was feeling out parts of the wall to see what areas would be good. Finally, he felt a soft pressure point, and it opened up a secret passage.

What he saw was a hallway that no one knew existed. As he walked into the hallway, a door on the very end opened. It was Freddy. Jon was smart or lucky. For a moment, he stared at Freddy. He waited for Freddy to notice him. He should have hidden or at least allowed himself the element of surprise. But Jon had waited far too long for this. He knew what he wanted to do.

Freddy had walked about 20 yards from Jon when he finally realized how close they were to each other. Jon watched as Freddy beamed at him with the look of a cat that ate the canary.

"Hello Jon," cried Freddy.

Jon pulled his gun at the same time Freddy pulled his.

"Not going to let you catch me off guard again. Put your gun down, kid," said Freddy.

"You first asshole."

"Mr. Caine has been asking about you," said Freddy. "How happy is he going to be when I tell him we got you."

Something occurred to Jon. Freddy was being more chatty than usual. That irritated him to the fullest extent.

"You stupid sack of crap."

"So hurtful," Freddy remarked.

"Go to hell."

"We'll both go together."

Jon just glared at Freddy. That was insulting. Jon walked methodically, with no fear, as he got closer to Freddy.

"Get back!" Freddy warned.

"Ten years ago, you shot a man named Robert Drake," said Jon. "Shot him in cold blood in front of his 12-year-old son."

"I shot many people…"

"You hit the car, then you walked over to the driver's side and you shot him in cold blood. You did that."

Freddy's face fell. It was then that he realized he could not intimidate Jon.

"You have a death wish."

"No, I only wish to hurt you real bad."

He fired his gun, deflecting Freddy's gun away from his hands with perfect accuracy. Freddy winced in pain. He charged at Freddy and grabbed his chest and held him against the wall. The pain from the gunshot graze allowed him to overpower Freddy, and he held the gun to the hitman's head.

"Now what are you doing to do to me?"

"You will do nothing. You wouldn't dare! I work for Alexander Caine! I am Freddy Hunter. I…"

Jon lowered his gun and shot Freddy in the kneecap, and the hitman howled in pain.

"You shot me you asshole!"

Jon grabbed Freddy by the throat.

"Where is Caine?!"

"I'm not going to tell you nothing."

"Really?"

"Really."

Jon shot Freddy in the left shoulder. Freddy cried out again as blood poured out of his shoulder now. He fell to his good knee.

"I hate you! Should have killed you back then!"

"Tell me where he is! Now!"

"You kill me and you will never see Jessica again!"

Jon pistol-whipped Freddy across the face. The man fell further to the ground. He stepped on his throat.

"I'm tired of this crap, Freddy!"

Jon stood over Freddy and put pressure on him with his boot.

"Take me to him."

Freddy then looked instinctively in the door's direction where he came from. Jon smiled and grabbed the hitman by the feet and started dragging him across the floor while he whined in pain. He normally might feel bad, but this man killed his father. Making him suffer seemed reasonable. He dragged Freddy, who was whining, across the hallway. He opened the door in which Freddy was looking at and entered the room and saw Caine standing there with Jessica tied up. Jon drew his gun.

"Let her go!"

"Jon, no!" cried Jessica.

Caine turned to Jessica, and then to Jon. The bald man looked at him with an arrogance only he possessed. The grin on Caine's face was telling.

"Glad you put the pieces together, Jon," Caine gushed as if he were some proud parent.

"Yeah, wasn't too hard," Jon exclaimed as he dragged Freddy and threw him on the ground in front of Caine, who did not react. Freddy continued to whimper in pain.

"Pathetic," Caine sighed, showing his disappointment with his subordinate.

Jon held his gun firm. Jessica watched with anticipation, not knowing what Jon would do. She knew how much Jon hated and Caine, and she supposed he was about to find out too. Caine did not seem to panic. He looked back at Jon after dismissing Freddy.

"You disappeared for ten years. Then you come back and confront me in my office, then you shoot at me in a public night club," Caine highlighted.

"What's your point?" Jon fired back.

"Why are you back in town, Jon?" asked Caine.

Jon adjusted the trigger. He still had his gun aimed at Caine, but Jessica was right behind him, so it was an empty threat. "You know why."

Caine just smirked. It irritated Jon.

"What's so funny?"

"You," Caine replied. "You are still crying over your daddy?"

"Your guy pulled the trigger!" cried Jon, pointing out to Freddy, who is still wincing on the ground.

"Do you have any proof?" asked Caine.

"I was there!"

"Who the hell will believe some lunatic who went missing for over a decade? And Jon, you were the one that blew up my shipment destroyed my compound aren't you?"

Jon did not answer. He had to be careful. There was no good from allowing Caine to get in his head.

"Yeah," said Caine. "You were. There is no one else who could penetrate my security. I don't know where you have been, but it looks like you have had training."

Jon still said nothing. He was not sure how to reply. He kept his gun focused on Caine, and the bald man did not act afraid at all. Caine probably figured Jon was not serious. Jessica stayed quiet throughout the entire ordeal.

"Here's my proposition," said Caine as he quickly knelt beside Jessica and pulled out a gun and held it against her temple. Jon's eyes grew as this happened. Jessica's eyes bulged a little, but she tried to not show it.

"Let her go!" Jon ordered.

"I have no intention of harming her or you," said Caine. "I only wanted information on you, and I got it. Now I have one warning for you. Leave me and my operations alone and I promise I, nor Frederick, will bother you."

"Let her go!" Jon ordered again, still maintaining his aim. He could shoot Caine's gun off, but he might hit Jessica. Jon would not put her at risk.

"Do we have a deal?" asked Caine.

"You killed my father," said Jon, trying to hold back tears.

"That's your word against mine. You are a deranged fool, and I am an industrialist who built half this town. Who the hell do you think the courts going to believe?"

Jon considered this for a moment. He hated it when Caine was right. There would be more opportunities to take the bald man down, but for now, he had no choice. Slowly, he lowered his gun and gently placed it on the floor. Caine smiled.

"That's more like it," said Caine, who lowered his gun. He untied Jessica and then shoved her toward Jon.

"Watch it, asshole," said Jessica, who did not appreciate being shoved. Jon caught her as she fell. They both knelt on the ground, looking up at Caine.

"Give my daughter my regards," said Caine.

"I'll tell her what a piece of shit her father is," Jessica shot back.

Caine shook his head. "You disclose anything to my daughter and I will bother you, and you won't like it when I bother you."

"Don't you dare threaten her!" Jon roared.

"I don't make threats, Jon," said Caine. "I make promises."

Jon and Jessica slowly picked themselves off the floor. Freddy continued to wince in pain. It disgusted Caine.

"Get off the floor," said Caine. "You're embarrassing me."

"How the hell do you expect to explain my disappearance?" asked Jessica.

"I already have that covered," said Caine. "Now leave."

Jon and Jessica looked at Caine, then each other. Then they sauntered away. Jon and Jessica left Caine Enterprises through the front gate. Security did not stop them.

Jon and Jessica made their way to the Orange Grove Police Station. Despite his misgivings, Jessica asked Jon to accompany her. Hudson saw his daughter and ran to hug her, and she returned the hug.

"Thank God you're okay, Jessie," said Hudson.

Hudson then saw Jon.

"Jon? What the hell happened?" he asked him.

A man in a suit stood in the corner. This was the district attorney of Orange County.

The district attorney's name was Dan West. He was a smug, large man in a power suit that thought he was God's gift to lawyers. He had a fat round face and a gigantic figure. He had won the election two years ago and would look for re-election soon. Jon hated him already.

Another man also entered the building with him. Jon recognized him too as the mayor. This was Mayor Jose Rodriguez. He was a slightly chubby man with glasses and curly black hair. The way they walked together, Jon could see these two as arm-in-arm in corruption together. He knew they were corrupt, based on the dirt he had dug on them while researching everyone in this town. They had been in Caine's pocket from the get-go, and Jon knew this.

"We have the man who did this," said West.

Jon gave them a curious glance, trying to see into their eyes, and saw nothing but emptiness. Hudson stepped in front of Jon.

"What the hell are you talking about? How could you have the man already?"

"My office got a call about a confession. Your officers are bringing the man in," said West.

"I wanted to be here to congratulate you on successfully capturing your daughter's captor," Rodriguez added.

This was suspicious to Jon. Why would the district attorney and the mayor suddenly show up at the police station at the same time? This was a power move by Caine. He had to know it. Caine was flashing out his power to show Jon and Jessica that he meant business.

"Nice to meet you, I'm Dan West," West extended his hand to Jon.

Jon looked at the man suspiciously. He extended his hand cautiously. West had a firm handshake. It was almost too firm. Rodriguez stepped in and offered his hand, and Jon reluctantly shook it. He hated both men, but he had to play nice, for now.

"So how did you find Jessica?" asked Rodriguez.

You already know you slimy piece of shit, Jon thought.

Before either Jon or Jessica could answer, two pollice officers hauled a man into the station. The man was fidgety and acting irrationally.

"I'm telling you they framed me! I didn't do nothing!" cried the man.

"Tell it to the judge!" the officer shouted back.

Thomas Martin walked in behind them, and Hudson approached his officer.

"What's going on?" asked Hudson.

"We caught the man who kidnapped your daughter," said Thomas.

Jon and Jessica stared at the man, who looked similar to Freddy. Suddenly, they understood everything. They now knew exactly what Caine meant. He had set up a patsy to take the fall. Jon understood just how powerful Caine was, and how much more difficult it would be to take him down.

Chapter 12: The Legion of Samurai

February 14, 1996, in São Paulo, Brazil

Many years ago, Vladimir was working as an honest businessman. He was the salesmen and his wife Ileana made all the items they sold. His wife was a very creative genius. She made beach clothing, gemstones, and copper cookware. It was a very simple way of life, but they made a good living off of it. They sold most of their products at the outside market on the streets of São Paulo.

Ileana walked into the area while Vladimir was manning the fort. He gazed upon her and stared. His wife was stunning to him. She had black hair that went just down to her shoulders, and she was in good shape. Her face was round and in perfect form. She was the mother of his children. They had a son named Ivan, and a daughter named Nubia. As Vladimir looked upon his wife, he felt a greater appreciation for her.

"Vladimir," said Ileana. She then took out a gem she finished making. "One more."

"You are wonderful, my love," said Vladimir as he kissed her on the lips. She returned the kiss with good measure.

"We are having a good day now?" she asked.

"Very well," he replied. "We will feed our children for weeks."

Vladimir packed some food into some containers when a man walked up to their table. He looked suspicious, dressed in dark clothing from top to bottom.

"Hello," said the stranger in fluent Portuguese.

"May I help you?" asked Vladimir.

"My name is Saul Salgado," said the stranger. "As you know, this area is owned by the Great Command of the Capital. We run much of Brazil and offer you a service."

Vladimir furrowed his brow. The Great Command of the Capital was one of the three major cartels in Brazil. They were as powerful as they were ruthless. The Great Command of the Capital had the most hold, the most weapons, and the most men. They also had a skilled leader in Carlos Cortez, along with a strong up and comer in a young man named Armando Escobar. Salgado was one of their top hitmen. Vladimir knew his reputation well.

This group was not old either. Vladimir remembered how they started just three years before 1993. The Great Command of the Capital originated inside a prison and during a football game. Despite their relative newness, they were already powerful by 1996. Their primary targets were police officers, as they had already killed hundreds of uniformed men.

Vladimir looked at Salgado with trepidation. He had to be careful about how he acted right now. Vladimir had his wife and children to think of right now. He had to tread carefully.

"What do you want?" asked Vladimir.

"Protection," said Salgado. "You pay a fee and we leave you alone."

Vladimir immediately understood. But it was not a situation he could partake in. If he allowed this man to charge him for "protection" he would forever be in debt to the cartel. However, if he refused, the cartel could come after him. He attempted to play the sad man angle.

"Please," said Vladimir. "I do not have the money to afford. We can barely feed our children."

Salgado shook his head.

"Pay us the money and you will have protection and we may leave you some crumbs if you have the need."

"Please, I cannot afford it."

"Pay! Or suffer!"

This set Vladimir off. He grabbed Salgado by the chest and braced.

"You threaten a poor man who cannot pay your fee! Leave now scum!" *cried Vladimir as he threw Salgado on the ground. The cartel representative picked himself off the ground in anger.*

"You will pay for this disrespect!" *he roared, and he took off in a huff.*

Ileana saddled next to Vladimir. She cradled him.

"Vladimir, what are we going to do?"

Vladimir and his wife were at home with their children. They tucked their children asleep as their bedtime was early. It was appropriate for children so young to sleep early to replenish their bodies. Ivan was barely four years old, and Nubia was two. But his children had already established outstanding personalities of their own. They were having dinner at their small table. Ileana had picked up bread from the store and actually could afford fish tonight too. She had cooked it up.

"This is delicious love," said Vladimir.

"Anything for you," said Ileana. She leaned in and kissed him on the cheek. As she did this, the door and front wall exploded. They fell back from the impact. There was smoke everywhere from the explosion, and now Vladimir heard his children crying. To his horror, he spotted Salgado, and two armed men enter the home with now no open door.

"I told you that you would pay for your disrespect!" shouted Salgado as he entered.

The two gunmen fired their weapons. Vladimir and Ileana took cover behind their small couch. He leaned in toward his wife.

"We must get the children," said Vladimir.

They kept themselves low and made their way to their children's rooms. They evaded the gunfire and made their way into the small rooms. Ivan and Nubia were crying at the sound of the gunfire. Vladimir scooped up Nubia and Ileana carried Ivan. They made their way out the backdoor as the gunfire continued.

"Come on out, you are dead anyway," said Salgado.

They were outside the house. Vladimir motioned for his wife to go toward the car. Then he noticed something terrible.

"You're bleeding," said Vladimir as he noticed Ileana had a bullet wound on her abdomen.

"I'll be okay," said Ileana. "We have to make sure the children are okay."

More gunfire ensued, and Vladimir immediately dropped and took cover over Nubia. Ileana put Ivan down and placed him below Vladimir's protection.

"I will get the car," she said.

Then Vladimir saw his wife quickly scatter toward the car. The next thing he saw changed his life forever. As Ileana stepped next to the car, it exploded, engulfing in flames, along with his wife. He wailed in despair.

"Ileana!!!!!!"

"Mommy!!!!!!" cried Ivan as Vladimir felt even worse.

Before he could mourn, more gunfire erupted. With tears in his eyes, Vladimir carried both of his children and scattered toward the forest and away from the explosion. His priority was getting his children to safety. Ivan was crying and so was Nubia, and he had to calm them down. For the moment, he had to shield himself from any emotions.

Vladimir was about 100 yards away from his home, and his car was now in flames. The current danger forced him to leave his dead wife's remains in the car as it burned. He needed to escape the assassins who wished to harm them.

"He's here somewhere," Vladimir heard Salgado say. "Kill him and his children."

For the first time in his life, Vladimir felt something he never knew. He felt unfiltered anger and vowed he would avenge his Ileana.

A few days later, Vladimir held a small ceremony for his wife. He had evaded the cartel, and he kept his children safe. However, they had stayed in shelters for the last few days, knowing that they could not return home. Vladimir kept his children safe, but he could not do this forever. He never recovered his wife's body. It was not safe. He had no choice. So instead, he made a small memorial at a cemetery nearby.

"Ileana," said Vladimir. "I'm so sorry."

There was a man near Vladimir. He had not noticed this mysterious man as grief consumed Vladimir. The man's hand touched Vladimir on the shoulder and he looked up to see.

It was an older man. He wore what appeared to be Samurai's clothing. He looked of Asian descent. The man had short-cropped hair and a small round face. His hood slightly obscured his face.

"May I help you?" asked Vladimir.

"It is you that needs help, my friend," said the Samurai.

"My wife," Vladimir began. "They killed her."

"By one of the great evils, correct?"

Vladimir nodded.

"My son, I am so sorry for your loss," said the Samurai.

"Thank you," replied Vladimir.

Vladimir extended his hand to introduce himself.

"My name is Vladimir."

"My name is Franco. But most call me the Samurai."

Vladimir looked at him curiously.

"What do you mean?"

"Come with me and I will show you."

The Samurai took Vladimir and his children into his home. Vladimir went with this stranger without hesitation because he had nowhere else to go. He had a feeling that this man could help him.

The Samurai showed Vladimir a magnificent fortress that no one would have ever known. They walked to the top of the Pico de Jaragua in São Paulo. The sight mesmerized Vladimir as he made his way into the fortress. He still wanted an explanation, and he was sure the Samurai would give it to him.

The Samurai and Vladimir entered the temple. They walked in and hundreds of men, all dressed in samurai garb, greeted them.

"Gentlemen, this is Vladimir," said the Samurai. "He and his children will stay with us. Treat them like you treat me."

The men greeted him without saying a word, and Vladimir was more curious than ever. He nudged the Samurai.

"I am confused, who, what are you?"

The Samurai smiled.

"My friend, we are the Legion of Samurai. Our goals in life are to hunt down the wicked that commit unspeakable acts of evil and wipe them off the face of the Earth."

Vladimir tried to comprehend this. This group was a modern-day terrorist group, in the form of an old Chinese inspiration. Vladimir looked around the room and spotted weapons of all kinds, mostly swords, daggers, and some guns. Another man appeared before Vladimir. The Samurai presented him.

"This is Diego Rivera," said the Samurai. "He is my second in command."

Vladimir shook Diego's hand. He looked at the man, and he was a sturdy man. He had an enormous round face with a lot of facial hair and medium length hair.

"Welcome to the Legion," said Diego.

Vladimir spotted a young boy in the distance. Diego realized Vladimir was looking at the boy.

"Ah, I see you have children," said Diego. "I have an adolescent son. Manuel. Perhaps they can play together."

Vladimir smiled. He felt like he was home.

Weeks passed, and Vladimir trained with the Legion of Samurai. They prepared his body, mind, and soul. The Legion of Samurai took him and his children in and treated him like royalty. But he understood that there was an insignificant price to pay. He knew that they wanted his services, and that was okay with him. Vladimir wanted revenge, and the Legion of Samurai were here to help.

April 1st, 1996, Saul Salgado's home

Vladimir and the Samurai made their way toward Salgado's home. They had made their way to the home after the Legion had tracked the address.

"This is where the man you seek lives," said the Samurai.

"Do you believe we two can take him alone?" asked Vladimir.

"Our records show Salgado has two men protecting him," said the Samurai. "We are skilled enough."

The Samurai handed Vladimir a sword.

"Do what is needed."

Vladimir looked at the Samurai, starting to have doubts.

"Are you sure? This man.."

"This man killed your wife! He tried to kill your children. Do not forget that."

They spotted the two men guarding the exterior of Salgado's house. The Samurai prepared something in his hand and threw it in their direction. It dropped in front of them and before they could react; it exploded in front of them, blowing them away. Their bodies went flying into instant death. The doors came off and smoke filled the air.

Vladimir and the Samurai approached the open door and Salgado emerged with a gun in his hand.

"You killed my men! You do not know who you are messing with!" he roared.

The Samurai flung his sword at the gun, deflecting it away from Salgado's hand, causing him to bleed. He cried at the pain. Salgado was unarmed and bleeding. The Samurai turned to Vladimir.

"Do what you came to do."

Vladimir methodically walked toward Salgado, who spotted him for the first time.

"You! You wouldn't dare you pathetic little man! I am in the Command of the Nation! They will come to you! They will kill you! They will.."

Vladimir stabbed Salgado in the heart, mostly to shut him up. He would worry about the consequences later. He now had an army behind him.

Salgado spotted the blood flowing everywhere, and his eyes bulged up. The cartel scumbag looked down at the blade, which was still in his chest, and then he dropped like a potato.

Vladimir looked at Salgado. He stood still and could not believe he had just killed a man. It felt horrifying and amazing at the same time. He had avenged his wife. While Vladimir did not feel better, at least he had eradicated one evil man from the world.

"Well done," said the Samurai.

Vladimir and the Samurai quickly left. They made their retreat to their fortress, where they were safe from the reach of the cartel. Vladimir continued to operate for the Legion of Samurai, and he aided them in whatever they needed. He was eternally grateful to them for helping him avenge his wife.

Part 2

Chapter 13: Frank Hudson

January 28th, 2016

  Jon and Jessica went their separate ways, and she told him she had an AA meeting to attend to that night. That was okay because Jon had some drinking to do. He went to the Orange Grove Bar and Grill and planted himself down on the stool. Scotti, the bartender and youngest child of Caine, made her way to his direction.

  "Ah look who is back? You survived whatever you had to go through?" she asked.

  "Tenfold Squatty."

  "The name is Scotti."

  "Yeah, whatever," he replied. "Just give me a whiskey on the rocks."

  "Dick," muttered Scotti under her breath. She went to grab the whiskey, and Jon sat there for a moment. He looked around his surroundings and then back in front. Scotti got the whiskey for Jon and handed it to him. He took a swig in one shot and slammed it down. Then, he pulled out a 20 dollar bill and handed it to her. She looked at it, unimpressed.

  "More, Dotty," said Jon.

  "Scotti!"

  "I can't be required to remember names! Just give me my shot!"

  Scotti did as requested and handed Jon the shot. He grabbed the whiskey and swigged it efficiently and then slammed it down.

  "God damn that feels good."

  "So what's got you bothered?"

  "Your piece of shit of a father."

  "Excuse me?"

  "You heard me," replied Jon. "Your father, the great Alexander Caine. Do you even know what he has been up to lately? Let me tell you. He kidnapped Jessica just to see who was targeting him. He used my Jessica, your alleged friend Jessica, to prove a point. That doesn't even include the part where he ordered my father's death."

  Scotti looked at Jon with disbelief.

  "Where the hell do you get off talking about my father?"

"Oh I forgot," said Jon. "You're the youngest. He's probably hidden the most from you."

"My father would never commit the unspeakable acts you are saying."

He broke out in laughter and slammed the table with his fist, taking Scotti by surprise.

"Listen, babe."

"Don't call me that," said Scotti.

He rolled his eyes, annoyed. He sighed.

"Listen you stupid bitch," said Jon, and her eyes grew large with anger. "Your father is a very shady businessman. Amy is starting to see it, but even she is in denial. So are you. Eventually, you'll see him for the scumbag he is."

Scotti slapped Jon across the face. He felt her hand come across him like a hammer, getting the point just right. He shook it off and saw that she was visibly angry.

"Get out of my bar!"

"Usually when women do that, it comes after some fun," remarked Jon.

"Get out!"

"Fine," said Jon, picking himself up. "Remember my words, little Miss Caine. Your father is dangerous."

Jon picked himself off and left, leaving Scotti standing there starring a dagger through him.

He stumbled into his apartment, still feeling some effects of the alcohol. The maps from earlier were still there. He shut the door behind him and just slouched off toward the floor.

"Get off your drunk ass, we got to talk," Hudson commanded as he revealed himself inside Jon's apartment.

Jon looked up to see the Orange Grove Police Commissioner towering above him. Slowly, with some hesitance, he pulled himself off the ground. He looked solemnly at Hudson, who was not smiling. Jon apathetically marched toward the couch and took a seat and made a motion with his hand for Hudson to do the same. The commissioner took a seat adjacent from where Jon sat and looked around.

"Nice dump you got here," Hudson remarked.

"How d'you find me?"

"I'm a detective, not a fool Jon."

He just looked at Hudson for a moment, trying to figure out why he was here. The two held their stares, with neither man wanting to move an inch.

"What d'you want to talk to me about?"

Hudson sat up, focusing on Jon. He leaned in, displaying that he meant business.

"Where were you on the night of January 25th and 26th?"

Oh, Jon thought. Hudson must have caught onto his activities, or at least he was suspicious.

"I was in my apartment," Jon lied. "I was tired from my plane ride in."

"Uh-huh," Hudson noted.

"You don't believe me?"

"I never said that."

"You implied it."

"I just confirmed what you told me."

He stood up immediately, straightened himself out. He turned his back to Hudson for a moment, then turned back.

"Are you accusing me of something, Frank?"

"I did some digging on you, and your past Jon."

Jon attempted to compose himself.

"What did you find?" he asked, inquisitively.

"I know you spent some time in South America. I know you spent some time in several jails down in Brazil."

"And why exactly were you looking up information on me, anyway?" The tone in his voice took Hudson by surprise. The tension built between these two, but he had to be a little careful around Hudson.

"Because you show up a few days ago, act all mysterious. Then, someone shoots at Alexander Caine at in the Orange Grove Lounge, an incident happens at Caine's Compound, then Jessica gets kidnapped and you help bring her back. Worse yet, someone saw a man that looked exactly like you at the lounge."

Uh oh, Jon thought. While there was no concrete proof that Hudson knew anything, but he was a good detective. Hudson must have felt something wrong, and as he placed his hand on his shoulder. "You've always been like a son to me."

He sighed, hesitating. "Things I have done over the last ten years are not easy to talk about."

"We've all done stuff we're not proud of. What we do from there usually determines who we are."

"Have you ever heard of the Great Command of the Capital?"

"One of the three big cartels in Brazil?"

Jon nodded slowly. It was now or never.

"Over the last ten years, I was a high ranking commander to one of the biggest drug lords in Brazil."

Hudson gave Jon an amused face, not believing him

"You're kidding, right?"

Jon said nothing, staying serious. Hudson's expression changed. His face fell flat as he went from slightly chuckling to now contemplating what Jon was trying to tell him. The older man's face fell flat as he stared at him, realizing.

"Oh my God, you aren't kidding."

"I wish to God I was," replied Jon. "The man that took me in was Armando Escobar."

"Was?"

"It's a long story," said Jon. "I believe he is dead."

"Why would you say that?"

"Because," said Jon with a coldness that chilled the room. "I watched his house burn down and he was inside."

He saw the pain in Hudson's face. The look of disappointment spread all over his face.

"Start at the beginning," he said to Jon.

"I was riding my bike one day near the Caine estate because even then, I knew that he had something to do with my father's murder."

Hudson's jaw dropped. "Jon, I'm so sorry..."

"Anyway," Jon interrupted. "I was riding my bike when I was taken by child traffickers. Next thing I know, I was in South America. They were going to sell me either into sex slavery or some other kind of perverted use for children."

"How did you end up with Escobar? Was he the leader of the sex ring?"

Jon shook his head. "No. He was the one that saved me from them. Killed every one of them."

Hudson thought about this for a moment.

"What was his motive for saving you?"

"He told me he had a soft spot for me and did not want to see a child harmed. Later on, I learned it was more about recruiting me for his army."

"So you worked for him then? From that point on?"

He nodded. "I was in the cartel from age 12 to 18 when I set fire to his house."

Hudson's jaw dropped, horrified at what Jon told him. "Why did you do that?"

"He was going to expand his operations to California because he knew about my connection," Jon explained. "He planned to strong-arm the government, starting small and then working his way up. I had to stop him. I could not let him harm the people I cared about. I knew how dangerous he was."

"How many people did you kill in that fire?"

Jon hesitated. "Roughly 25 men were in that house on the night that it burned to the ground."

Hudson's face said it all. The look he gave Jon could kill. He looked appalled and shook his head sadly. Jon instantly regretted telling Hudson, because now the man had a different opinion of him.

"How many men have you killed in total over ten years?"

"I'm not sure," replied Jon.

"How many men!?"

Hudson's louder voice shocked even Jon. Hudson's anger stunned Jon, even if he partially expected it. Finally, he gave in.

"57."

"57 men? You killed 57 men?"

"To be fair, they were all evil men."

"That doesn't matter," replied Hudson. "You took away many lives. What the hell happened to the boy that used to visit my house all the time? What happened to that boy?"

"That boy died along with his father," Jon's eyes were cold and unapologetic. "And his death was sealed when a certain police officer did nothing to put the murderer away."

Hudson stood up angrily, his hands shaking.

"You realize you just confessed to multiple murders to a police commissioner, right Jon?"

"Not in your jurisdiction."

"I could have you extradited. You would go to prison for the rest of your life. And it would not be an American prison, it would be a Brazilian prison. Not as nice."

Jon felt betrayed. He had poured his heart out to Hudson, and instead of sympathy, he got judgment. He now knew telling Hudson was the wrong move. Jessica understood him and related to him. Her father was judgmental.

"Go ahead. I could just disappear again," he said to Hudson.

Hudson thought about this for a moment, then something occurred to him. He glared at Jon.

"You did all those things," Hudson noted. "You tried to kill Caine too."

"Yes," Jon did not want to deny it anymore. This was who he was. Hudson was the first person he had been brutally honest with.

Hudson stood up abruptly. The look on his face displayed such disdain and disappointment. He shook his head and made a foot toward the door.

"You are not the boy I knew," he blurted out.

"No, I'm not," replied Jon.

"Your father would have been disappointed in you."

Those words from Hudson stung Jon. As the commissioner made his way toward the door and opened it, he turned around.

"Next time you break the law, I will arrest you."

Jon did not reply. He just watched as Hudson opened the door and slammed it shut exiting the apartment.

Chapter 14: Recovery and Renewal

January 29th, 2016

Jessica was with her support group. She still hated these people. Shondra led the class once more, and she looked at Jessica with a relaxed face. She seemed a little hesitant to call on her, but she knew she had to. She was okay with that. They wanted her to talk, she would talk her mouth off.

"Okay, Jessica," Shondra began. "It's your turn. Let's try to keep it civil this time."

"No promises, doc."

"Just try."

Jessica sighed. She had been here for ten minutes, and they already annoyed her.

"Well," she cleared her throat. "My old friend who I used to have a crush on just came back to town after ten years of being presumed dead. The whole reason, aside from my mother being murdered, for me becoming a crack and alcohol addict and going into a terrible downfall in my life. It's pretty much the whole reason why I became this bitter pill of bitchiness. He is back, and he is driving me crazy, and I find myself drawn to him more than ever."

Everyone stared at her with their jaws open. Jessica had captured all their attention, and it privately gave her joy.

"So I got kidnapped the other day," she went on. "The men who took me told me if I ever told anyone, they would murder me and my entire family. Well, the only family I had left. Jon saved me. I find myself hating him and loving him at the same time for all of this. He brought this madness into my life by coming back."

"I'm sorry, did you say you were kidnapped?" asked Shondra, genuinely shocked.

"Oh yeah," replied Jessica. "Alexander Caine and his boy Freddy Hunter."

"The billionaire industrialist? But he seems to be…"

"Refined? Elite? This is the exact reaction he knew it would get if I ever told anyone. Well, everything here is confidential. Don't tell anyone I told you guys this, or he will you know, kill me."

"I'm not sure that's how that…"

"Anyway," she cut Shondra off and then cleared her throat and continued. "I haven't had the urge to drink, shoot up any drugs, or do anything to harm myself in years."

"That's wonderful news, Jessica," replied Shondra, genuinely showing joy in her voice.

"I have however had the urge to stab someone! After seeing the injustice first hand and the power that Caine held, I want to be the one that brings him down once and for all."

"I think that's quite enough for today, Jessica.."

"Same time next week, doc?"

The support group kicked her out again. She picked up the dust off her feet and scuttled out. The next morning, Jessica was in the coffee shop and she waited for her appointment to show up. She had done some investigating of her own and knew she had to have the perfect person to help her find her mother's killer. The situation with Jon had distracted her for a while and she could not afford it anymore.

Before Jon's return, Jessica had paid a visit to the Newport Beach Police Department. The whole point of that trip was to gather some information on her mother's murder. While it was a cold case, she hoped that there was something.

The Orange Grove Police Department had worked with the Newport Beach Police Department to figure out the person who killed Jessica's mother. But there had been politics preventing anything from getting done. The Newport Beach Police Department never solved the murder. They called it a hit-and-run accident. But Jessica hoped that there was something else that could change that verdict. In her heart, she knew something else had happened.

She met a rogue ex-officer that helped her. This woman had not only elected to help Jessica but also put her in connection with a shady friend of hers. She helped Jessica get access to the remains, and then when that happened, they accessed the cause of death. When the results came back a couple of days ago, it appalled Jessica at what she found out. It turned out that her mother did not die from being hit by a car as the report originally stated. Instead, Jessica's mother Rachel Hudson was shot several times. This confused Jessica. Why had that not been in the original report? Did her father know? Jessica remained quiet for the time being and not confront her father about it. Instead, she hired a private investigator.

She told the private investigator to meet her at the Harbor House Diner where she worked. It was low key enough that no one would pay attention, and her coworkers did not bother her much when she hung out here.

The private investigator walked into the coffee shop. He was a fit man, but Jessica could tell he was an older man. He had some brown hair, likely dyed, that was balding. He sported a brown, grayish beard around his face. The man had toned muscles all over, showing he worked out frequently, probably too frequently. He wore a suit, black and blue. Jessica stood up to greet him with a handshake and a smile.

"You must be Jessica," he greeted her.

"I am, you are Patrick Carlin."

Patrick had a briefcase in his hands. Jessica had a manila folder, which contained the information she had learned. Now, she was hiring Patrick to take that information and run with it. There were many things that a private investigation firm could do that she could not always do.

"Have a seat," she said.

Patrick did as Jessica requested, making himself comfortable in the booth across from her.

"Thank you for meeting me," said Jessica.

"No problem," replied Patrick. "Now that we have the pleasantries out of the way, please enlighten me as to why you requested a meeting with me for my services."

She handed him the manila envelope. Patrick took the envelope and opened it up. He observed the contents for a while. Jessica studied his face as he did this. She knew what was in the envelope and all the material. Patrick was the first person other than her to look at the contents. She had not shown it to her father, Ulisez, Amy, Scotti, or even Jon.

"I am investigating my mother's death," said Jessica. Patrick kept his eyes on the files.

"I'm listening," he replied.

"When I was 12 years old, we were walking in Newport Beach and she was violently run over by a car and left for dead."

"Oh, I'm sorry."

"The thing is," Jessica went on. "I think it was intentional and I think she was killed before she was hit."

"Do you have proof?" he asked.

Jessica took out more content from the file. Patrick stared at it with astonishment, not believing what he was looking at.

"How did you get these?"

"I'd rather not say," replied Jessica.

"You're in pretty deep, aren't you?"

"She was my mother. I have to know the truth."

"What do you think happened?"

She hesitated for a moment. She felt like Patrick could understand everything based on the toxicology reports, but wanted to hear it from her. That was her impression on how things went, and she was sure he knew enough to recognize what he saw in the report.

"Four bullets in her body according to the toxicology reports," she told him.

"Do you believe she was shot?"

"Absolutely. I know she was shot."

"Have you told anyone else about this?"

Jessica shook her head.

"What do you need from me?" asked Patrick.

"I need you to help me find out where the bullets came from," she said. "Once we do that, we can find out who manufactured the gun. Once that happens, I will have the evidence I need."

"This happened ten years ago. It can be difficult."

"If anyone can do it, you can," replied Jessica.

"I appreciate the vote of confidence,"

"And I'd like some secrecy on your part."

She pulled out another envelope and slid it across the counter.

"Of course," said Patrick. "Not a word. I'll have some information as soon as I can."

They shook hands, agreeing to a partnership.

A little later at Jessica's apartment, there was a knock on the door and Jessica went to answer it and Jon was standing there. She could tell he looked uncomfortable.

"Hey," her voice rang with awkwardness.

"I wanted to check on you."

"Two days later."

She motioned for Jon to enter the apartment. And he did. They walked inside and Jessica closed the door behind her.

"I should probably explain," said Jon.

"You think?"

"My life is complicated."

"Complicated usually means being screwed up from something. You are literally trying to kill a man!"

"Well, not trying.."

"Oh, I forgot, you're just blowing up his property. Baby steps right Jon?"

"To be fair, they're bad guys with lots of guns.."

"And that makes it right?"

"What are you, the morality police?"

She placed her hand on his head gently.

"What the hell happened to you?"

"A lot."

She released her hold on him. She had a lot of mixed emotions. A part of her wanted to beat the crap out of Jon, and the other part wanted to kiss him.

"What are you going to do next?" she asked, not knowing if she wanted the answer.

"He knows my connection to you," said Jon. "I have to make sure he never goes after you again."

"I can take care of myself, Jon. My dad gave me self-defense lessons when I was young."

He shook his head. "Caine's power does not care about your self-defense."

"Worry more about yourself, Jon. I'm fine."

Jon sighed. "Just please be careful."

Before he could leave, Jessica grabbed Jon's arm. "Something else is wrong, what's up?" Jessica could tell that he had something to say, but was not sure of how to go about it. She placed her hand on his face, and he pulled back for a moment as if he were afraid.

"What's up with you? Why did you react like that?"

"I'm sorry," he apologized.

"There's something you're not telling me."

She scanned his face and sensed something. Jon's face stayed still, not showing anything. Jessica could admit he had a good poker face.

"I spoke with your father earlier," Jon said.

"Oh? What about?"

"I told him about some of what I did when I was in South America."

Jessica listened, not daring to say a word. She wanted to hear what Jon had to say, as she too was curious.

"I was kidnapped by sex slave traders," Jon continued, and Jessica placed her hands over her face in horror. "A man named Armando Escobar saved me. What I told your dad, simple enough; Escobar killed them. He killed them to save me. Out of some twist of loyalty, I guess, I stayed with him for six years."

"I don't understand," Jessica interjected. "Who was this guy?"

She saw Jon pause, taking a breath. He resumed.

"He was Armando Escobar, the leader of the Great Command of the Capital, one of the largest cartels in Brazil."

"Was?"

Jon nodded. "I believe he is dead."

Jessica grew uncomfortable. She studied his face and noticed some regret, but mostly sorrow.

"What did you do, Jon?" she asked very matter of fact.

"I burned his house to the ground."

She watched him as he said this and noticed no movement or sign of any regret. The boy she knew and loved once did not exist, replaced by this shell of a man. But was Jon trying to come back to her in his little way?

"What did you do for the next four years?"

"I worked as a bounty hunter for a guy named Ram," Jon replied.

Jessica touched Jon on the shoulder. He looked up at her, confused.

"Why were you so damn nervous?"

"Your dad didn't take all this well, Jess," said Jon, itching his forehead a little. "I did some bad things with some bad people. Stuff I regret."

She continued to comfort him, but now she was curious.

"Why did you come back now?"

"I already told you to destroy Caine."

"No," Jessica shook her head. "I mean, why did you wait until all this time?"

Jon hesitated. She knew that there was something else. If there was one thing Jessica did very well, she could read people. She also could control her temper, unlike her father. The plan was to understand Jon, not to shun him away.

"I met a man named Vladimir Ramirez," Jon recalled. "He bailed me out of a Brazilian jail and helped fortify some of my skills. He sent me here."

Jessica took this in. Now, she knew the truth. She had wondered what Jon had been up to all those years, and now she knew. The guy did not have a choice; he had to be in the cartel or they would have killed him. There was some curiosity about the bounty hunting thing. What must that have been like?

"Where is he now?" she asked.

"I don't know," was what he said, and Jessica knew that he was telling the truth.

She was not sure what to do. Jon looked down in sadness, and she saw a side of him she had not seen since childhood.

"I'm so sorry you went through all that," Jessica consoled him. She placed her hand on Jon's shoulder. For a moment, it was that. Something happened. She felt something inside her grow as if it were butterflies. This could not be love, she was positive she did not love Jon, least not yet. However, at that moment, she felt something tender for him and wanted to share it with him as much as she could.

Her entire body tingled. Her eyes met Jon's, and they stayed quiet for a moment. Suddenly, the darkness in her life did not matter. They locked eyes, intense and focused. They both leaned in and their lips met.

She felt the sensation as she kissed Jon. Her eyes closed as she enjoyed the tender moment. She felt him press forward, and the feeling of his lips against hers sent a wonderful shiver down her spine.

They pulled apart and just stared at one another for a moment. This was a moment she had not seen coming, but one she had fantasized about. This little stare down continued for a moment, and it was like they were having eye sex. Jon stood up, and Jessica continued to look at him.

"I have to go," he lamented.

Jon stood up, and Jessica watched him open, and the door and leave. She felt more secure in her feelings for Jon but more confused about what they were now.

A couple of hours later, there was a knock at the door and Jessica went to answer it. Hudson stood at the door. Jessica made a motion with her right hand, signaling him to come in. She shut the door softly behind him and he turned around.

"You know why I am here right?" Hudson inquired.

"To warn me about the evil Jon Drake," Jessica replied sarcastically.

"Cut it out Jessie Bear," Hudson's voice was sharp. "He is a killer."

"Oh, he's a killer now?" Jessica played this game with her father several times, so this was not new. "Because he told you about some things he did in South America? So that makes him a bloodthirsty killer?"

"So he told you?"

"Yes, he told me, dad. Jon has been nothing but straightforward with me."

"And you're okay with this? You're okay with the fact that he has killed people?"

"Jesus, dad! He hasn't killed innocent children, he killed cartel members."

"And that makes it okay?"

Jessica scoffed. "You judge him too harshly."

"I cannot condone his behavior."

"Condone? Or course you wouldn't condone anything, dad. You're too blind to see that Jon wanted to confide in you, and you turned on him."

"I did not turn on him."

"Yes you did," cried Jessica. "You didn't even give him a chance to make amends when he was opening up to you."

"Were you aware of the fact that he is targeting Alexander Caine?"

She said nothing. She was not sure if Hudson was acting as a father or as a detective.

"So you are," Hudson noted. "You were aware of it and you didn't notify the police, me or even Ulisez."

"Would you turn me in?"

Hudson hesitated. She scoffed again. She walked over to the kitchen sink and got some water for her father and returned to hand it to him. Hudson took the water and nodded in thanks and drank it.

"You have to know he's dangerous," Hudson warmed.

"He's Jon, my Jon, your Jon," Jessica countered, then made a motion with her hands. "Our Jon. I am not just going to abandon him because you don't like what he had to tell you."

Hudson just stared at Jessica like she was speaking another language. He shook his head and sighed. Jessica sat beside him.

"Jon is someone you cared for at one point," she continued. "You adopted him. Sure, it was not official yet, but he lived in our house for a month after they killed his dad. He was like a son to you.

"Do you really want to cast him out? Do you really want to turn your back on him after he made his way back to town?"

"He's back in town to kill Caine," Hudson corrected her.

"Which is why we need to be equally vigilant in our efforts to help him," she insisted.

"I want to help him," Hudson conceded. "But not if he will keep trying to kill Alexander Caine."

"At least he's making a move against Caine," Jessica fired back. "What have you done?"

"I have tried my best to bring that evil bastard down," Hudson protested.

"Not good enough."

"You don't understand how powerful he is. He is connected with the right people and it makes it difficult to bring someone like him down."

"And while you have allowed him to escape prosecution on a technicality, many other people have suffered at his hands. When will it end dad?"

Hudson did not answer. Instead, he stood up and headed toward the door. He opened it and shut it behind him, leaving a loud thud as he closed it behind him. She worried about her father sometimes, but most of all, she worried about whether he could ever forgive himself for allowing her mother to die.

Chapter 15: The Deathstalker

That Same Day

Vladimir made his way into his new home in Laguna Beach. He had made the transaction in secret and under an alias. While he admired Jon Drake, he did not completely trust him. There was also another reason Vladimir was in town. Someone had alerted him that there would be an attempt on Jon's life, and it would not be from any normal thug. It would be from a ruthless mercenary who was efficient as he was deadly.

So Vladimir had bought the home in Laguna Beach. They would not be here for a long time. He did this to have a place to stay, and one for his warriors to inhabit.

The house had seven bedrooms, seven bathrooms, and was about 9,500 square feet. The house was on a small hill next to the ocean, with a 40-foot drop directly below. The main bedroom on the second floor had a large glass window overlooking the ocean. There was also a balcony parallel to the master bedroom. Vladimir's master bedroom was toward the back of the house, while six bedrooms were on other sides. He had purposely bought this property because it was the best place to house his warriors. He could not put his people at a hotel, for risk of arousing suspicion. There would be no renting either. He bought the house for $22 million. The Legion of Samurai had gained a lot of money over the years, mostly through investigative jobs. While they were a secret organization, there were a select few that knew of them and paid them handsomely for favors. Vladimir had turned the Legion of Samurai from a small army in the mountains to an extensive empire with many affiliates. They had been around for centuries but now contained unlimited wealth.

He stood in one bedroom, used as a training room. Manny stood beside him. Two men and a woman entered the room. The first man was Kareem, a lanky, skinny black man with no facial hair or hair on top of his head. He wore black all over his body, hiding his skinny frame. The next man was Bao, a Vietnamese man with a strong build, a bald head. He wore a muscle shirt and black pants. The woman was Elicia, a beautiful blonde-haired woman with a face that could seduce any man, and quickness that could just as easily destroy him. She wore black pants and a tank top to match. These three were among the most talented members of the Legion of Samurai.

He faced them and waited as they finished their training. They looked at him and knelt obediently, including Manny.

"You have one job today, find the one they call the Deathstalker, and bring him here," Vladimir commanded.

"Your wish is our command," Kareem responded.

Then, like obedient soldiers, they all vanished. Vladimir sat on the chair in the training room and closed his eyes. He meditated, closing his eyes and letting himself become one with the world.

His senses enhanced during the process and he felt the inner peace flow through him. He was not aware of how long he meditated when he opened his eyes.

He sat in his training room. He sensed something or someone behind him. He did not turn around immediately as there was nothing to fear.

"You need to know your place, Deathstalker," his voice boomed, yet his eyes remained closed.

A man emerged from the shadows. A.J. "The Deathstalker" Walker was a large black man with graying black curly hair and a salty beard that encompassed his face. He wore camouflage armor from top to bottom and he sported a scar on his left cheek, showing a memento from the past. He sported a cap similar to what the British Special Forces wore.

The tension in the room was palpable as the Deathstalker held his weapon of choice; a PKM, a machine gun that could do a lot of damage.

"Call off your men mate," Walker ordered in the most polite way possible. He had an accent when he spoke from the United Kingdom. Vladimir always believed the man was likely from Manchester or Glasgow, but he never could tell.

Vladimir turned around and faced the man holding him at gunpoint. Within seconds, Manny, Elicia, Bao, and Kareem all emerged and stood around Walker with swords drawn. Vladimir motioned for the four of them to stand down, as he lifted his arm in the air to signal authority. Walker held his stance, and Vladimir smiled.

"Tell your people to not come after me," Walker commanded calmly.

"Your assignment conflicts with my vision," replied Vladimir.

"My assignment is one that will land me a lot of money," Walker answered.

They just looked at each other blankly for a moment. Vladimir kept his cool, although he had a PKM aimed at him. Walker could shoot him dead, but there was a greater chance that his soldiers would avenge him, no matter how skilled the Deathstalker was.

"Do you remember how you got that scar?" Vladimir had changed the subject and pointed out the scar on Walker's cheek. The Deathstalker frowned.

"Yes," Vladimir continued as if Walker had answered him. "I searched for you after you killed the Samurai. At the time, it was personal. I looked for you, I found you, and I beat you within an inch of your life. I stabbed you across the face and the only reason I allowed you to live is because you provided me information on my enemies.

"Now, I am asking you Deathstalker, do you really want to cross me and interfere with my plans now?"

Walker said nothing. He held his stance while scanning the room, looking for an escape. Although Walker had a gun aimed at Vladimir, he was the one truly was in danger.

"No, you will not interfere," Vladimir maintained. "You will do what you are told and stand down."

Walker smiled. "Do you know why they call me the Deathstalker?" After I left the British Special Forces, my buddy Rava and I started a business. It didn't do well. We went broke. But then Rava and I came upon a brilliant idea, use the skills we learned from the British Special Forces and put them to good use.

"We started in Palestine. We got involved in the Israeli-Palestinian conflict and they hired us to eliminate bad people. We didn't discriminate. We took jobs from both sides. But the reason I kept getting hired was because of my ability to eliminate every target they assigned me. I never failed to finish a job. They nicknamed me the Deathstalker after the deadly scorpion.

"By that point, I was getting hired by the biggest hard men on the bloody planet. I'm not your regular Joe Bloggs, nor some josser, I'm the Deathstalker, and I always finish the job and I always kill my target.

"Now this manky man paid me a packet to take down the lad and he'd be miffed if I didn't finish. I got no time to muck about. A man hired me to do a job, just like with your master, who I shot in the noggin."

Vladimir did not react to Walker's comment. He just stared at him dead-eyed with a look of ferocity.

"Do what I say," Vladimir ordered.

"I don't look being told what to do," Walker shot back.

"It would be in your best interest to do so this time."

He could see Walker was considering his options. With precision, Walker put his gun down slowly. He packed it into his large holster. Vladimir knew that would happen and had every ounce of confidence that Walker would not shoot him. However, he always prepared to die and if it happened, the Legion of Samurai would continue.

"Do we have an agreement?" he asked.

Walker smiled and then reached into his pocket and threw something at the ground before he could react. The room filled with smoke everywhere, and he placed his hand over his nostrils to prevent himself from being knocked out. The tear gas spread throughout the room and he stood in his place as it rose. After a few seconds, the smoke cleared, and Walker disappeared. Vladimir smiled. He found it ironic that Walker had disappeared using a technique made famous by the Legion of Samurai. He would keep his eye on Walker and make sure he did not kill Jon Drake.

After the Deathstalker confrontation, Vladimir made his way into Thomas's house. His sudden appearance surprised the detective. Then Thomas acknowledged him.

"Lion," Thomas looked at him. "I did not expect to see you so soon."

"There is a slight problem, Panther."

There was a history between these two that was familiar, as Thomas knew exactly who Vladimir was and that he had been coming.

"I have been monitoring Jon Drake just like you requested, sir," Thomas insisted.

"Jon Drake is not the problem, at least not yet directly. We have an additional problem, or an old one, as you may recognize."

"What is it, sir?"

"The Deathstalker has returned, and he has a contract from Alexander Caine to kill Jon Drake."

Thomas's face sponged up, and his brows furrowed. Vladimir understood the feeling as the Deathstalker had humiliated Thomas in a fight once, and he surely wanted his revenge. But he had to make Thomas understand that this was not about revenge, but about the mission at hand.

"We should have killed him when we had the chance," Thomas remarked.

"Be that as it may," Vladimir replied. "We must prevent him from killing Jon Drake."

"Why do you care so much about Jon Drake? He's a loose cannon. I don't even think he will accomplish his mission."

"Jon Drake has too much potential to simply give up on. And I believe he is too smart to betray me right now."

Thomas did not reply. He knew that Thomas did not like Jon, but he knew that the Panther did not like a lot of people. It was in his nature to dislike everything.

"You were once a loose cannon," Vladimir reminded him. "Then you joined the Legion of Samurai and found a place, a home where you could channel that anger. Now, look at you."

Vladimir and Thomas stared at one another, with each giving a knowing glance. He placed his hand on the detective's shoulder.

"You are one of my best," he told him.

"I will do my best to keep him alive," Thomas reassured him.

Chapter 16: The Samurai

July 15th, 2007 Inside the Legion of Samurai Fortress

Vladimir meditated with the Samurai. He had known this man for 11 years now and had fully ascended to the third in command of the Legion of Samurai. The Samurai was still the beloved leader of the Legion of Samurai, and Diego was the second in command. Occasionally, there was tension between the two, but Diego respected the Samurai and vice versa. There would be no plans of treason or double-cross. Besides, the Samurai was in his late 60s anyway, so they expected him to retire soon and pass the mantle to Diego and Vladimir, anyway.

In his 11 years with the Legion of Samurai, they had taught him every fighting technique possible. Vladimir had ascended quickly and even raised his children here. Ivan had grown so strong, as he was now 15 years old, and quickly training to be a member of the Legion himself. Nubia would be 13 later that year, and Vladimir encouraged her to educate herself on everything possible. He did not want this life for his children, so he encouraged them to further their interests. They did not remember their mother much, and that broke Vladimir's heart. Vladimir did his best to raise them, and he had a lot of help from members of the Legion. Diego had become a sort of a surrogate uncle to Ivan and Nubia. The Samurai had almost become like a grandfather. Manny had become like another brother to them. The only thing disappointing to Vladimir was the lack of women in the Legion. Vladimir did not wish to remarry or anything of that sort, but he wished his children had a motherly influence.

He continued to meditate. It was his favorite thing to do before training. The Samurai had taught him so much over the years, but meditation had been the best thing. It allowed Vladimir to clear his mind, and his soul. He still felt a lot of anger about his wife's murder, despite avenging it. Meditation helped set him right. The Samurai being there also helped.

He continued this practice, and the Samurai stood up. Vladimir opened his eyes slowly. The Samurai standing up usually meant the session was over. He reached over and placed his hand on Vladimir's shoulder.

"My friend, you have come a long way since your early days," said the Samurai.

"Thank you, Samurai," replied Vladimir.

"Come," said the Samurai. "I wish to give you something."

He followed the Samurai into his private quarters. The Samurai took out a lockbox and opened it, bringing out a necklace. He gazed at the necklace in awe and the Samurai handed it to him.

"This is a necklace that has been part of the Legion for centuries. The previous leader handed it to me and I am handing it to you," said the Samurai.

Vladimir took the necklace and held it in his hands with care. No one had ever given him anything of sentiment to him before. He looked at the Samurai and hugged him, taking the old man by surprise.

"Thank you, sir," said Vladimir.

"You are welcome, Lion," replied the Samurai.

As they stood there, the sound of an explosion rang outside their fortress. Vladimir and the Samurai took cover. Then the Samurai looked at Vladimir.

"Make sure the children are secure, we are under attack!" say,

The Samurai and Vladimir left the private quarters and headed for the main halls of the fortress. More explosions rang out and Vladimir saw his children running toward him along with Manny.

"Dad! We're being attacked!" said Ivan.

"Go hide in the basement, you too, Manuel," said Vladimir.

"But dad, I want to..."

"Do what I say, Ivan," he ordered his son.

Ivan looked at Nubia and Manny, and that was the sign to go. The young teenagers headed toward the basement. Vladimir and the Samurai prepared themselves and armed themselves with swords and knives. Diego emerged and stood in front of them.

"What is the meaning of this?" asked the Samurai.

"Sir, we are under attack by two assassins! They caused the explosions!" replied Diego.

As they said this, a man entered from the stairs. Vladimir, Diego, and the Samurai turned to face him. The man had someone with him.

Vladimir looked at these men and knew them based on reputation. The tall black man in camouflage gear was A.J. "The Deathstalker" Walker. His friend, an English Indian, was Rava Blackwell.

"We're only here for the old man," said Walker. "Step aside and no one else gets hurt."

Diego charged toward them both before Vladimir and the Samurai could react and Blackwell sidestepped him and they both went down the stairs, tumbling while punching each other. Vladimir faced off with Walker, intending to fight. Vladimir and Walker exchanged sword swipes, with each matching the other. Walker nudged him off.

"You're good," said Walker.

"Better than you," said Vladimir.

"Not quite," replied Walker.

They again exchanged sword swipes, with each clanging the other's weapon, neither drawing blood. Finally, Walker moved back a few feet.

"I don't got time for this," said Walker.

He took out a Baretta 92FSS handgun gun and quickly fired hitting Vladimir in the leg wounding him. The Lion fell to the ground in severe pain as the blood started gushing out. He screamed in agony as this happened. The Samurai bent down to tend to Vladimir, then he stood up and faced off with the Deathstalker.

"Finally, the main event," Walker boasted.

Walker stared down at the Samurai for a second and grinned as the old man picked up his Katana sword. He gripped it while the Deathstalker drew his Baretta.

Walker fired off another round and the Samurai leaped off the ground in catlike fashion, evading the gunfire with precision. Vladimir watched as this unfolded, seeing this almost 70-year-old man jumping to avoid getting shot.

The Samurai pressed forward with his sword and swung it at Walker, barely missing him. The Deathstalker then connected with a blow to the midsection, knocking the old man off balance.

Vladimir, while tending to his pain, watched in horror at what happened next. Walker grabbed his Baretta and looked at Vladimir.

"Watch this, you'll learn something," said Walker.

Walker fired several rounds into the Samurai's chest, mortally wounding him as Vladimir screamed. The Samurai coughed up blood as his stomach bled out all over the place. He clutched his stomach to stop the blood, but that proved pointless. Vladimir watched as the Samurai stumbled, losing his balance, before collapsing to the ground, dying from his injuries. Walker turned to Vladimir and stood on him, with his boot pressed to Vladimir's chest. He was helpless to do anything.

"I would kill you, but I don't do that for free," said Walker. "Consider yourself lucky."

Walker took his boot off and walked away. Vladimir watched as Diego and Blackwell came back up the stairs and then Walker clobbered Diego across the face, knocking him out on the stairwell, but still alive. He watched as Walker and Blackwell left as quickly as they arrived. And they had crippled the entire Legion of Samurai beyond belief.

Vladimir crawled over to the Samurai and knelt next to him. He ignored the seething pain in his leg and just had a moment with a man he considered a father. Vladimir cried as he laid on top of the Samurai's lifeless body, knowing things would never be the same.

The Legion of Samurai held a ceremony for Franco "The Samurai" Yuan. The Legion of Samurai was without a leader and it was a unanimous decision to have Diego take over. Vladimir had no issues with it. He loved Diego like a brother and fully supported him. There would be no fight over the title of leader.

The Legion of Samurai and all their warriors lined up in a circle around the crypt where the Samurai laid to rest. Diego led the ritual and Vladimir was second-in-command.

"Our beloved Samurai is gone," Diego began in Portuguese. "But we will go on. We will continue to fight the good fight and destroy all the evil and wickedness in this world. I have tasked myself and Vladimir with finding out who ordered the kill. Catching the killer is not as important as catching the men that gave the word. But mark my word, we will."

Diego unleashed some smoke, which was a tradition with the funerals held by the Legion of Samurai. Vladimir found it odd that Diego did not want to catch the man that committed the crime. But then he figured that there were at least three cartels that could have potentially ordered the hit. The Legion had been actively sabotaging the Brazilian cartels as much as they could over the years. This was their way of fighting evil on the ground. Their other affiliates around the world worked to fight other cartels, and they were growing every day.

Vladimir realized that they likely would have to deal with them all. The best way to deal with the cartels was swift violence. That was the only method that evil men understood.

Following the ceremony, Diego and Vladimir meditated. Now, as leader of the Legion of Samurai, Diego collaborated more with Vladimir. There had been a rumbling at the front door. Vladimir feared the worst.

Vladimir and Diego made their way out slowly, expecting the worse. Instead, they saw their men walking in side by side with another man whom they did not recognize. Vladimir noticed the man. He was a strong viral black man. The man probably was about 18 years old. He walked over to the man and motioned for his men to let the man go. "State your case, young man," said Vladimir.

The young man looked up at Vladimir. The Lion could see that this man was distressed, even without displaying it so much on his face.

"I have searched long and far for this place,"

"State your name," said Vladimir.

"Martin. Thomas Martin."

"Why are you here?" asked Vladimir.

Thomas put his head down. There was sadness in his demeanor. Something terrible had happened to him. Vladimir sensed it.

"I am here to forge a path to destroy all evil," said Thomas.

"As we all are," replied Vladimir. "What are your demons?"

"My brother," Thomas began. "My baby brother, they killed him."

Oh, Vladimir thought. He had expected something like this. No one comes to the Legion of Samurai without some element of tragedy in their background. Everyone in this room has either lost someone or watched someone they cared for die. Vladimir placed his hand on Thomas' right shoulder. The young man had a lot of anger in him, and Vladimir knew he had to help him channel it. Thomas looked up at Vladimir.

"You are now our brother, we will help you. We will mold you and we will strengthen you. You will never feel the pain you feel ever again," said Vladimir to Thomas.

Vladimir placed his hand on Thomas. He turned to face the warriors, and Diego emerged. He approached Thomas. Diego extended his hand.

"Welcome to the Legion of Samurai, Panther," said Diego.

Thomas acknowledged his new nickn1ame. He returned the handshake. The two men embraced with Vladimir looking on.

Chapter 17: The Blindside

January 30th, 2016

    Jon was at the shipyards in Newport Beach. Caine was still up to his old antics. Jon could not stay away. He had to destroy this man. Caine killed his father, and there was no way Jon would let that stand. He studied these men, monitoring every single person's movement. Jon picked a discreet location, a block away. He had not yet decided what he would do. There had to be a way to take down these men and set their supplies on fire. Before Jon could do anything, a shot rang out, and out of instinct he ducked. A bullet went right through his windshield, destroying it. More gunfire rang out and Jon took cover. He crawled out the passenger window. He felt that he had no choice. If he stayed in the car, he was a dead man. The gunfire stopped and Jon took cover behind the car, looking everywhere, trying to locate the source.

    "And I thought I was hard to kill," said a familiar voice.

    Jon turned toward it and instantly recognized who it was. His eyes grew large with horror and anger. He could not believe it.

    "Deathstalker," he confirmed.

    "Are we going by code names now Drake? Or should I say, White Warrior?"

    Walker stood in front of Jon with a gun in hand. They had met nine years ago when Jon was 13 years old, and a little before his 14th. They encountered each other again in Rio when Jon became a bounty hunter at 18 years old. That encounter was not as friendly as the first, as Jon was to prevent Walker from assassinating someone. It did not go so well. By that point, Jon knew exactly what type of man A.J. Walker was. He had learned that the man that saved his life at 14 was a contracted killer. That was when he knew him by the name Deathstalker, the scorpion that delivers the strongest poison in Africa. Jon learned about this when he met Walker the second time.

    Everything Walker touched died. He had a perfect kill record.

    "Why are you here, Walker?" asked Jon.

    "It's simple," said Walker, positioning his PKM machine gun. "Some slap-head wants you dead. Now hold still lad and don't be a prat."

He rushed the assassin and tackled him to the ground, attempting to take him by surprise. Walker threw him off and retook control. The Deathstalker got on top of Jon and punched him in the face. He felt the blow of the large man's fist connecting with his face and blood spurt out.

Walker connected with an elbow to the face, drawing even more blood. The Deathstalker then pummeled Jon with repeated blows, and there was not much he could do as he felt the brush of his fist hit him over and over, in a fluid motion. Walker had meant to shoot him. It was clean and it was simple. But Jon had avoided getting shot. This current situation was Walker improvising. He did what he could to cover his face, but Walker kept removing his hands and continuing the beating. He felt his eyes swell up, and his face felt like an old catcher's glove. Walker was relentless in the attack, and Jon knew this. This was why they called him the Deathstalker.

He could not let Walker kill him, he had too much to do. Now, he realized exactly why the Deathstalker was here. He rolled out of the way of another punch and unleashed a flurry of kicks that took Walker by surprise. The assassin backed off slightly as Jon made contact. Walker took out a Baretta handgun and began firing. Jon evaded each shot with precision, but one bullet grazed him in the shoulder, causing him to yelp in pain. He looked at the shoulder and checked for any blood and cursed silently to himself for getting grazed. He then took cover behind another car. Walker kept firing. Jon wondered how much ammunition this guy had.

"You are only delaying the inevitable, Drake."

"Nothing inevitable here, Walker."

"It's not personal lad, I have a job to do."

"Killing me sounds personal to me."

Walker was like a machine, and he would not relent. Jon was in terrible pain from the beating he took from the Deathstalker. He could blackout at any moment and he knew that there would be no coming back if that happened. There had to be a way to get out of this situation for now. There was no good staying here.

He would have to retreat for now until he was better prepared. Jon took out what was in his pocket, and it was exactly what he needed. He flung it in Walker's direction and smoke started spewing out. Walker calmly put a mask on.

"Really, Drake? Tear gas pellets? Are you pickled again? Did you forget who I am?"

The smoke continued and when it cleared, Jon was in front of Walker. He grabbed his claw gun and flung it at Walker, and it struck the assassin in the left eye, wounding him. Jon yanked on the grapple and pulled, causing Walker distress.

"Ah!!!" screamed Walker as Jon took it out after making contact.

The Deathstalker was bleeding a little from the eye, and Jon had to make a choice. He could continue to engage in a fight with Walker and potentially risk getting hurt more. Or he could retreat and heal himself. He chose the latter. There would be another day to fight Walker now that he knew that the assassin was in town and that he was working for Caine. Walker did not have to tell him that, but the implication was enough to speak volumes.

"Until next time, Deathstalker," said Jon.

Jon pounded on the door and Jessica opened it and it horrified her to see him standing there bruised and beaten.

"Oh my God, Jon!"

She held Jon in her arms and he passed out. Jessica looked at him and noticed all the bruises and the injuries he had suffered all over his face. He did not know how long he was out when he woke up to Jessica staring down at him.

"What the hell happened?" asked Jon.

"Obviously someone beat the crap out of you," said Scotti.

Jon sat up and looked around and spotted Scotti and Amy. They had been there the whole time.

"Hey slutty is here," said Jon.

"It's Scotti you stupid piece of shit!"

"I honestly stopped caring five seconds ago."

"Asshole," replied Scotti.

Jon smirked at Scotti. He turned to Amy.

"You're here too? This is like a Caine kids reunion. Missing the brother though."

"Why are you such a dick?" asked Amy.

"Who did this to you?" asked Jessica.

"Deathstalker," replied Jon.

"An African scorpion?" asked Scotti.

They all turned to her, surprised.

"What? I read," she replied.

"No, it was a man they call the Deathstalker," said Jon. "His name is A.J. Walker. I met him when I lived in Brazil. I encountered him a few times. He's a paid killer."

"What's he doing here? Why did he do this to you?" asked Jessica.

"Caine paid him to kill me," said Jon.

"You got to be kidding me," said Amy.

"Not this bullshit again," said Scotti.

"Can these two leave?" asked Jon to Jessica. "They're going to annoy me."

"Screw you, Jon! You're the one accusing our father of attempted murder!" said Amy.

"Yeah, what are we supposed to do? Take it up the ass?" added Scotti.

"Can you guys leave us to talk, please?" asked Jessica.

Amy and Scotti gave Jessica a look.

"Are you kidding me?" asked Amy.

"I'll text you later. I promise," said Jessica.

Amy scoffed. Scotti grabbed her leather jacket and put it on. The sisters left without saying another word. They slammed the door behind them. Now, Jon and Jessica were alone. She turned toward Jon, who was still on the couch, laid out.

"Okay, the truth now," she commanded.

"About?"

"How were you in a position to get the shit beat out of you like this?" asked Jessica.

"Because I get a thrill out of being beaten," joked Jon.

Jessica chopped his chest. He yelped in pain. She knew he was still in pain.

"What the hell was that for?!"

"For being cute with me," she said.

"So you think I'm cute?"

Jessica smiled. "Don't flatter yourself." She grabbed the washcloth and applied it to his wounds. There were many wounds. "We all loved your dad, Jon. But this approach you're taking is just asking to be killed. Look at all these bruises. How did this Deathstalker get the jump on you?"

"I never knew he was coming."

"How are you still alive?"

"I stabbed him in the eye with a claw gun. Was able to get away."

"Wow. Just when I thought you have told me everything, you…"

"I had no choice, Jess. It was either do that or stay there and get killed."

"Jon listen," she began. "You have to change your approach. Maybe I can help?"

He shook his head. "No one can help me. Caine needs to pay for what he did."

"Jon, you know what happened to my mother. I am looking for justice. Justice is your best goal, not revenge."

"That's you, Jess," said Jon. "But that's you. I need to do what works for me."

"And is destroying Caine's empire and killing him going to bring your father back?"

It was a good question. He figured someone would ask him that, eventually. He did not expect it to be Jessica. He did not respond to her question because he hated that question.

"Jon," she went on. "I am hiring a private investigator to look into my mother's murder."

This intrigued him. "How long have you been planning this?"

"For quite some time," she replied. "She was murdered and the case still hasn't been solved nearly a decade later. I want answers and I want justice."

He slowly sat up. She did not stop him this time. He grabbed the washcloth from her hand and used his hand to place it on his forehead.

"I wish you could go my path," she said. "I don't want you locked on this suicide mission."

He listened intently. He stared at her face and realized how beautiful she was. Jon had always known she was beautiful. Even back then, Jon knew she was a pretty girl. Jessica had grown into a beautiful woman, only she did not seem to see that.

"And this is something that might be bigger than you," she went on. "I just want you to.."

He kissed Jessica on the lips, mainly to stop her from talking. But he enjoyed it. At first, Jessica did not appreciate this. But after a second or two, she fell into it. After kissing him back, she pulled away.

"What the hell are you doing?"

"I couldn't help it," he sheepishly admitted.

Jessica slapped his shoulder and he groaned in pain.

"You're lucky I like you."

"You're lucky I tolerate you."

She grabbed the washcloth from Jon and resumed cleaning his cuts. He looked at Jessica the entire time she did this, admiring her.

He spent the night sleeping it off on her couch and then left of his own accord. He did not want to be occupying too much of her time. So he sulked. The city was pleasant at this time of year, as it was not too hot and a little chilly. Jon had learned to enjoy walking back in Brazil, and he continued that tradition back home. While there were many options like ride shares, he preferred to use his feet.

Around lunchtime, he made his way into the Orange Grove Bar and Grill. He seemed to have established a second home here.

Jon sat at the bar at the Orange Grove Bar and Grill. He unloaded on a beer or two. He had been soaking up his wounds since yesterday. After he had left Jessica's apartment, Jon had gone home to recover from Deathstalker's attack. He still had the bruises all over. Jon wondered why Walker was here. After their last encounter, Jon figured he earned Walker's respect. They were not always on the same side, but there was a mutual understanding between Jon and Walker. The White Warrior and the Deathstalker had gone to battle a few times, and Jon had lost each time. Not that Jon was bad, far from it. The British Special Forces had trained Walker, and the Deathstalker had over-matched Jon every time. He never beat the Deathstalker, and that weighed on his mind.

He stared at his shot glass with the alcohol. The alcohol was all that helped him when dealing with immense pain, either literal or figurative.

He pounded another shot and Scotti appeared before him.

"How does your liver not explode?"

"Years of practice, Sloppy."

"Scotti."

"Whatever."

He took another shot. He was not sure how many he had drunk by this point. The alcohol went down smoothly compared to the old days. He did not care anymore. Jon's wounds still hurt, but the alcohol numbed it down.

"You still look like shit," said Scotti.

"You're not exactly a beauty queen yourself," He shot back.

Scotti flipped him off. Jon returned the gesture. As this happened, Ulisez slid into the bar and sat next to Jon.

"Calm down One-Beer Jon," he said. Ulisez turned to Scotti. "Can I get a beer, Scotti?"

"Sure thing Ulisez," said Scotti, her demeanor changing from toxic annoyance toward Jon into respect and admiration for Ulisez.

As she went to get the beer, Ulisez patted Jon on the back. This kind of annoyed him, but he took it since it was Ulisez.

"What do you want?" Jon grumbled as he sipped his rum.

"I heard about you getting your ass kicked. Heard it was A.J."

Jon grunted in annoyance. He had forgotten that Ulisez met A.J. Walker once before. Jon was there when it happened.

"Yeah, Deathstalker is back and he wants me dead," said Jon as he took another shot. The rum went to the back of his throat as he swallowed it on one take. He was actively trying to get drunk, but it was not taking. He figured getting drunk would help him with the wounds that Walker gave him.

Scotti came back, flashed Ulisez a smile, and handed him his beer. He nodded thanks and she returned it with her eyes. Their eyes met for a moment and Jon noticed an attraction between the two. Scotti smiled again, then shyly walked off.

"Uh oh," said Ulisez, almost mockingly.

"Yeah uh oh is right," said Jon, slightly groaning. "Walker wants to kill me."

Jon motioned for Scotti and she came back. Her expression was less enthusiastic for Jon than it was for Ulisez.

"Another Sloppy," said Jon.

"For the thousandth time it's Scotti you alcoholic piece of shit," she said.

"That's not exemplary customer service," replied Jon mockingly.

Scotti rolled her eyes. She grabbed another shot of rum over the rocks and handed it to Jon. He admired how much disdain she had for him and how he could drive her nuts. Jon knew her name was Scotti but got a rise out of purposely mispronouncing it to see her reaction. What could he say, he was an asshole. He took pride in it.

He gave her a folded up 20 dollar bill and then motioned for her to keep it. She did this without smiling. Scotti went back to helping other customers.

"What are we going to do?" asked Ulisez.

Jon took his shot of rum. He downed it quickly before Ulisez even knew it was there. The alcohol just soothed every bruise. It tasted terrible, but it did the trick.

"We are not going to do anything," replied Jon, emphasizing the high pitch in the word 'we'. "I will figure this out and get Deathstalker off my back."

Jon abruptly left Ulisez sitting there with his beer. He had to do this on his own. After a while, Jon departed the bar and left Ulisez to attend to his own devices.

Chapter 18: The Walker of Death

July 11th, 2007 in São Paulo

Jon knew his 14th birthday was near. But that no longer mattered. He had lived and trained with cartel leader Armando Escobar for about 17 months now. It had been a rough transition at first, but Jon knew no other life. Escobar, despite his ruthlessness, offered him the opportunity to go home. Jon told him that there was not a home to go back to. That was not the truth. Jon still had Hudson, Jessica, and Ulisez back home. Escobar and the Great Command of the Capital had trained him on everything. They taught him how to properly run drugs across certain checkpoints, how to spy on rivals, and how to defend himself. While Jon still was a teenage boy, he already had gained some adroit moves. Escobar conducted most of Jon's training, with some help from his number one guy, Geo. Jon liked Geo because he was not much older than him. Jon believed Geo was about seven years older by his count.

Jon walked into the Historic Center, acting on instructions from Escobar and Geo. He was told to look for anything suspicious, or anyone that might be a potential rival. Tourists were everywhere, but this was also a popular spot for spies and people associated with the other cartels.

Their major rivals were the Orange Command. There were three other cartels, but Jon did not know much about them. Escobar had briefed him a little on them but stated that they posed only a minor threat to their army. Jon felt great being part of an enormous army, even if it was one that killed people. He stopped caring about all that long ago when Alexander Caine murdered his father senselessly.

As he walked through the Historic Center, he noticed two shadows near him. Jon moved forward, without running, to evade them. The two shadows were on his tail, moving closer the further Jon went. Finally, he turned into an alley and was almost to the other side when one man got in his path. Then he turned around and noticed the other man had blocked his exit. They trapped him!

He looked back and forth toward each man's direction. Jon spotted something on their bodies. They were orange tattoos, displaying that they belonged to the Orange Command. Jon had never felt as much fear in his life as he did right now. Escobar and Geo were nowhere near him, and he had nowhere to go. Jon realized he may die right there and then. Suddenly, he heard two gunshots. He flinched when this happened and covered his eyes. Then, after a few seconds, Jon opened his eyes only to realize that the two men were on the ground. Someone had shot them down and they plopped to the ground like sacks of potatoes.

He looked everywhere, searching for the source of the gunshots. He heard a clanging of a ladder and looked up to see a looming man sliding down the ladder from above. Jon was in awe as he watched this all take place. It was a large black man with broad shoulders. He wore black camouflage from head to toe. The clothes he wore included a shirt, a jacket, and black tactical pants. The man had short black hair with a trimmed beard. He approached Jon, who backed away slowly.

"Take it, easy lad, I'm not going to hurt you," said the man. Jon recognized the accent, as it seemed British. "My name is A.J. Walker."

Walker extended his hand and Jon looked at it and then shook it after some hesitation.

"Jon," he replied. "Jon Drake."

They shook hands for a moment. Then Walker released.

"What's a young lad like you doing here in Orange Command territory?" asked Walker.

Jon was not used to anyone speaking English to him down here. Escobar had arranged for several people to teach him Portuguese and even Spanish. He rarely used English these days. So it was odd to see this black British man appear out of nowhere too. It also was convenient that he saved his life from these two men, who would likely kill him.

"Thank you for saving my life," said Jon, ignoring his question. Escobar had warned him that the cartels always had someone potentially spying for them, just as he spied for them. While Jon was grateful that Walker saved his life, he did not trust him. There was something off about him.

"You're welcome," said Walker in a calming voice.

Walker did not move. Jon noticed all his weapons, at least the ones that were visible. He noticed a gigantic sword over his right shoulder, and two guns in his coat pockets. There were a couple of knives also layered inside his jacket, hidden from view, but Jon could see them.

"Who are you?" asked Jon. The question took Walker by surprise. He gave Jon a look.

"I told you, lad. My name is Walker. A.J. Walker."

"No," Jon shook his head. "I mean who are you?"

Suddenly, Walker understood the question perfectly. He smiled, admiring Jon's courage and his curiosity.

"I am an independent contractor."

"What does that mean?"

Walker smiled. He placed his gun over his shoulder and clinched it.

"What's a lad like you doing on the streets, anyway?"

"My boss sent me," replied Jon.

"Boss?" asked Walker, curious now. "Aren't you a little young?"

"14," said Jon.

"14, huh? I have a son that is your age. Only he's back in London," said Walker.

"Is that where you're from?" asked Jon.

Walker nodded. "I'm here for work. I am after someone. Maybe you can help me."

The man took out a photo and it was a picture of an old man. Jon did not recognize it. Later, he would realize that Walker had shown him a picture of the Samurai, the leader of the Legion of Samurai.

"Very well then," said Walker. "Stay safe, lad."

Walker left Jon to his own devices. The young man watched as the intimidating man walked away.

Chapter 19: The Cliff

February 1st, 2016

  Jon made his way to Brea. A man was working on some audio tracks. He had dirty blonde hair and glasses to cover his brown eyes. He had a tooth that was a little darker than the other teeth, and it looked cracked. The man was tall, standing at about six feet two inches. He wore a simple v-neck gray t-shirt and black khaki pants. But that did not matter. This was his studio. The man was listening to some people playing instruments and it was boring him. But he plodded on because he was getting paid.

  After a few minutes, the session was over and the man saw them off. He walked back into his office when he noticed a shadowy figure. Jon Drake showed himself to the man, startling him.

  "Who are you? How did you get in here?"

  "Are you Mike Wilson?"

  Mike nodded

  "I heard you are the best at everything sound, whether it comes to preparing live events, and other sound qualities that could be useful," said Jon.

  "How did you get in here?"

  Jon ignored the question.

  "I want to hire you, I need a guy like you. Someone that can get things done like that."

  "First, before I agree to anything, tell me your name, dude," said Mike.

  "Oh sorry," Jon extended his hand. "Jon Drake."

  He shook Mike's hand. He could feel the strong firm grip and had decided that Mike would be perfect. He wanted someone on his team that was smart, capable, and strong.

  "What can I do for you?" asked Mike.

  "Have you ever created audio equipment that can fit in small rooms?"

  "Yes," replied Mike. "But I usually confine most of my work to large sound stages and big shows."

  "I need your services," said Jon.

  "I'm not exactly into that type of work.."

Jon did not say another word. He just pulled out wads of 100 dollar bills and threw it on the table in front of Mike. The musician looked at the money and his jaw dropped. It was clear he had never seen that much money in his life, and Jon threw the entire world at him.

"10,000 dollars to start for the first month," said Jon. "You will get an additional 10000 every month after."

Mike continued to stare at the money. He touched the money, eyed it, and then looked back at Jon. He nodded and extended his hand, and Jon returned it. Jon had a new employee.

After that, Jon went home and slept. When he slept, it was like eternal darkness and he did not dream as much as he used to. Whenever he had some kind of dream, it was usually a nightmare about his dad being shot, or of his time in Brazil.

He must have been in a deep sleep because he heard his cell phone ring. At first, Jon mistakenly thought it was an alarm, but then remembered that he never used alarm clocks. Jon could wake up without warning. He had taught himself how to be vigilant over the years while working for the cartel.

The only person who had his number was Ulisez. He had not even given it out to Jessica or Hudson. He stared at the phone for a moment and saw Ulisez's name pop up. This was weird to Jon because Ulisez never called him. Ulisez usually texted him. He knew that because Ulisez hated calling anyone. If he had to reach Jon, he sent a text message. That is why Jon took a moment. Finally, he answered.

"What do you want?" asked Jon.

"That's not an acceptable way to greet your friends, Drake," said a voice on the other line that was most definitely not Ulisez. Jon recognized it instantly.

"Walker."

"Ah good, you remember me, lad," replied Walker.

He still felt the bruises and the cuts from Walker's last attack. His fight with the Deathstalker had taken a lot out of him, and he still had not recovered. But now the question on his mind was simple: why did Walker call from Ulisez's phone? Something was wrong.

"Where is Ulisez?"

"Was wondering when you would ask lad?"

"If you hurt him, I will—"

"You will what mate?"

Jon hated when Walker called him 'mate' or 'lad' or any other slang from England or Ireland, or wherever the hell he came from. Walker acted like they were old friends most of the time, basically to piss him off.

"Where is he?"

"He's alive, and I have no intention of killing him," replied Walker. "Provided you make your way over here."

"And where exactly is here?"

"Come on lad," replied Walker. "That would be too easy. But I am sure you can trace it and track me down. Looking forward to seeing you."

Click. Walker hung up the phone. Jon recorded every call, but he did not need that here. He had placed a tracker on Ulisez's phone when they last met. He went to his phone and looked up the settings, and then activated the tracer, pinpointed the location, and it shocked him to what came up.

Ulisez and Walker were in Corona Del Mar. But they were not just in Corona Del Mar. According to the tracer, they were on a cliff in Corona Del Mar. That could not be right. Jon wondered how they were on a cliff. The next question he had in his mind was why Walker would want to meet on that cliff.

Jon decided he had done enough thinking. Sometimes, one had to go with the flow. He packed all of his stuff that he knew he would need. Walker would not catch him off guard this time. Jon also knew that the Deathstalker would expect him and be ready. But Jon was the White Warrior. He also had a reputation for being brutal, and he needed to use every ounce if he would save Ulisez. Jon knew that Walker must have taken Ulisez to get to him. But then again, that was not Walker's style. He rarely took hostages. Walker was a mercenary that only went after his target and nothing else. This was not his ordinary way of doing things. Jon shook that all aside.

He started his drive down Jamboree Road, noticing all the trees hunched over. In California, the trees did not fall or wither during the wintertime. The weather was so great that the trees stood standing in California. This week, it had been 90 degrees. Jon felt like he was in the desert. He wondered how this was winter.

There was some traffic on the way down to Corona Del Mar as it had been four o'clock. Jon hated people, even more, when they drove, then when they were in his face. People were stupid, but especially more when they attempted to drive. They usually slammed on their brakes for no reason. He almost crashed into them many times.

He finally got to Pacific Coast Highway after a while. He waited at the light for a moment and wondered where all these people were going. He made a left turn and headed for the coordinates on his tracer. He drove a few blocks until he came upon Poppy Street. There was an area on that street where you could park without someone randomly giving you a ticket or towing you. He did that and then walked down Poppy Street and made his way on the beach.

The sand was mushy as he stepped on it. Growing up, he had never gotten the chance to enjoy the beach. His mother used to take him when he was younger, but after she died, he never went again. Robert, Jon's father, was too heartbroken to do anything with Jon after that. Once Robert died, he found himself in Brazil and stuck in the Great Command of the Capital. Cartels were too busy peddling drugs and killing people to take one of their soldiers to the beach.

As he stepped on the sand, he turned his head left and started walking toward the coordinates. Jon walked a good few blocks and even found himself at the end of the beach. Only, it was not the end of the beach. There were rocks that he had to overcome, and he did. He climbed over these hurdles and made his way past that obstacle. Finally, the beach returned and it was now just private homes. This was Corona Del Mar, where people had a beach in their backyard. The beach was empty mainly, as it was just rocks leading onto the shore. Jon finally glimpsed what he was looking for. The cliff was massive. He knew this area was Cliff Island. The rock itself was Ladder Rock. Jon assessed the situation and the height of the rock. He estimated it was about 25 to 35 feet at length. There was no way to get to the cliff without swimming. So he swam. The swim was decent, as there was not much current. The water was a little cold, at approximately 59 degrees Fahrenheit. Jon learned how to swim from his mother, but he never had time to train his body to withstand cold water. Tropical climates had dominated Brazil, and the water barely went down to 72. He forgot about the cold water and just swam. Finally, Jon got to the edge of the cliff. He climbed. The climb was easy for him, as the Great Command of the Capital had taught him how to climb cliffs. At least Jon could give them credit for one good thing. He finally made his way to the top after a five-minute trek. As he made his way to the top of the rock, Jon glimpsed where his coordinates ended. Walker stood there in all his armor, and Ulisez was sitting down looking like a truck had hit him. Jon scanned him and noticed he was awake, just bruised and battered with cuts everywhere. Walker did this. Jon huffed a little, as the climb had tired him out a little. He looked at Walker.

"What's the big deal about doing this on a cliff Walker?" asked Jon.

Walker smiled. He looked down at Ulisez, then shoved him down in front of him. Jon watched as Ulisez hit the ground with a thud. He did not react. He kept his eyes fixated on Walker.

"I got a job to do, Drake."

"Who is paying you to kill me?"

"Surprised, you don't know. Large bald man, lots of money."

"Caine. How could you do this, A.J.? You know me."

"Like I said before, it's nothing personal," said Walker.

"Me dying feels a little personal to me," said Jon.

Walker chuckled. Then his expression changed. It got real. Walker stared a hole down at Jon. The two seemed to be in an ever-present showdown. Ulisez crawled over to Jon, who looked at him with disdain.

"Get up," said Jon.

"Uh oh," said Ulisez as he continued to stagger.

"Time to die, Drake," said Walker.

"You first, Walker," said Jon.

Both took out their guns and began firing wildly while Ulisez crouched down, covering his ears. He took cover behind a rock as the gunfire sprayed near him.

"Very well done lad, but you're still not as good as me." Walker fired off several more rounds and Jon could hear the Deathstalker getting closer, his footsteps clanking loudly on the gravel as the smoke from the gunfire spread through the air. He peeked over and fired a shot, but knew he hit nothing.

He realized his best chance to get Walker was to cause him to lose his gun. He moved further back, past the rock and around another hard edge.

"Where are you, Jonny boy? I got a present for you, lad," Walker called out like a father coming home for Christmas.

"No one wants your garbage presents, Walker," he heard himself shout out amid the gunfire.

He crept around the rock and finally noticed an angle he could use. Walker ambled methodically around the edge of the other rock, his gun firmly in his hand ready to use.

With every ounce of strength and courage, Jon leaped off his feet and ran shoulder-first into Walker's side. The Deathstalker did not see it coming and lost the grip of his gun.

The two engaged each other in a fistfight, with Jon clobbering the assassin with right fists before Walker recovered and took over, using his head and his left hand for a powerful uppercut. Both men sprung to their feet and Walker took his out PKM Machine Gun.

Shit, Jon thought. He forgot that Walker used three guns.

He never expected the man bringing all of them on top of a cliff. He tried to think of something, anything quickly, as he had a deadly machine gun pointed at him.

"End of the line, lad," said Walker.

Walker aimed his weapon and prepared to fire. Then a shot rang out. Walker's eyes gouged up and Jon noticed him drop his sword. Someone had shot him in the back. Walker looked back and stumbled, and both he and Jon saw the shooter: Vladimir Ramirez. Walker turned around to face Vladimir.

Vladimir fired his gun again, sending a bullet into Walker's chest. The Deathstalker stumbled even more so until finally he lost his balance and fell over the cliff. Jon crawled over and saw Walker fall 25 feet and hit the water, but he could see nothing after. The riptide had grown and everything grew choppy. The waves were intense that day, and Walker's body did not show.

Jon turned back toward Vladimir.

"Vladimir?"

"Hello, Jon," said Vladimir.

"You… you.."

"Avenged the Samurai, my master. I have finally taken the Deathstalker down."

"You shot him! You killed him!"

"I despise using guns," Vladimir tossed the gun over the cliff in disgust and then turned back to Jon. "But it had to happen."

Jon staggered to his feet. He shook his head, attempting to make sense of what happened.

"I believe the words you are looking for is 'thank you'," Vladimir boasted.

"I had it under control!" roared Jon.

"Sure you did," said Vladimir.

"What are you even doing here?"

"I am here to ensure that you are doing what I sent you here for," said Vladimir.

"These things take time."

"Time is of the essence, Jon. You need to finish your mission."

"Got a little sidetracked by the top mercenary in the world trying to kill me!" his voice rose in anger.

"You need to focus."

Ulisez finally staggered to his feet. He leaned next to Jon, who had also picked himself up. Vladimir still had his gun out. Then Ulisez made a mistake.

"He just killed a man," said Ulisez. "I have to, have to, bring him in."

Vladimir smiled. "Fool, I saved your lives."

"It doesn't matter, you have to.."

Ulisez slowly made his way to Vladimir. He faced off with him, but Vladimir used his quickness and wrenched his arm.

"Let him go!" cried Jon.

Vladimir shook his head. "I am tired of games."

Then Vladimir grabbed Ulisez with full force and before Jon could do anything, he hurled Ulisez over the cliff. Jon watched in horror as his best friend went over the edge.

"What the hell!" he roared.

"You have two choices, Jon," said Vladimir. "Bring me down, or save your friend."

Jon looked over the edge and saw Ulisez land in the water. He seemed like he was okay, but then he started seeing him struggle. He turned back to Vladimir.

"Why did you do that?"

"To show you how ruthless I could be," said Vladimir. "You have one week to finish off Caine. If you do not, expect great consequences."

He wanted to punch Vladimir, to take him down. But then he looked over the edge.

"You better save your friend," Vladimir taunted him.

He ran toward the edge and leaped off the cliff. He felt the wind flowing through him as he made the jump. Finally, he hit the water and felt the rush of the cold water. He swam frantically, looking for his friend, and saw something floating in the water. He swam toward it and noticed it was Ulisez. The waves continued to pound him relentlessly. Finally, after a few minutes of struggling, Jon clamped onto Ulisez. He noticed that his friend was unconscious. The urgency suddenly rose. He swam with all his might and Ulisez on his side. His friend's weight was a little larger than his, but he had learned long ago how to carry above his weight. After several more minutes of struggling, Jon plopped Ulisez onto the shore. He started compressions on his chest.

Come on, damn it, Jon thought. He delivered CPR to his friend and after a few minutes, Ulisez coughed out water and started croaking all over the place. But he was alive. Jon fell over to his side from exhaustion. Ulisez looked over, still laid on his stomach. They stared at each other for a moment, both feeling like death.

"Why are all your friends crazy?" asked Ulisez.

"You're welcome for saving your life, you sack of shit," replied Jon under tired breathing.

A moment passed and both looked at the waves, which kept pounding the shore. Jon and Ulisez laid on the rocky sand, not caring about the discomfort. They looked up at the cliff and could see nothing. Vladimir was not there. Walker's body had not surfaced.

"What next?" asked Ulisez.

Jon did not know. He pondered the ultimatum that Vladimir gave him and wondered how he would get out of this. Most of all, he regretted getting into business with an ecoterrorist. Now he was in between Caine's criminal enterprise and the Legion of Samurai, and that was not a good place to be.

A little later, Jon sat in his apartment, disheveled and disoriented. He needed a drink badly. He wished he had one in his hands right now. He had to go buy more rum, and possibly vodka. He did not have much food in his cupboard. The only thing that made up as food in his apartment was crackers. He usually went to a diner or other places to eat, when he was not drinking himself to death.

His wounds were still fresh from his brush with Walker. But he also now had mental wounds associated with Vladimir's ultimatum. He had to deal with this situation and he wondered how he would. Ulisez was better now, as he was resting. Jon had ensured he would live another day. But he did not know what happened to Walker, or if he was still alive. There were a lot of questions, but he had to see what he would do about Vladimir. There was a knock on the door. Jon carefully walked to the door. He looked through the peephole and noticed it was Ulisez and opened the door. Ulisez walked in without being invited. Jon felt a little peeved at this.

"What the hell, man?"

"I'm jinxed. I'm jinxed man," replied Ulisez.

"How did you find out where I lived?"

"You brought that psychopath to town," said Ulisez, ignoring his question.

"Which one?" asked Jon, feeling like a smartass.

"Both of them! Deathstalker! Now Vladimir! I'm having PTSD with my hand because of what A.J. did to me and then feeling worse because of being thrown off a damn cliff!"

Jon hesitated, then shrugged his shoulders. "Well, I guess that was my fault."

"My hand keeps shaking for no reason," said Ulisez as he pressed his hand out slowly to show Jon.

"Well then," said Jon. "Stop shaking your hand."

"I can't One Beer Jon! I can't."

"Whoa, okay, let's calm down."

"I am calm!" cried Ulisez and Jon did everything he could to restrain himself from laughing.

"Jesus, you act as you have never gotten the shit beat out of you before or thrown off a cliff."

"I have never been thrown off a cliff before!"

Jon just looked at Ulisez. "But I know you have been shot before, and I know Walker beat you up before."

"That's not the point!"

"Hey, don't blame me! I warned you to stay out of this!"

"Don't use logic against me."

"Let me check it."

"What?"

"Let me check it."

Ulisez held out his bandaged right hand. Jon cradled it with ever-loving care.

"It's fine, you will be okay."

"Yeah?"

"Hey, buddy?"

"Yeah?"

"Sorry."

"For what?"

Without warning, he grabbed Ulisez's right hand and slammed it onto the table with a hard thud. Ulisez screamed in horrible agony as the pain from his injured hand clanging the table pressed. He clutched his hand. Ulisez looked up at him, angry.

"What the hell was that for?!"

"For being a pussy," replied Jon. "Now stop being a little bitch and get up! I will need your help to take down Caine and soon, Vladimir."

Ulisez staggered. He used the table to balance himself. Ulisez grabbed the edge of the table with his left hand.

"Come on buddy, you can do it," he mocked his friend, cheering him up.

Ulisez finally got to his feet and stood up facing Jon. "When my hand heals, I am going to kick your ass."

"Cedo, you couldn't kick my ass with both of your hands healed and one of my hands tied behind my back."

Ulisez gained the energy to chuckle. "We'll have to put that to the test someday."

Jon motioned for Ulisez to sit down with him, and they sat down on the table. Jon pulled out a piece of paper and a pen.

"We got work to do," said Jon.

Chapter 20: Jessica's Investigation

February 2nd, 2016

Jessica opened the door to let her father into her apartment. He walked into the place with some trepidation.

"You called me?" asked Hudson.

"We got to talk," replied Jessica.

Hudson walked in and Jessica closed the door behind her. She knew she had to tell her father about this because he would find out, eventually. It would be better for him to find out from her instead of anyone else. She needed to do this. She did not enjoy talking to her father, as they still had a strained relationship. But this was important.

"So what's up?" he asked.

"Before I tell you, promise you won't get upset," said Jessica.

"I can't promise that."

"Dad, just humor me."

"Okay," said Hudson, sighing. "I promise."

"Good."

"Now what's this all about?"

"I hired a private investigator to look into evidence I found on mom's murder."

She knew that he might not take this news well. She had expected it. But for the first few seconds, Hudson said nothing at all. He kind of just stood there without an expression on his face. Jessica studied her father's face, waiting for something, anything that showed emotion.

"I thought I told you to let this go."

"You did," replied Jessica. "But you have not been completely honest about mom's death from the get-go."

"Your mother died of a hit-and-run car accident."

"It was not a hit and run, and it certainly was not an accident!"

"Yes, it was…"

"How dare you stand there and tell me it was an accident when we both know it was a murder!"

"Watch your tone, Jessie!"

"No, dad. I am tired of the hiding and the non-answers. My mother's killer deserves to be brought to justice."

"Your mother was killed in an accident—"

"My mother was murdered! I now have proof that she was murdered in cold blood! She was shot several times, and you did nothing to solve it!"

"You will never understand—"

"Understand what? That you let yourself be intimidated? How does it feel to know you are a coward?"

Jessica heard those words coming out of her mouth, and it even shocked her. She had always had a somewhat volatile relationship with her father, but it had never escalated like this, even when she was high on drugs. Hudson shook his head again. He stood up to leave.

"I will be going now."

"We are not finished!" Jessica blocked his path as she was livid. Hudson glared at his daughter.

"Yes, we are," Hudson put his foot down. He shoved Jessica aside and opened the front door and slammed it behind him, leaving his daughter in a huff.

She knew her father had a hard head and could be an ass. But she stood up for what she had to do.

Later, she invited Ulisez over. He was still recovering from his injuries suffered at the hands of A.J. Walker. The Deathstalker had beaten the crap out of him and he felt helpless. Jessica had heard what happened to Ulisez from Jon. She invited him over and they ordered some chicken wings, his favorite. She figured that the chicken would help her friend a little. Ulisez dug into the chicken wings with the ferocity of a lion. It used to disgust her watching her friend eat, but she had gotten used to it over the years. She did not eat any chicken, as she preferred other food.

"Thanks for the wings," said Ulisez as he kept biting into every piece.

Jessica looked at her friend and his pummeled face and wondered how he felt during the beating. Jon and Ulisez both had scrapes and scratches all over their bodies when Jessica saw them. She could not remember ever getting into a life-threatening fight when she was younger, but she had some scuffles. Her father taught her not only how to use a gun, but how to defend herself. Jessica looked at Ulisez's hand and realized he had swollen it somehow.

"What?"

"Did Jon really slam your hand on the table?"

"What?"

"He told me," said Jessica. "Told me you were whining about a bruised hand."

"Yeah, then the jerk slams my hand on the table."

"Were you crying?"

"What? No.. I… what?"

"Oh my God! You totally cried! Like a little bitch! Just like he said!"

"The wounds are still fresh!"

"Jesus, don't get all emotional."

"My hand isn't shaking anymore, and that's the least of my issues."

"So Jon helped you?"

"In his own psychotic way."

"So, dad knows about my investigation."

Ulisez stopped eating his wings.

"How'd that go?"

"About as well as you would expect. Jon told him about his past too."

"Well…"

"Well, what?"

Ulisez bit into another wing and then spoke with his mouth full of chicken. "Least everything is in the open now."

Jessica sighed. "I never thought I'd miss rehab right about now."

"Can you pass me some ranch?"

She walked to the fridge and grabbed a bottle of ranch and threw it at Ulisez and he caught it. He squeezed the bottle onto the plate and then dipped the wings into it and took another bite. She smiled as she watched her friend chow down.

She met Amy for dinner at a sushi place in Costa Mesa. They decided to meet because Jessica felt she owed her friend some form of explanation after the situation with Jon. They greeted each other with a hug as they met in front of the restaurant.

The sushi restaurant was not too large, but not a small dive either. It had enough room for about a couple of groups as there were roughly nine tables. The restaurant also had a bar where a person could sit and order straight from the chef. The owners were a wonderful Japanese couple who had welcomed them into their restaurant for years. Their names were Ken and Tatsu Tajiri.

"Hi guys," Amy exclaimed joyfully as they walked in. The husband and wife owners waved back at Amy excitedly. They took their seat as Mrs. Tajiri handed them menus and greeted them. Jessica and Amy took their menus and looked at them for a moment. There were lots of options for delicious sushi.

Jessica scanned the menu and searched for something appetizing to order. She had always loved eating sushi with Amy. It was their thing they did when they needed to see each other for no reason.

"Dragon roll, what's that?" Jessica asked.

"That's an inside-out sushi roll," Amy explained. "Some shrimp tempura and cucumber on the inside. It's fantastic."

Jessica checked down the box that said 'Dragon Roll' with the mini pencil on the table and added that to what she would order. Then, she marked 'Vegas Roll' and 'Salmon Sashimi" and placed the pencil back down.

"I'm ready," she informed Amy.

"Great," replied Amy. She motioned over to Tatsu, who walked over and greeted Amy warmly. "I'll have these things, a glass of whatever you have on draft, and she will have that."

Tatsu took the menu orders from Jessica and Amy and walked off. There was a moment of silence now as Jessica and Amy just sat there, not knowing what to say.

"So," Jessica began. "Are we going to talk about the elephant in the room?"

"Which one?"

"Well for one, your father tried to have Jon killed," Jessica pointed out.

"You don't have any evidence that—"

"Oh come on Amy," Jessica interrupted her. "Jon comes back to town, and an assassin shows up and is being paid a lot of money. The assassin implied that your father paid him a lot of money to kill Jon."

"Why are you both so quick to believe every bad thing about my father?"

"Why are you so quick to turn the other way and ignore the evil things your father does?"

She knew that question would sting Amy a little, and she did not care. She saw as her friend went frigid from the question, potentially thinking about an answer. There was no correct answer. Caine had done a lot of shady and disgusting things over the years, some proven and some rumored. That always made her friendship with Amy and Scotti a little tense. Amy was someone who was smart enough to see her father's misdeeds and did not want to appease him at all. Scotti was someone who did not yet know what type of man her father was. She was constantly trying to prove her worth.

"You don't know or understand what it's like to grow up as his daughter," Amy said.

"Then help me understand," Jessica declared.

She placed her hand on Amy's, to comfort her. They were almost in tears, and Jessica saw that her friend had a shell she had been hiding in for years. Being the daughter of Alexander Caine could not have been easy. This was their friendship. They could bite each other's heads off one moment and cry together the next.

"You saw firsthand how the Caine family can move people around like chess pieces when you met my mother," Amy said.

"Regardless," Jessica responded. "I need your help to—I don't know—help me out. I have to tell you something, Amy.

"I have recently hired a private investigator to look into the death of my mother. I believe it may involve your father."

Jessica watched Amy's face, looking for a reaction. Tatsu arrived with the sushi and placed it neatly on the table. Amy did not look up and kept her face stoic while waiting for Jessica to say something else. She grabbed her chopsticks and picked at the sushi without saying a word.

"And I wanted to let you know," Jessica went on. "If I find evidence against your father, I will come after him. I wanted to make sure you're not standing in my way when the time comes."

Amy nibbled on the sushi. Jessica could tell that she was processing the information, thinking carefully about what she would say.

"I came to you out of respect because I love you and cherish our friendship," Jessica paused for a moment, then went on. "You have always been like a sister to me and I never want you to forget that."

Amy took another bite of her sushi and then swigged a drink of her beer while maintaining eye contact with Jessica. Finally, she broke her silence.

"Thank you for informing me," was all she said.

Amy continued to eat her sushi, and Jessica was not sure if her friend wanted to snap at her or not. This was all nerve-wracking. It almost made her want to snort crack again. She used to lose herself in the drugs, and that was partially how she met Amy. It was when she would go on a Molly binge with Rion Caine. But had she gotten over that? A person who suffers from drug addiction is never really 'over it' and is just on the brink of relapsing. It is usually not even the drug or the alcohol that causes it, but an event.

"I just hope this doesn't affect us," said Jessica.

"No," Amy shook her head. "We're okay. You do what you got to do and I will do what I have to do."

"What does that mean?"

"Jess, I love you," replied Amy. "But he is my father. If they charge him with something, no matter how horrible it may be, I have to stand by him."

At first glance, it appalled Jessica. How could Amy stand with that monster? After thinking about it for a few moments, she suddenly understood.

"Look, I get it," Jessica lamented.

Jessica took a bite of her sushi and savored the taste. There was nothing like good sushi to curb the taste of bad news. For the rest of their time, they quietly ate their sushi.

A little later, she went to Santa Ana and visited the district attorney. She walked into his plush office. That was no doubt paid for by some corrupt blood money. West stood up to greet her, and she shook his slimy hand with caution. While Jessica knew that West was corrupt, she wanted to see just how far gone he was.

"What can I do for you, Ms. Hudson?"

"I want you to reopen the Rachel Hudson case," she was direct and straight to the point. She studied his face to see if there would be any reaction. When her mother died, West had been the district attorney, so he was old enough to remember what had happened. His eyes shifted as if wanting to be anywhere else.

"What's wrong, West? You look spooked," Jessica teased. She saw West give her a look that signaled annoyance. She patiently waited.

"Jessica, that case has never been closed, but it's—it's cold."

"Uh-huh," replied Jessica. "And how did such a violent death on a public street go so cold?"

Jessica had not intended to come here to interrogate West, but that seemed to be where they were going. She already had her investigation opened, but she wanted to see if West would budge. The district attorney tapped his desk nervously, which was a clear tell for how he was feeling. Jessica sensed the fear in him, but it was not Jessica he feared. West feared Alexander Caine.

"Something wrong?" she inquired, further nudging him.

"You don't understand how these things work—"

"Don't patronize me you slimy piece of shit," Jessica had finally lost her temper. "I am Frank Hudson's God damned daughter. I picked up a thing or two from him and I know the legal system up and down."

"Yet you are nothing more than a waitress who is a former drug addict," West sniped. Now he was getting nasty. Good, Jessica thought. The gloves were off.

"My past issues have nothing to do with an investigation that you are too much of a pussy to pursue," Jessica hissed.

"Some tongue you got on you," West rebuked. "You come into my office and make demands. Someone ran your mother over like a dog. The fugitives are still at large and we are working on it."

"Ten years later, Jessica scoffed. "Someone was paid off."

"What are you insinuating?"

"You know damn well what I am insinuating," Jessica shot back. "I know about Alexander Caine's arrest and I also know about your unwillingness to press charges back then. Why is that West?"

She watched as he sweated a little. Good, Jessica thought, let him squirm a little. West cleared his throat.

"Lack of evidence," West insisted. Jessica rolled her eyes. She knew he would say something ludicrous like that. She had expected it. The seeds of corruption were deep in this county, and it was hard to fathom who else was in on this. Regardless, she persisted.

"That's bullshit and you know it," she shot back.

"Oh really," West chuckled now. "And what the hell are you? Some kind of wannabe CSI?"

"I know enough to realize when something is shady. I have started an investigation of my own and wanted to give you a fair warning that the day of justice is coming."

It was probably not the smartest thing in the world to tell a corrupt district attorney that she was conducting her investigation. In the best-case scenario, he would laugh it off. In the worst-case scenario, he might tell Caine. She wanted that privilege.

"The first thing you should investigate in your little investigation is how a privileged little girl falls so easy into drug addiction," West mocked her.

Oh good, Jessica thought. He had chosen option A. That gave her some time.

"Now if you don't mind, I have work to do. Get the hell out of my office," West ordered.

"Gladly. I feel disgusting just being here," she replied.

Jessica left without saying another word. West was another person she wanted to bring down. Everyone involved in her mother's murder would pay for their crimes.

Chapter 21: The Lion

February 6th, 2016

    Vladimir's deadline that he gave Jon was quickly approaching. It was not one that he looked forward to, as he had expected Jon to be obedient. When he took Jon out of that jail, Vladimir had saw loads of potential in the man. He believed Jon to be among the best fighters he had ever seen, and could easily mold him into one of his warriors. He was even willing to look past Jon's transgressions in the past. But the one thing that brought them together was the fact that they both came from a place of pain and tragedy. For Vladimir, it was his wife. For Jon, it was his father. They had both been witnesses to horrific crimes. Vladimir took a chance on the young man, believing him to be a potential competitor to the throne as leader of the Legion of Samurai. While Manny did not approve, Vladimir did not particularly care. He believed that his heir should have to earn their place, and he even molded this in his children.

    He meditated in his training room. The last time he had done this, he received an unexpected visit from the Deathstalker. He was almost positive he would not be receiving any visits from A.J. Walker soon. If Walker was alive, he would surely pick up his wounds.

    The door opened, and in walked a young man and a young woman. The young man was Ivan Ramirez, Vladimir's son. He had a round face with black facial hair around that he groomed neatly. His short black hair was curly and neatly placed. He had a body that was muscular, but not too much to be odd-looking. He sported a black t-shirt with some cargo shorts. Ivan was sporting the 'Californian in Winter look'.

    Standing next to Ivan was Nubia Ramirez, his daughter. She sported a V-Neck black shirt and black yoga pants. Her eyes were green and inquisitive, and she had a square, triangular face that fit her features perfectly. She possessed long-flowing dark raven-colored hair that went down to her shoulders. Her face looked unassuming as she entered the room with her brother.

    Vladimir knew his children were in the room but did not stop his meditation. They had learned by now to wait for their father to finish his work. Finally, after a few moments, he completed his meditating. Vladimir stood up and looked at both of them.

Every time he looked at Ivan, he saw a little of Ileana in him. The young man had his mother's face. But when he looked at Nubia, he saw himself. They shared similar features and the same hair.

Nubia had green eyes like the Cheshire cat. Her hair was long and flowing, extending past her shoulders. She wore a blackish-red lipstick and very little makeup as she made her way into the room with her brother. A part of her seemed shy and unassuming. She was very much like Vladimir, but he also saw his wife when he looked at her. Like Ileana, Nubia had her heart.

"Hello, father," Nubia called out.

"Hello, daughter," Vladimir spoke to Nubia. He turned to Ivan. "Where are we, boy?"

Vladimir referred to Ivan as 'boy' a majority of the time. He could tell that it irritated Ivan a little but did it to test his loyalty.

"We have scanned the Caine Enterprises perimeter. You should have access and we will join you," Ivan informed him.

Vladimir smiled. Ivan was the tech-geek of the family. His son could handle cameras, rewire camera networks, and also handle any other video or audio-visual equipment. It was something that the Legion of Samurai had never had before, but it was a skill with value in this day and age.

"Excellent," Vladimir replied. "We will pay him a visit later this afternoon."

Ivan and Nubia stood there for a moment as if waiting for their father to dismiss them. Vladimir held out his hand. Despite how proud he was of these two, he would never tell them. Now, he had a bigger test.

"I want to see that you are ready," Vladimir declared.

Ivan and Nubia looked at one another in confusion. Vladimir stared at his children blankly. Then they understood immediately. Ivan and Nubia turned and faced off against each other as if they were about to battle. They waited for Vladimir's command.

"Begin," Vladimir ordered.

Within seconds, Ivan and Nubia began to viciously exchange chops and punches. Their motions were fluid and near perfect as both were a match for each other. Ivan laid the first shot when he poked his sister in the eyes. A cheap shot, but effective. Nubia reacted from the eye poke, crying out. Vladimir rarely approved of dastardly tactics, but it was an excellent training tool. His children had to prepare for everything, and what better way than to try it against each other?

Nubia recovered from her eyes being poked and glared at her brother. Ivan spat on the ground to show contempt toward his sister. She scanned her potential moves, and Ivan waited for her action.

Vladimir observed this keenly as he waited for what would happen next. She charged toward her brother, and Ivan brushed her aside by grabbing her by the hair and throwing her face toward the ground, smashing it.

Vladimir shook his head; that was a foolhardy move by Nubia. She picked herself off the ground, frustrated. Ivan stared down at Nubia with some pity. She stood up and faced him. Nubia made some motions with her index finger, taunting Ivan, telling him to bring it. He smiled, and Vladimir could tell his son was enjoying this. Ivan walked toward Nubia and reared his right arm back and swung. She ducked his punch and then delivered a backhand chop to the midsection. Ivan felt the blow as the arm contacted his groin and struggled to stay afoot.

Vladimir chuckled and was silently proud of her for taking the initiative. Nubia then grabbed Ivan's head and yanked it down onto her knee and stuffed his face. His head ricocheted against the knee and fell backward. Nubia took the initiative and then leaped into the air and delivered a roundhouse kick, contacting Ivan's face, sending him down to the ground with a thud. Ivan fell to the ground with a thud and Nubia stood tall, the victor. Vladimir applauded, and Nubia bowed gracefully to her father.

"Now help him up and shake hands," Vladimir commanded his daughter.

Nubia did as ordered. She knelt beside Ivan and helped him get to his feet. She extended her hand and shook Ivan's hand, and he reciprocated grudgingly. Nubia kissed her brother on the cheek, and anyone who watched this would not have believed that she was the one who knocked him to the ground. He shoved her off of him for a moment, then Vladimir glared at his son. Ivan saw his father's look and then grabbed Nubia and hugged her. Vladimir smiled, approvingly.

"Come, children, we have work to do," Vladimir said.

A little later, Vladimir made his way to Caine Enterprises along with Manny, Nubia, Elicia, Kareem, and Bao. Nubia got to go with them because she won the fight, and Ivan stayed back to maintain surveillance. It was what he was better at, anyway. Nubia was his warrior, and he did not hesitate to use her beauty to his advantage either. Enemies often saw a woman and took her lightly because they thought with their penis instead of their brain. That was usually a fatal mistake, and having Elicia and Nubia on his team was a benefit. He had trained them efficiently, and they could hold their own.

Getting into Caine Enterprises was easy for them. They would not be going through the main entrance. While Vladimir felt that his team could go through the front entrance with no issues, he wanted to be as delicate as possible in his approach. There were vents on top of the company's headquarters. He had them approach from the top and make their way down. People rarely looked up when walking. He took advantage of the carelessness of others.

Vladimir and his forces entered through a vent in the ceiling and made their way down. They walked methodically through the top chambers and left through another vent in the attic that placed them firmly in the middle of a hallway on Caine's top floor.

His team landed right in front of the ditzy receptionist from earlier. Before she could react, Elicia grabbed her and covered her mouth, and then injected her with something. The receptionist dozed off, falling asleep quickly. The six of them made their way into Caine's office and they saw the bald industrialist sitting at his desk with Freddy Hunter by his side.

"What the hell," Caine exclaimed.

Freddy reached into his pocket and pulled out a gun, and Bao threw a dagger at him, deflecting the gun away. Manny, Nubia, and Elicia surrounded Freddy with swords. Vladimir calmly walked toward Caine, with Bao and Kareem flanking him. Caine looked at him peculiarly. It was not a look of fear, but one of confusion. There was also some intrigue or curiosity on his face.

"Who are you?" Caine asked.

"At last we finally meet Mr. Caine. Allow me to introduce myself. I am Vladimir Ramirez, the head of the Legion of Samurai. I am certain you have heard of us."

Vladimir waited and saw Caine's face fall, and it was as if he suddenly remembered that he had anywhere else to be. He watched as Caine's eyes shifted, potentially to see if there was any help to come in. There was no one coming. Vladimir's team had sealed the entrances off to prevent any interference.

"The Legion—Legion—" Caine stuttered. Vladimir recognized the speech tone, and it usually occurred when someone recognized what they were and what they were capable of.

"Yes, Mr. Caine, the Legion of Samurai," Vladimir smiled, acknowledging Caine's sudden fear. He watched as the bald billionaire tried to compose himself.

"I thought you were an urban legend?" Caine inquired, and it was not a question, but a tactic used to buy him some time.

"No, I assure you we are quite real," Vladimir emphasized exquisitely as he touched the penholder on Caine's desk. He attempted to gauge a reaction from Caine but found none.

"What do you want?" Caine went straight to the point, and Vladimir preferred it that way.

"I want peace on Earth and all men of evil to die."

Caine chuckled nervously. Vladimir turned away from Caine for a moment and glanced at Freddy, who was being held in check.

"This is your best man, is it not? He's nothing more than a hired thug, someone who can be contained or destroyed easily. You prioritize this man for all your evil deeds and stand back and pretend you have done no wrong.

"You use this man to carry out all your incomprehensible actions and then act like nothing can touch you. Then you attempt to hire a man to kill Jon Drake when this man cannot do the job."

Caine's eyebrows rose. Vladimir saw him flinch a little at the mention of Jon Drake's name. He turned back toward Caine.

"I have taken care of your Deathstalker," Vladimir assured Caine.

"I don't know what you're talking—"

"Do not pretend to be ignorant with me. I am the Lion. I know all and I will use everything you have ever done and destroy you quickly."

Caine got irritated. "How dare you? Do you know who I am? I am Alexander Caine!"

"You are nothing more than a man," Vladimir exclaimed. "And men can be destroyed. The history books will show that a coward named Alexander Caine bowed down to the Lion, and his empire that he had spent over 20 years building will be destroyed in an instant."

"I do not appreciate being threatened," Caine was getting angry, forsaking any fear he had.

"I do not make threats, Mr. Caine, I make promises," said Vladimir.

Vladimir nodded and Elicia, Nubia, and Manny backed off of Freddy and allowed him to stand there incompetently. Bao and Kareem inched back a little, and Vladimir made a motion with his hand.

"Be warned, Mr. Caine. You have one week to leave down or I can guarantee you will not like what happens next," Vladimir's voice went dark and menacing and then he threw something on the ground and smoke filled the room.

While Caine and Freddy were helplessly coughing their lungs out, Vladimir and his team made their way out. Smokescreens were old but effective, and Vladimir had no issues using them. They made their escape hastily the same way they entered the building from the top. The top of Caine Enterprises was the last place the authorities would have thought to have looked. A helicopter made its way to the top of the building, and Vladimir latched onto the rope and waited for his team to climb aboard. Then he was the last one to climb aboard. The helicopter made its escape into the distance.

Vladimir took the initiative. He made his way to the city hall. There was business to attend. He made his way into the mayor's office. Security had not been tough to pass, as Vladimir did not take any weapons. The time for that was not now. They allowed him in and he walked toward the mayor's office. The secretary was a Hispanic woman, probably Mayor Rodriguez's effort to show that he was a man of the people by hiring fellow minorities. She looked up pleasantly.

"May I help you?"

"My name is Vladimir Ramirez. I have an appointment with Mayor Rodriguez."

She scanned through the computer and pointed at something with her finger.

"Of course," she said pleasantly. "I will let him know you're here."

Vladimir waited patiently. He was not used to being on someone else's time, but this was the exception he would make. It was about a full minute before the secretary summoned him and he entered Rodriguez's office.

The mayor greeted him by extending his hand, and Vladimir shook it. Now it was time for business.

"Nice to meet you, Mr. Ramirez," Rodriguez beamed as he shook Vladimir's hand excitedly.

"Likewise Mayor," replied Vladimir.

"I was very intrigued by your call, Mr. Ramirez," Rodriguez said.

Vladimir took it in. The mayor was a typical political weasel, out to make the extra buck while pretending to care about the community. This was the type of man that rode around in SUVs and then parked halfway down the block to ride in an energy-efficient car to make himself look better to the public. Then, to make things worse, he would leave the SUVs running, thus destroying the environment even more. Vladimir detested him but had an agenda that required the mayor.

"Yes, Mr. Mayor," said Vladimir. "My company has been promoting energy-efficient ways of transportation. I would in simple terms like to build a train."

Vladimir watched as Rodriguez's eyes lit up. It was a weird, wet dream by politicians in California to want to build public transportation and have everyone take it. They wanted to convert California into New York and every major metropolitan area in the world. The only problem was that the state of California did not adhere to this way of transportation, and Vladimir knew it.

He believed in these ideals, but to a different extent than Rodriguez. Riding a train would not save the world. It did not matter what people rode or drive. What mattered was how they responded to their environment and how they cared for the world. That, Vladimir believed, is what the people of California and everyone on the left side of the political spectrum did not understand or were too stupid to realize. As much as he hated the Republican Party in America and detested everything they stood for, he detested the Democratic Party just as much because they always lied about who they were. He could see the evil in the conservatives, while the liberals pretended to play on some misguided ideals.

But Vladimir preyed on this. He wanted to ingratiate himself into this city, and the first step was appealing to this weasel mayor.

"That sounds—that sounds amazing," Rodriguez gushed.

Vladimir smiled. Then, he took out a pen and started scribbling down a number on a piece of paper and handed it to Rodriguez.

"I will trust this would be a good amount to start," Vladimir announced.

He watched as Rodriguez's eyes rose. The weasel was probably thinking dollar signs and figuring out how he could scam up more vanity projects with the money.

"This is amazing, Mr. Ramirez," Rodriguez exclaimed.

"I would like to continue doing business with the city. Potentially build new opportunities."

"I agree wholeheartedly," Rodriguez bellowed.

"I have a plan that would unite Orange Grove with Costa Mesa and Newport Beach. It would be a nice commuter train that would travel from the five freeway to Pacific Coast Highway," Vladimir explained.

"That type of project sounds years away," Rodriguez was somber a little.

"My people can make it happen along with cooperation from your city," said Vladimir.

"Mr. Ramirez, I only have so much pull," said Rodriguez.

"It can be done, all we need is faith. I have faith in your leadership and you have faith in our new friendship."

Vladimir studied Rodriguez and knew that the man was contemplating his offer. He had a way of being very convincing for getting things he wanted. There was a grand scheme at play here, and the train was the least of what he was planning. Orange Grove was just the beginning and he eventually would make his way up the state and take everything piece by piece. He watched as Rodriguez looked at him and then saw the slow smile creep in. The mayor extended his hand.

"I'm all in Mr. Ramirez," he announced.

Vladimir returned his hand and shook it.

"Excellent. I look forward to future opportunities and you will get a check soon."

Vladimir left the mayor's office soon after. He had one more stop to make and made his way into Thomas Martin's house. He took the detective by surprise, and Thomas dared to draw his gun on him. Then he realized who it was and stood down.

"You shouldn't scare me like that, Lion," Thomas's voice rose.

"I do not appreciate your tone," Vladimir reprimanded him.

"What is your business here, sir? I have done everything you have asked," Thomas insisted.

"It seems you have," He acknowledged and glanced at the picture frame on Thomas's desk. It was a picture of Thomas's brother and mother. Every time he saw this picture, it reminded Vladimir of how much he had lost over the years. Thomas was his brother and both had lost someone. In Thomas's case, it was his only family.

"Does it still pain you?" Vladimir asked him.

"Everyday sir, I do not go a day without thinking about it," Thomas lamented.

Vladimir patted Thomas on the back. "Good."

Thomas looked at Vladimir curiously, potentially misinterpreting what he meant by that.

"You need to hold on to the pain," Vladimir went on. "It is the only thing that will strengthen you and once you become powerful enough, you can do anything you put your mind to."

"There is another reason you are here," Thomas was smart enough to see through the lines.

Vladimir nodded. "There will be something that occurs. It will be tragic and you must be ready."

"What does that mean?" Thomas understood the ominous words that Vladimir uttered but wanted more details.

"It is best you do not know the full details," Vladimir replied. "I wanted to share with you the fact that it may happen soon and I best prepare you."

Vladimir turned to walk away, and Thomas held onto him from the shoulder. Had anyone else tried that, it would have offended Vladimir, or he might have even thrown them to the ground. But he had too much respect for Thomas.

"You need to give me more than that," Thomas insisted.

"Let's just say that you were right about my experiment. I have put an end to it, or at least force that experiment to go along with what I want," Vladimir said.

He turned away and walked off, and Thomas did not stop him. Now their next plan was in full motion and no misguided idealist would stop them. While the conservatives and the liberals in modern politics would argue and moan about climate change, Vladimir would actively do something about it. Their plan was in motion and the Legion of Samurai would enforce their will on everyone that stood in their way. Now, their first goal was teaching Jon Drake a lesson.

Chapter 22: The Warning

Orange Grove Bar and Grill-February 7th, 2016

Jon was back on his stool, this time looking at an empty glass in which he had consumed his first shot of alcohol. He stared at the glass with a look of disdain, wishing the alcohol could make him forget everything that had transpired over the last few. He played with the glass for a few moments, analyzing it for no reason at all.

Scotti stood there in front of him, looking at Jon with her usual stare of irritation and disgust. She mostly saw him when he ventured to her bar, except for the time he walked into Jessica's apartment all battered and beaten.

"Why do you look like someone killed your puppy?" she asked him.

"Why do you always look like someone who's been rejected by life?"

Scotti flipped him off. He returned the bird. It seemed to be their thing. Their conversation was free-filling hostility.

"God, who shit in your cornflakes?" asked Scotti.

"This whole damn universe," said Jon.

There was a moment of silence. Jon stared hopelessly at the empty glass, and Scotti noticed.

"You want another?"

"Yeah, make it the strongest you got."

"You already got the rum…"

"Give me a vodka," said Jon.

"Anything in it?"

Jon shook his head. Scotti obliged without protest. He resumed staring at the glass, as it was his thing now. Scotti returned and gave him a glass of vodka, straight up. Jon swigged it as Scotti watched, horrified. He slammed it back on the table.

"Easy," she said.

"I'll go easy when I want to go easy."

"Is drinking really going to help you?"

"Is talking really going to help you?"

"Fair enough."

Scotti grabbed the Vodka bottle and poured more into Jon's empty shot glass. He took another swig.

"So what's wrong with you, anyway?"

He groaned, annoyed.

"Do I really look like I want to talk Scotti?"

"Holy shit, you said my name correctly, you're not a complete idiot."

"I do that for your amusement."

"But yeah, you look like you want to drink, or stab someone, not sure which order."

"I definitely want to stab someone."

"Me too."

He smiled, Scotti grinned back.

"You should, it's so liberating," said Jon.

"If only."

Jon scoffed. "Hasn't stopped your father."

"My father is…"

"Was attacked yesterday by a group calling themselves the Legion of Samurai."

Scotti gave him a peculiar look as if to say 'how did you know that'.

"Your father is a dangerous man, but he has a lot of enemies who are equally dangerous," said Jon.

Scotti poured Jon more vodka. He lost count of how much he had drunk already. Was it three, four, maybe five glasses? The alcohol was taking its effect, which was good. Jon needed it.

"My father may have a lot of skeletons, but he's still my father, and someone tried to kill him yesterday," said Scotti.

"Yeah," replied Jon. "I was accused of it. But I had an alibi. I was home picking my wounds."

Scotti poured herself a drink, this time with Jon. They clanked glasses and drank together.

"To more shitty days ahead," Scotti toasted.

"Cheers," Jon slammed the shot down.

A little later, he stumbled out of the bar. He drove nowhere, so he was okay with being almost blackout drunk. Only he never got blackout drunk. He toed the line.

He felt someone, or something, watching him. He stopped short, analyzing the area, and closed his eyes to visualize the area. Out of instinct, he lunged into a nearby bush and clamped his hands together and pulled something out.

Thomas came stumbling out of the bushes. Jon reared his hand back and punched him in the face. The corrupt cop stumbled back as the fist connected with his face.

"I told you once before Martin, don't follow me!" cried Jon.

Thomas touched his face gingerly. "Your right hand is pretty damn solid, Drake."

"What do you want?"

"I came here to offer you a proposition."

"Hell no!"

Jon and Thomas know each other from before their encounter here. There was a great disdain shared between them.

"Let's be clear Drake," said Thomas. "You know who I am, and what I can do. And I know who you are."

"What did they call you in South America? The Sex Panther or some stupid name like that?"

"Just Panther dipshit."

"Same shit."

"And like a Panther," said Thomas, ignoring Jon's remark. "I can kill anything at lightning pace."

"God, you Legion of Samurai and your ridiculous names."

"We're not the only ones 'White Warrior'."

Jon smiled. "What can I say? I'm ferocious and the people felt that I deserved a nickname."

"Of course you are."

"So what then? Are you now Vladimir's lapdog?"

"I'm my own man."

"Not from where I am standing."

"You don't know jack shit, Drake."

"No, I don't," replied Jon, almost sarcastically. You are a corrupt cop giving information to Caine. You also are a member of the Legion of Samurai. Just whose side are you on Martin?"

"The same side I have always been on, my own."

"A part of me respects that, and the other part of me wants to beat the shit out of you right now."

"I'd like to see you try."

"Cut to the point Martin! What's your proposition?"

"I don't always agree with Vladimir, but there is a way to avoid his wrath while not working directly for him if you catch my drift."

"Are you suggesting a partnership? Jesus, I didn't know you cared."

"I don't," replied Thomas. "For all I care, you could get shot a thousand times, and I'd just sit back and enjoy with a bag of popcorn."

"How sweet of you," said Jon sarcastically.

"But I believe a partnership could be more effective than either of us trying to go about it separately."

"Let me think about this," replied Jon. "I will pass. Hard pass. You're a human piece of shit."

Thomas shook his head.

"You'll regret that."

"Next time you follow me, Martin, I won't be so forgiving."

Chapter 23: The Loss

February 8th, 2016

Jon entered the Harbor House Diner and saw Jessica waiting for him. She looked radiant, even drinking a cup of coffee and her hair all messy. He walked toward Jessica and sat across from her. She looked up at him through her cup and smiled.

"Glad you could make it," said Jessica.

"Why wouldn't I?"

"Well…" Jessica interrupted herself by sipping some of her coffee. "You never know with you."

"I will always make time for you, whether it's for coffee or if you want to do some fun naughty stuff."

"Jon!"

"I'm guessing this isn't one of those times?"

"No!"

"Okay, then what's on your mind, Jess?"

"Dad told me."

"Told you what?"

"Everything."

Jon looked at her, lost like a boy in the woods.

"You got to help me out here."

"He told me the truth about my mother's death."

His jaw dropped, actual surprise.

"Well, don't keep me in suspense."

"Alexander Caine. He ordered my mother's death as retaliation for my father arresting Freddy for your father's death."

He felt saddened now. But when he looked at Jessica, he saw coldness. It was the same coldness he felt every day. Only the coldness was for the world.

"I now understand you a little more. I understand the hatred you feel for him. We share a common enemy now."

Jessica extended her hand. He received it. The sadness that they shared for a long time now was mutual. They held hands for a moment, taking because they were now in this together, to the bitter end.

Jon left the diner and Jessica because he had to go see her father. Hudson had called him about something important, and Jon was curious. He rang the doorbell this time, and Hudson opened it and welcomed him inside. The two had come to an understanding, and Hudson wanted Jon over to discuss something. He walked over to the couch and sat on the table.

"Do you want a beer?" asked Hudson.

"When do I not want a beer?"

Hudson smiled. He walked over to the fridge and grabbed a beer and handed it to Jon.

"Now let's get onto why I called you over here."

"It wasn't to lecture me, was it?"

Hudson shook his head.

"No. I am over that. I understand now that you did what you had to do to survive. I don't like it, but I understand. That's not what I called."

Jon leaned in.

"Well, color me curious. Not drunk yet, but curious."

"Hold off the getting drunk part until you hear what I have to say."

Hudson took out his laptop and showed it to Jon. There were case files of Alexander Caine and his entire network on it. Jon looked at Hudson curiously.

"What is this Frank?"

"I am going to finally lead the team to bring down Alexander Caine and his cronies."

Jon studied the files and their contents. There were many dates and write-ups about Caine here. Much of this was speculation, but some of it was minor crimes against people who allegedly worked for him. But nothing concrete to tie to Caine. Some of these files actually may have had enough evidence to convict, if there was a district attorney brave enough to prosecute.

"Why are you showing me this?" asked Jon.

"Because I want to create a secret task force that finally brings down Caine once and for all," said Hudson.

He looked at Hudson, taking it all in.

"Why did you want to show me this here? Instead of at the police station?"

"Because I am not fully confident my office is secure," said Hudson.

At once, he understood. He knew about the corruption but always believed that it was just Thomas Martin. Hudson believed that there was over one mole in his department.

"What do you need from me?" asked Jon.

"I need all the skills you gained from the cartel and everyone who ever taught you anything, and we will bring Caine down."

Jon extended his beer and clinked beer bottles with Hudson. "To a better future."

"To a better future."

They both took a swig of their beers. They drank, and then Jon looked at Hudson. He sighed.

"Sometimes Frank, I think about my father."

Hudson said nothing, just staring at him for a moment. Jon went on.

"I remember how much I loved him."

"And he loved you a lot, Jon."

"Let me finish."

"Sorry."

"It's fine," said Jon. "As much as I loved my father, things were never really the same after my mother died. He seemed to put more of himself into his work until he ended up dying."

"He was doing the best he could to support you as a single father. I could relate to that."

"No, I get that," replied Jon. "But it seemed like he became emotionally distant, almost out of some weird sense of guilt. It's weird."

"I'm sure that wasn't the case.."

"Well whatever it was, when my mother died, I think my dad did too."

"Jon, did you see Freddy shoot your father?"

"You know this, Frank."

"How about your mother? Do you know how she died?"

Jon shook his head.

"I was eight years old. Dad told me she got sick. But I think something else could have happened."

"Jon, what are you trying to say?"

"I don't think my father told the complete truth about what happened to my mother. I think he hid something --- something terrible."

Hudson looked at him and noticed something unusual from him. Tears flowed down Jon's face. He was crying. Hudson grabbed Jon and hugged him, and all the emotions from years gone by finally came rushing out. He shook his head and wiped away his tears.

"No time for this."

"It's okay, Jon. It's okay."

"You know what I missed about home the entire time I was in South America?"

"Me?"

"No, of course not."

Hudson laughed. Jon smiled an actual genuine smile.

"Evan at a young age, you knew this, and I knew this. Man, I always loved your daughter. She is what kept me alive."

Hudson nodded, acknowledging his approval. Despite his disdain for Jon's actions, he respected the man he once cared for.

"She is the reason why I have tried to mend my ways a little," Jon went on. "If we're being honest here, I came back to town to get revenge on Caine and eventually kill him."

"I know."

"And I know you don't enjoy hearing that."

"But it's not a surprise."

"But the reason I haven't been able to kill him is because of my love for your daughter. It's the sole reason I haven't been able to do that."

"Jessica has always been strong-willed, like her mother."

"And you."

Hudson shook his head.

"Jessica is much stronger than me. I have always been afraid. Afraid of losing her the way I lost her mother. That fear has made me a coward."

"You are not a coward."

"I am," said Hudson. "I could have brought Caine down years ago. Instead, I let him harm more people."

"You were protecting your daughter. It's understandable."

"And now's she trying to find out who killed her mother."

"Any ideas on that?"

Before Hudson could respond, something blasted the doors open! The explosion was sudden and all-encompassing and sent Jon and Hudson tumbling to the floor. They both groaned as the smoke lifted from the explosion. They were on the ground, knocked from the couch, and in some pain. From the corner of his eye, he could see footsteps walking. He noticed a cut on his leg and one on Hudson's arm. Then he saw the footsteps emerge.

Vladimir, Manny, and other armed warriors entered the gaping hole that used to be the front door.

"Vladimir?" asked Jon weakly.

Vladimir motioned to Manny, who walked over toward Hudson and yanked him up by the right arm. Hudson screamed in pain as Jon watched helplessly from the floor. Three Legion of Samurai warriors held Hudson up. Two held his arms, and one punched him across the face, drawing blood. Vladimir walked toward him, with Manny by his side, and leaned into him.

"Hello, Jon."

"Vladimir. What are you… what are you doing?"

"I warned you that you had one week to finish off Caine. You did not heed my warning."

"I… you haven't given me enough time."

"Plenty of time. You should have realized that there was no going back."

Hudson lifted his head as the two warriors held him. He looked at Vladimir and finally saw the man that Jon had talked about.

"You must be Vladimir Ramirez," said Hudson.

Vladimir smiled. Freddy held Jon off with a sword, and Vladimir walked over to Hudson.

"How great it is to make your acquaintance Commissioner Hudson," said Vladimir.

"I heard about you, I know what you and your people are," said Hudson.

"All you need to know Commissioner Hudson is that this is the beginning of the end. I intend to destroy every living being on this planet and once I am finished, a new human race will rise. We will be clean again."

"You can't!" cried Hudson.

"I can and I will," said Vladimir. "But first…"

Vladimir turned back toward Jon. The two men holding Hudson rushed toward Jon and held him down while one remained with Hudson. Vladimir leaned in and punched Jon in the stomach. He moaned in pain. The warriors held him down. Vladimir turned back toward Hudson, who bled all over.

"It is funny how you continue to associate yourself with people of no significance, especially this man of justice," Vladimir said to Jon while looking at Hudson the entire time.

"Please Vladimir, your quarrel is with me. Let Frank go," said Jon.

Vladimir turned back toward Jon. He put on some black gloves. Then he pulled out a Katana sword.

"Vladimir don't do this!" cried Jon.

The two warriors hit Jon, and he fought back. Manny stepped in and used his fist and connected with Jon's face, a small measure of revenge for him. Jon fell with a thud to the ground. More blood poured out. He was still aware of his surroundings. The two other men clobbered Jon over the head with closed fists, and he felt every blow. Manny motioned for them to stop. They grabbed Jon's hair and held it toward Hudson.

"It's a shame this is not Jessica. But close enough. Sins of the father," said Vladimir.

Vladimir rushed Hudson with a force so quick, it happened in seconds. He grabbed Hudson's face with his palm. Hudson showed no fear, but anger instead. He glared at Vladimir with a hatred he had not shown toward anyone except Alexander Caine.

"Mr. Hudson, did Jon ever tell you the story of how I began my quest against evil?"

Hudson did not say a word. He struggled as Vladimir's large hand gripped him tightly. The warriors held Jon back as he struggled.

"My great love Ileana was killed in an explosion. The cartel was trying to kill me and my family as a way of showing their power. They killed my wife. Do you wish to know what I did?"

Hudson did not respond, nor could he, as Vladimir held him tight. Jon continued to struggle.

"I trained with the Legion of Samurai and then avenged my wife. I killed the cartel boss that ordered my wife's death and began my quest to eradicate all the evil in the world. Compared to a coward like you, I did something. You stood by and watched as Alexander Caine destroyed everyone in your life."

"I couldn't! He would have killed my daughter," said Hudson, despite Vladimir's palm covering his face.

"Coward! A coward is a man who deserves no sympathy!"

"Please," said Jon, as he continued to struggle. "Please Vladimir, he's innocent."

Vladimir burst into laughter. He tightened his grip on Hudson.

"Only a fool would believe that anyone is innocent. Evil lives in all of us and it's up to me and the Legion of Samurai to eradicate it, starting with your friend."

Hudson shook his head, holding back tears. Vladimir leaned in even closer.

"Tears are for the weak. It will be all over soon."

Without warning, Vladimir plunged his Katana sword into Hudson's chest. Jon screamed in horror as this happened, as tears flowed down his face. Vladimir twisted the sword deep into the commissioner's chest, and the blood flowed out like a volcano. Hudson's eyes bulged up as Vladimir clenched the sword. Then he immediately removed the sword from Hudson's chest. The commissioner staggered for a moment, then slowly fell to the ground. The three warriors let Jon go, and his first instinct was to kneel on the floor beside Hudson.

"Stay with me, Frank! For the love of God stay with me!"

Hudson's eyes fluttered. He felt weak, desolate. He reached out to Jon.

"Please… take… care …"

"Save your energy. You will be okay."

"Tell Jessica I love…"

Hudson convulsed. He looked on in horror as he saw the man go into a mini seizure. Then finally, the suffering ended, Hudson's eyes flickered until finally, it was over. He held Hudson's lifeless body now and silently wept for a moment. He thought of everything in his life now. Slowly, he turned toward Vladimir and felt more rage than he had ever felt before in his life.

"You will pay for this you monster!"

"I highly doubt that," said Vladimir.

He rose to his feet and Vladimir, Manny, and the three warriors quickly surrounded him.

"I will finish you all right now," said Jon.

"Good luck," replied Vladimir in an amused voice.

The three warriors instantly attacked Jon, and he fought back with vigor. He held them off, deflecting their swords, then knocking them out with precise strikes. Manny rushed Jon from behind and Jon clobbered him with a forearm, causing him to stumble back.

Vladimir emerged from the side, and Jon used his right hand to block the strike. Vladimir attacked Jon's cut arm and wrenched it, causing him to scream in agony. The Lion leaned into the White Warrior and whispered.

"You are and never will be any match for me."

Vladimir struck him across the face with his forearm, causing him to drop to the ground like a sack of potatoes. He did not remember what happened next because everything went black.

His eyes flickered and he groaned in serious pain. He could not remember how long he must have been out for. As he rose slowly, he suddenly remembered what had transpired. He heard the sirens outside the house. He paid no attention to it. He saw Hudson's body and wept.

"No. No. No. No. No. No. No!!!!! I'm so sorry Frank! I am so …"

Jon did not finish. He wept beside Hudson and crawled around him.

"I am so sorry! I am so…. sorry!"

As Jon did this, officers entered the house. Ulisez and Thomas were among those officers as they had their guns drawn.

"Drake?" asked Thomas.

He looked at them all, then kept weeping. He placed his head on Hudson's lifeless body.

"Oh my God!" said Ulisez as he saw Hudson's body.

"Drake!" cried Thomas as Jon continued to weep.

"Jon, what the hell happened here?" asked Ulisez.

"Vladimir," said Jon. "He did this. He killed Frank."

Thomas glanced at his other officers, while Ulisez kept his eyes locked on Jon. They all still had their guns drawn, except Ulisez.

"We were talking," Jon continued. "Then Vladimir…."

He could not go on, as his tears continued to flow out.

"Start from the beginning," said Thomas.

"I --- I --- can't," said Jon.

"Calm down, Drake," said Thomas.

He gave Thomas a look of death. "I can't calm down, you piece of shit! My friend is dead! Can't you see that?"

One officer next to Thomas snickered. "Looks like we get a case of a man killing a cop who came out to arrest him."

Jon turned toward him, angry. He recognized him. This cop's name was Bobbie Freewald. He was a white man with short blonde hair and freckles that never went away. He was as corrupt as Thomas was but much worse. Freewald did not have a Legion of Samurai to attach himself to, he just was on the take and enjoyed delivering swift brutality. He was the same height as Jon and had disliked Jon since Jon came back. The other officer, the one who said nothing at the moment, was Saul Santos, a Hispanic-American man with short black hair who was just as corrupt as Freewald was. He usually delivered police brutality beatings alongside Freewald.

"You don't know what you're talking about, you stupid little bitch!"

"What did he just call me?" asked Freewald.

"I think he called you a stupid bitch. Are you going to take that?" asked Santos.

"Both of you shut up!" cried Jon.

"Oh you're going down," said the Freewald.

Ulisez stepped in between Jon and Freewald to prevent an altercation.

"Stand down," said Ulisez to Freewald.

Freewald did not listen. He charged Jon and attacked him. Freewald punched Jon across the face and the blow pushed him back. Jon recovered and then delivered a swift kick to the legs, dropping him. Santos grabbed Jon's arm, attempting to restrain him. He twisted free and slammed his elbow into the officer's kidney. Santos circled him with newfound respect. Then he attacked again, delivering a sweeping head kick, knocking Jon off balance. Thomas remained still and Ulisez screamed for them to stop. Santos punched Jon across the face and then charged him. Jon fell backward, then drove his legs into the air and propelled the officer into the air and onto the floor with a hard thud.

"Enough of this!" roared Ulisez as he grabbed Jon and held him.

"What are you doing?" asked Jon.

"Calm down!" cried Ulisez.

"I didn't do anything!" replied Jon.

"You just struck two police officers," said Thomas. "And I am pretty sure I can find some things that can stick."

"Right back at you, Panther," said Jon to Thomas.

Ulisez released his grip on Jon and then stood in front of his friend. He did not have a choice.

"Put your hands in the air, Jon."

"You realize I can escape right?" asked Jon.

"Just do it," said Ulisez.

Thomas aimed his gun at Jon. "Don't force me to shoot your bitch ass."

"You'd like what wouldn't you?" asked Jon.

"There is one thing I would like," replied Thomas.

"Yeah, what's that?" asked Jon.

"Tell me in plain terms. How did Frank Hudson die?"

Santos stepped back in. "Come on, Lieutenant Martin. It's obvious he killed Commissioner Hudson."

"Shut up!" cried Jon to Santos. He turned back to Thomas. "I already told you I would never do that. I would never do anything to hurt Frank. He was like a father to me. I would never hurt him."

"Where is Vladimir?" asked Thomas.

"I don't know," said Jon.

"Do you realize how flimsy your story sounds?" asked Thomas.

"It's time. Why would I lie?"

"I don't know Drake. Why would you lie? It seems to be what you well," said Thomas.

"Hey Thomas, have you heard of pot meets kettle?"

"Lay off Thomas," said Ulisez. "Jon isn't responsible for this."

Thomas turned toward Ulisez. "A man you consider a mentor is dead on the ground."

"That isn't Jon's fault," replied Ulisez.

"Regardless of if he actually killed the guy, it doesn't make it any less his fault," said Thomas.

"Unlike you, I am not corrupt!" claimed Jon.

Thomas turned back toward Jon and then slugged him in the face. Jon crouched down to the ground from the blow. Ulisez rushed to intervene, but Freewald and Santos stood in his way.

They blocked his path. Thomas grabbed Jon by the throat, lifting him with power, and then punched him again, sending him down to the ground with a thud.

"Pick his white ass up," said Thomas.

Freewald and Santos shoved Ulisez aside. Then they both grabbed Jon up and held him. Thomas faced Jon.

"Commissioner Hudson was killed by a man who paid you. That makes you an accomplice to the crime," said Thomas.

Jon shook his head. "No."

"Jon Drake. You are under arrest for being an accomplice in the murder of Frank Hudson. You have the right to remain silent. Anything you do can or will be held against you in the court of law."

Freewald and Santos placed handcuffs on Jon, elbowing him in the back while doing this.

"You have the right to an attorney. If you cannot afford one, one will be appointed to you."

Freewald and Santos held Jon. Thomas looked at Jon. Ulisez still had a look of shock on his face, and could not believe what he just witnessed. He felt impotent.

"Do you understand the rights as read to you?"

Jon nodded reluctantly. Thomas grabbed Jon and took him outside. At this occurred, a car drove up and the worst person who could have arrived came upon the scene. Jessica stepped out of the car. Ulisez tried to intercept her. Jessica noticed Jon in handcuffs.

"Jon? Ulisez? Thomas? What's going on? Where's my father?"

"Jessica, there is something you got to know," said Ulisez.

Jessica looked at the gaping hole in the wall of what was her father's house. An overwhelming feeling of horror came upon her. Something was wrong, wrong. She spotted Jon and turned back to Ulisez.

"Why is Jon in handcuffs? Where is my father? What the shit is going on?!!!"

"Jess. Do not go in there," said Ulisez.

Jessica shoved her friend aside and walked toward the gaping hole that was her father's front door and meandered toward the scene and saw the horrifying scene of her father lying on the floor bleeding from his wounds, dead. She shook her head, crying silently. She fell to her knees and sobbed next to her father before it slowly turned to uncontrollable wailing. Some men, possibly paramedics or officers, tried to restrain her, and she nudged them off forcefully while crying over her dead father's body.

Thomas entered with Ulisez and watched as Jessica sobbed over her father's body. Ulisez placed his hand on Jessica's shoulder. Jon was still in the room being held by the two rogue cops.

"I'm sorry," said Ulisez.

"Who did this? Who killed my father?" asked Jessica with a coldness in her voice that meant business.

Ulisez looked back at Jon, who shook his head.

"Whatever they tell you, whatever they say about what they think I did, you know me and know I would never do this," said Jon.

Jessica's face was still in tears. She locked eyes with Jon as if to show that she believed him, no matter how terrible she felt right now.

"Get him out of here," said Ulisez.

Jessica watched as the officers placed Jon into the squad car and drove off. She saw Ulisez and Thomas following in their patrol car. The medics arrived soon and took her father's body, and she followed to give the details they needed.

As they placed Jon in the squad car, he thought of his situation and how he ended up in this situation. Regardless, Jon knew that he had to make things right. He would find a way out of this situation and make things right for Jessica and everyone else. But he had unfinished business with Alexander Caine, and now, especially with Vladimir Ramirez and the Legion of Samurai.

Chapter 24: The Birthday Present

July 18th, 2008

It was Jon's 15th birthday, but there would be no celebrations today. Jon trained with Escobar in a dungeon. The Great Command of the Capital had trained him for the last two-and-a-half years. Jon stood in front of Escobar. The cartel leader had helped mold him into a living weapon with boundless energy.

"Deathstalker killed the leader of the Legion of Samurai," said Escobar.

Jon reacted. He had met A.J. "The Deathstalker" Walker a year before. The British man had befriended him, and Jon would learn later that he had used him for information. That rubbed Jon the wrong way. While he was grateful that the Deathstalker had saved his life, it irritated him that Walker had used him.

"They are our enemies, so this is good news, right?"

"Yes," replied Escobar. "This happened last year. Since then, they have rebuilt their army and are preparing to attack all the cartels. They wish to exterminate us."

"We can handle them," replied Jon with bravado.

"Perhaps," said Escobar with hesitation.

"What are you saying?"

"This organization is as powerful as ours. They hunt down cartels and execute without hesitation. They will be ready to strike."

"So we have to strike first?"

"That depends…"

"On what?"

"I took you in when you were a mere 12 years old. Today you are officially 15. You are almost a man. I have trained you in everything I know and every form of survival and combat. But there is one thing you have yet to do."

"And what's that?"

"Take a life."

There was a moment of silence between them. Escobar was right; Jon had killed no one yet. The idea had never crossed his mind. But it was something that happened in cartel life. It was a way of life and there was nothing anyone could do about it.

"I'm ready," said Jon.

"Are you sure?"

"Why do you keep asking me that?"

"Because once you kill, it cannot be undone. Once you taste a man's blood, the sanctity of life you stole from him, there is no going back. Once you end someone, you cannot bring him back."

"I, I understand."

"I sincerely hope you do Jon Drake because a war is coming and you must be prepared. Are you ready to fight the enemy?"

Escobar looked at Jon. He handed Jon a nine-millimeter gun. The teenager held the gun, his first time holding one. Escobar smiled, and Jon smiled back at him. Jon nodded. Then something came to him.

"How did you find out about the Samurai?" asked Jon.

"It's simple, Jon," said Escobar. "I paid the Deathstalker to kill the Samurai."

The revelation shook Jon to the core. He now fully understood the business he was in, and that there were consequences to everything.

Escobar's Estate-A Few Hours Later

Jon and Escobar were training when an explosion rang out in the background. They immediately stepped into action. Escobar gave Jon a gun and nodded.

"It's time, we either survive or we perish," said Escobar.

Jon crept near the doors and could hear voices. There was a tank outside that fired at the door, blasting anyone that stood in its way.

"Time to avenge the Samurai's death!" a man shouted.

"The Samurai's death shall be avenged with the destruction of the Great Command!" another man chimed in.

The tank blasted again, and the doors collapsed. The Legion of Samurai warriors charged the entrance and an all-out war began!

Inside, Jon watched as the Legion of Samurai charged into the entrance and brawled with the Great Command of the Capital. Escobar grabbed Jon, and they headed into the dungeon, presumably to take cover.

"This room shall buy us some time. Are you ready?" asked Escobar.

Jon nodded.

"It's time to fight for your life. Be prepared."

They scurried inside. Throughout the chaos, they somehow got separated. Now Jon was alone. A shadow emerged, and a man confronted him: Diego, the leader of the Legion of Samurai.

"You there, boy," said the man holding his sword. "Tell me where Escobar is and I may just let you live!"

This was Diego Rivera, the leader of the Legion of Samurai. Jon looked at Diego, fear in his eyes. What could he do? If he betrayed Escobar, death would follow. If he fought this man, he also surely would die. There were no real options. Jon was between a rock and a hard place, and it was not a good place to be. He shivered on the inside, terrified of what may come. Diego was not a tall man, standing at about five foot nine inches. But he was the leader of the Legion of Samurai, which made him the most dangerous warrior of them all. Was he stupid enough to confront the leader of the Legion of Samurai? He pulled out his sword. What the hell was I doing, he thought. He felt nothing but unbridled fear, and the terror raged through every fiber of his being. Diego gave Jon a bemused look.

"Really? Do you want to challenge me? Do you know the forces you are messing with?"

Jon did not know the forces he was messing with. He was merely improvising. In his mind, Jon figured if he had to die, he might as well die like a warrior than like a coward. Plus, dying would not be so bad. His parents were both dead, so he might as well join them.

"Do you?" Jon asked Diego.

Diego laughed. Despite how much he amused the sword-wielding maniac standing before him, he knew that Diego did not feel bad for whatever he had to do now. He would strike down Jon as if he were an equal.

"A lot of loyalty for a man that would probably trade your life if given a chance," said Diego.

"Escobar saved my life," replied Jon. "The least I can do is try to protect him."

"Then you, my friend will die."

Diego attacked. He was relentless, swinging his sword. Every instinct in Jon allowed him to defend himself against every swing. He clanked swords with Diego for a good 20 seconds. Jon was on the defensive, not knowing how to attack. He survived every brutal shot. There was no sign if it was his training, or if he was just getting lucky. Their swords met, and Diego stared him down.

"You have had impressive training."

"I was prepared for you and your kind!"

"Answer me one question," said Diego. "How did Escobar corrupt such an adolescent mind? You seem so full of energy and a force… one that I cannot define properly."

"It is the anger that drives me, the pain that I cannot escape from."

"Let me make you an offer you cannot refuse," said Diego as he forced himself off Jon and they separated. "Join my cause. Join the Legion of Samurai and help us destroy the wickedness in this world starting with Escobar and help us cleanse all the evil there is."

It was a tempting offer. Jon briefly considered this. Was the Legion of Samurai the right move for him? He had spent two-and-a-half years with Escobar and was losing his grip on morality. He had watched Escobar kill men and steal from others. Escobar told him he was a liberator. But even at his age, Jon knew the truth. This was the largest cartel in Brazil. They were deadly, and they took many lives. Was this the life Jon wanted for himself? What would his parents think? Or was Jon in this cartel to punish himself for his parents being gone? Despite the offer and all its potential benefits, Jon shook his head.

"I'm afraid I cannot do that. I am too far gone."

"As you wish," said Diego. "Prepare to pay for your sins."

They engaged in another sword fight. This time, Diego took the initiative. He clanked Jon's sword, deflecting it away. Jon was without a sword now. Diego held his sword to Jon's chest. The leader of the Legion of Samurai seemed to toy with Jon.

"It is over," he said.

"You are correct," said Escobar as he emerged out of nowhere to slam Diego in the head with a baseball bat. Jon watched in horror as Diego fell to the ground from the impact of the bat connecting with Diego's temple. His head connected with the ground and blood oozed out. But Diego was still conscious, groaning at the impact of the bat to his head. Jon shook, and Escobar stood there. The leader of the Great Command looked at his apprentice and handed him a knife.

"Finish him now," said Escobar.

Jon looked at Escobar with trepidation. Now, it seemed like he made the right choice turning down Diego. Was Escobar there the whole time? Many thoughts raced through his mind now as he attempted to figure out what to do. He looked at Escobar's cold, hard eyes. Jon knew if he did not do what Escobar asked, he would kill Jon. There was no going back now. He was not confident in Escobar being fond of him to avoid the possibility of death. Escobar would kill him now that he was a man.

Jon looked down at Diego and saw his helpless body on the ground. He shook his head and held back tears. Finally, he launched his knife into Diego's neck and more blood oozed out. Diego seemed to have a mini seizure as the knife plunged into his neck. Jon gripped it despite being hesitant. He looked away, not liking the sight of the blood, or that he was about to end another's man's life. Finally, with his eyes closed, Jon pulled out the knife.

Jon looked down at Diego, who was still alive but losing a lot of blood. It would only be a few mere moments. Escobar nudged Jon out of his trance.

"Come on, we must go," said Escobar.

Escobar yanked Jon's arm and led him away, causing him to drop the blood-soaked knife.

Later at Escobar's Estate, Jon sat at a makeshift table. They had made their way to this hideout, where they would slowly rebuild their empire. Jon ate breakfast slowly and solemnly. Escobar approached him.

"What is wrong?"

Jon looked up. He was afraid of what to say. There was no going back, and no changing things. Jon had killed a man. He had taken away a man's life and taken away everything that the man would ever be. But there was still fear. He now knew the genuine fear of his life and what it entailed. One could say that Jon made his bones, but he wished he had not. Diego had made him an offer, and this implied that Diego was not a bad person. The Legion of Samurai claimed that they fought evil, and that was something Jon supported. But now Jon had become part of that evil. He knew in his heart that his father would be ashamed of him. Jon was ashamed of himself. He could not believe what he had allowed himself to become.

"Does it ever get easier?" he asked Escobar, a pathetic attempt to make himself feel a little better. But it was an empty question.

"Does what get easier?" replied Escobar, as if he did not understand what Jon was implying.

"Killing a man. Does it ever get easier?"

"As in, easy to find someone and kill them?"

Jon shook his head. He understood now that Escobar no longer felt any remorse, if he ever did, for anyone he had killed in the past. He was the wrong person to ask about this topic. But Jon pressed on.

"No," Jon said meekly. "I mean the feeling of knowing you took someone's life and the feeling of knowing you took away everything the man will ever become."

Escobar sighed. Jon suddenly became fearful. He wondered if this would be what triggered Escobar to finally kill him. Part of him expected Escobar's men to rush in and execute him properly He wondered how they would do it. Perhaps they would all take turns beating him like a piñata. Maybe they would just shoot him in the head. That would be quick and painless, and it would reunite him with his parents at least. This was the second time in as many days Jon pondered about dying. He had just turned 15, and while most 15-year-olds were thinking about learning how to drive soon, Jon's thoughts went dark most of the time.

"Listen," said Escobar in a soothing voice. "It's natural to feel something like you are feeling. But the feeling is something your enemies will not share. They will not hesitate to kill you if given the chance."

Jon gazed at Escobar with curiosity.

"What do you mean?"

"Was he not fighting you?"

Jon nodded. "Yeah."

"Did he not have the aim and the ability to kill you?"

"Well, yeah.."

"Then why do you find it so difficult to move on knowing this?"

Jon did not answer. Escobar had a point, but it did not erase the guilt. Diego Rivera was the first man he had ever killed.

"Our line of work offers no chance for weakness," said Escobar. "You must eradicate it."

"What I fear is something worse," replied Jon. "Something that might consume me, corrupt me. When you saved me from those horrible people, I was grateful and willing to show how appreciative I was. But now... I, I am not sure."

"You listen to me Jon, There is a reason I saved you and it was not just because of honor. I saw something in you, something that I knew could be tapped into. You are a warrior, someone that I consider excellent. You already are one of my top men. I see a bright future for you."

He heard these words, and they calmed him down a little.

"So what now?" asked Jon.

"We lie low for a while and then plan our next move. We make plans for the future and reclaim our power. You did well for your first kill."

Jon hesitated. Then something came to him, he was not sure why.

"Did Diego have any children?"

"I am not sure," replied Escobar.

He glanced at Escobar's eyes and did not believe.

"You're lying," he said.

Escobar became irritated and grabbed him by the throat, reminding the teenager about who is in charge here. He gasped for air as he felt the cartel leader's hands around his throat.

"You need to stop being so emotional, boy!" Escobar roared. "You are in this world and you are not going anywhere! You need not know answers to stupid questions. It does not matter and you need not know!"

He continued to gasp for air. "You're... choking me."

"Your loyalty starts and ends with me. Understood?"

Jon slowly nodded. Escobar released his grip on Jon's throat. Jon coughed, finally being able to breathe. He now fully understood everything. Jon had no choice. He was a soldier in the Great Command of the Capital, and nothing more. Jon would toe the line, or die.

Chapter 25: The Truth

February 9th, 2016

Jessica had to deal with the aftermath of the fact that Ulisez arrested Jon for allegedly murdering her father. She did not believe that Jon was guilty of this and knew in her heart that someone framed him. There was still a part of her that believed he was capable of it. However, she brushed such thoughts away for the time being. Despite all that, Jessica had something else to do that day. She would visit Jon in jail, but for the time being, there was something more important. Patrick had returned to her and gave her the first piece of evidence that she needed. Cobra Holdings, which was a subsidiary of Caine Enterprises, was the registered name of the truck that ran her mother down like a dog. Jessica had to go confront Alexander Caine.

When she arrived, she scanned the environment. Jessica walked up to security, and they did not give her a second look. They must have assumed because she was a somewhat attractive woman, she would be no threat. They were wrong. Jessica walked through security and headed to the top floor where Caine's office was. A ditzy big breasted blonde haired receptionist was sitting there playing with her phone. She looked up when Jessica entered and flashed that smile that a lot of women do when they want to pretend to be nice.

"Hi! May I help you?"

"I'm here to see Mr. Caine."

"Name?"

"Jessica Hudson."

The ditzy receptionist clumsily looked through the list, trying to locate Jessica's name. She fumbled through the pages.

"I don't see your name."

"Just mention my name and if he responds, I will meet him. If he says no, I will leave."

"Okay," replied the receptionist.

Jessica stood off to the side and waited for the receptionist to give her the signal. After a few moments, the receptionist waved her in.

She walked through the doors of Alexander Caine's office. She felt some nerves but otherwise was okay. Jon knew she was here, and that gave her some comfort. Jon was the only person who knew she was here. But Caine did not need to know that. She entered with confidence and sat at the chair in front of Caine. She looked for Caine's lackey, Freddy, but he was nowhere in sight. Something told her that Freddy was close by, in case Caine needed him.

"Jessica, what a surprise it is to see you here."

"Things look clearer when you don't have a hood over your head or a gun to against it."

"Oh my dear, are we remembering our little event?"

"You call it an 'event'. I call it kidnapping."

"Your word versus mine. Who would everyone believe, a well-known philanthropist or a former drug addict?"

"Of course," said Jessica. "That's the type of belief that allows you to get away with all of your crimes."

"Before you rant, I want to give my deepest condolences on the death of your father."

Jessica scoffed at him. "You're just mad you didn't get a chance to kill him first."

"While your father and I had our disagreements, we had reached a mutual understanding lately."

"The only understanding you two had was that he was to not go after you. I won't be that scared of you, Caine."

"Let's cut to the chase. What do you want?"

"I know Caine. I know."

Caine looked at her, curiously. "Excuse me?"

Jessica leaned in, almost over his desk, and within a few feet of Caine. "I know."

Caine looked at her like she lost her mind. He chuckled, apparently amused at this.

"I'm quite sure you know a lot of things, my dear, but run along as I am busy."

"I know!" cried Jessica a little louder now, startling Caine. "I know what you did to my mother!"

Caine's body language shifted. He went from being amused to slightly being annoyed. He did not show concern, not yet, about this claim. Caine glared at Jessica.

"I do not know what you think you know, but you surely don't know a damn thing."

"My mother was killed!"

"Yes she was," said Caine. "It was a car accident. A hit-and-run driver roughly ten years ago."

"No! That is not how she died!"

"Of course it is! It's public record."

"No! She didn't die from the impact of the vehicle. She died from a 22 caliber gunshot wound. Several to the chest."

Caine smiled, amused. He still did not feel the need to worry. This was just a mad woman's ranting. She had no tangible proof.

"And why would you believe that?"

"Because I discovered the truth when I examined her remains and discovered the bullets."

Caine looked at her but said nothing.

"So I assumed that the shooter had to be the person in the car and that my mother's death was no accident."

"Okay. Why the hell should I care?"

"You were temporarily arrested for the murder."

"I don't know what the hell you are talking about."

"My father told me. He arrested you."

"Did he also tell you they forced him to release me due to lack of evidence?"

"Yes, he did," said Jessica. "But all the evidence that the cops did not bother to check, points to you. You and my father had this hatred and quiet war that no one knows about. What better way to hurt him than to kill his wife?"

"All speculation my dear without a shred of fact attached to it."

"But there will be. I will prove what you did and I will put you away for a long time."

"Good luck."

"Your time is almost over. Enjoy it while you can. I'll show myself out."

Jessica stood up and turned to leave. The side door opened, and Freddy quickly blocked her path. Jessica saw him and wondered what took him so long.

"You're not going anywhere, my dear!" said Caine.

She sneered at Freddy, as he still disgusted her. He leered at her breasts, and she felt the urge to hit him. But she resisted because she knew that would probably cause her to end. She turned to Caine.

"People know I'm here. You do anything to me and they will hunt you down."

"I will do nothing," said Caine. "But you need to sit your cute ass back down and listen. It's time for an educational lecture on the way the world works."

She was not sure what she hated worse; Caine's vulgarity or his mansplaining. But she could not say it surprised her. Jessica looked at Freddy, then back at Caine. She walked back over to the chair and sat back down.

"This is ridiculous. You can't just hold me against my will."

Caine fumed. "I think after all this time, you of all people should know I can do whatever the hell I want."

"I said what I came here to say."

"But I haven't said mine."

"Whatever you have to say, just say it."

Caine snickered a little, and this annoyed Jessica.

"Well, my dear, you seem to think the world is as simple as black and white, that it is only good and evil. That is simply not true."

"I think I would classify you as evil," said Jessica.

"But I am not a bad guy," claimed Caine. "I am just a businessman that has to be ruthless. I do whatever is necessary to get the job done."

"Like killing my mother?"

"Your mother was a fine woman, one of the best to ever live. But she was collateral. I don't hold any grudges against her."

"How dare you speak about my mother that way!"

"Your mother was only part of the plan."

She raised her eyebrows. "What are you talking about?"

"Surely you don't think she was the target do you?"

Her eyebrows rose. This was Caine's way of admitting something without actually confessing. But what was he saying?

"Me?" she asked.

Caine nodded. "Tell me, my dear, what could be more painful than losing a child?"

She finally realized everything. At that moment, she now knew exactly what the truth was. They had not meant to kill her mother, but her. Caine and his goons wanted to kill Jessica to teach Hudson a lesson.

"I was meant to die," she trembled from the realization. She suddenly had survivor's guilt. Her mother saved her life that day by pushing Jessica out of the way. Rachel Hudson must have seen the gun and knew that someone was trying to shoot her. Tears flowed down her face, and she hated it. She did not want to show emotion, but could not help it. She did everything she could to hold back the tears. She shook her head sadly.

"I was meant to die. My mother knew it. She saw the gun…"

Jessica could not finish. Her tears overtook her, and she wiped them away. Caine leaned in. And now he was more terrifying than he had ever been. She saw the coldness in his eyes.

"Jessica Rachel Hudson, you are so naïve. You were on this quest to destroy me and you didn't even realize the ultimate goals I strived to accomplish."

"And what was that?"

"To show Frank Hudson what happens when someone opposes me!"

Jessica looked at Caine with some uneasiness.

"You seem a little nervous. What's wrong?" asked Caine with a hint of condescending attitude in his voice.

Jessica did not respond. Her mind was racing. Caine was a master manipulator, and he just used her mother's death to get her to emotionally respond. This angered her. She hated this man with a passion and understood why Jon wanted to kill him.

"Geez, maybe I need to lighten up the mood," said Caine. He summoned Freddy, who walked up and pulled a chair over and sat next to Jessica. She looked at Freddy, and suddenly, without knowing why, she did not feel frightened anymore. She felt irritation, and suddenly some courage.

"Do you know what I just realized?"

"Enlighten me," said Caine.

"You thrive off fear. That's something that gets you going. It's something that enables you to keep your power. It's what turns good men like my father into cowards. It's what turns a system broken. People like you…"

"You're rambling, my dear."

"The point is; fuck you and your intimidation tactics!"

"That's not very ladylike."

"I am no ordinary lady, you vile piece of shit!"

"You have been hanging around Jon Drake way too much," said Caine.

"That's a good thing," replied Jessica. "He taught me that there is always something worth fighting for. And right now, I am demanding you let me go or else."

"Or else what?"

"Because if you don't, Jon will be here and you have already seen what he can do. Can you imagine what Jon would do if something were to happen to me?"

"Jon? Jon is in jail, my dear!"

"Do you honestly think a little jail cell would stop Jon Drake? Think about it, Caine."

Caine considered the idea, and Jessica could tell he was going over all his options.

"It's your move, Caine. You going to kill me and see what happens next. My father may be dead, but Jon still is very much alive. And I know you fear him. You feared him enough to sick one of the best assassins in the world on him, and that assassin got shot off a cliff. That would probably happen to your bitch boy here too."

Freddy growled in anger, like a dog. She smirked at this. She could see he was still recovering from the damage Jon inflicted on him. Caine took out his gun and aimed it at her. She did not flinch. She would not give him the satisfaction.

"I am Alexander Caine, you insignificant little cunt! No one speaks to me that way!"

Jessica smiled. She got a rise out of him. "Losing your temper, Caine?"

"I should have killed you years ago, you little slut!"

"Then do it! It's your move, Caine. What are you going to do?"

Caine's finger was near the trigger. He itched toward it but did not make a move. Instead, he put his gun down. She did not change her expression. Her bluff had worked!

"Get out of my sight!" roared Caine.

"But boss…" Freddy began.

"Frederick, get Ms. Hudson out of my sight immediately," said Caine to Freddy, ignoring his plea.

Jessica glared at Caine. Freddy yanked her off the seat and pulled her up. She yelped at the sudden pain. Freddy led Jessica away. Then she wriggled away and reared back and slapped Freddy across the face. He winced in pain, then he focused again and grabbed her again. He led her out of the office and then out of the building and threw her out of the building and onto her ass. Freddy flipped her off and then headed back inside Caine Enterprises. Jessica groaned in pain.

"Never doing that again."

She arrived home later and just broke down in tears. Jessica had been so focused on confronting Caine that she had almost forgotten to grieve. Now, she could no longer hold it in.

She clutched a photo of her father. She had not slept a minute since her father died. How could she? All she could think of was his horrible, bloodstained body. She had spent parts of the day crying. Her tears were still fresh on her face, and she was not sure when they would be dry. She had planned to go see Jon at some point later but did not have the heart to do so yet. She knew in her heart that Jon did not kill her father. However, Jon's prescience in Orange Grove was a huge reason someone had killed her father. From what Ulisez told her, a man named Vladimir Ramirez killer her father. He was the leader of the Legion of Samurai, which was an ancient vigilante group that went around the world attacking criminal enterprises. So why had they killed her father? That was the big question on her mind as she pouted. Why was her father targeted when he was not a criminal? She figured that perhaps Jon would know the answer, and she would get it out of him. She placed the photo down and heard a knock on the door. Jessica had not expected company, as Ulisez, Amy, and Scotti had already visited her earlier in the day. She walked over to answer the door and opened it to reveal a man with blonde messy hair.

"May I help you?" she asked.

"Are you Jessica?"

"Who's asking?"

"My name is Mike. Mike Wilson. I work for Jon Drake. I heard on the news about Commissioner Hudson. I am not sure how to tell you this but…"

"Yes?"

"Frank Hudson was my father. I'm your half-brother."

She stared at Mike, her jaw dropped. So much went through her mind at the moment. She grieved for her dead father, who she still harbored some resentment toward for everything that transpired with her mother. It was a mixture of sadness and anger. There was no room for additional feelings. She did not need this in her life, not right now. Many things went through her mind, but she said nothing.

"I know it's hard to believe—but if you let me explain…"

"Come on in."

Mike stepped inside and she closed the door behind her. She was hesitant to move around him and studied his face for a second to examine what she would say. What could she say?

They walked inside and Jessica motioned for Mike to sit down. He plopped himself down on the couch and made himself comfortable. She took a deep breath and gathered her thoughts, attempting to decide what to say next.

"So we're—I'm—you're.."

She would not find the words. Mike nodded.

"Yes. We are. I'm sorry to drop in on you like this, especially after he just died."

"Where have you been all this time?"

"My mother raised me, well, she and her husband, my step-dad, raised me."

"And you showed up after his death?"

"Well, not exactly."

"Then what's your story?"

"What do you mean?"

"Why are you here, Mike? My father didn't have a lot of money."

Mike shook his head. "I'm not here because of money, not at all."

"Then why are you here?" she asked, her voice rising a little.

There was silence. It irritated her just to be having this conversation. He almost reminded her of the people she came across in therapy. His voice was soft, like a beach surfer. She imagined he was a beach surfer in the mornings. He was probably the guy that caught every wave.

She slightly felt bad that she kind of yelled at this guy who claimed to be her brother. But this was also the most random thing to possibly happen today in the aftermath of her father's death. Recently, she thought Caine would kill her. This felt worse than that. At least with Caine, she could shout at him and sound tough. How the hell could she shout at this guy? It did not matter anyway.

"I found out recently. Last week. I was going to tell him but never got the chance," said Mike.

"So what do you want, Mike? Do you want to get to know me? You want to talk to his dead body?"

"I–I'm really sorry—I know how hard this must be.."

She got furious now. "You don't know a damn thing about how I'm feeling! You don't know me! You never knew me! You never knew my father!!"

Mike grew somber, a little dejected now. "You're right, I didn't."

"So for you to come out here out of the blue because what–you felt guilty? Well sorry Mike, I will not help you out with your guilt!"

"Please–I just want to know about the man that was my father.."

"The man that impregnated your mother is dead. He's fucking dead! My father is dead."

"Listen–I know you're angry.."

"You don't know the half of it! You coming in and telling me that my father had an affair!"

"I am 28. It happened before your father married your mother.."

She fumed now. "Get out!!! Now!!!!"

Mike stood up sadly. He slowly turned to leave. He looked back at her. "For what it's worth, I am sorry. I live in Costa Mesa. If you ever want to get in touch–I am around."

She pushed him out the door and slammed the door in his face. She had finally come down from her anger. Finally, her eyes welled up. She melted toward the floor and broke down sobbing.

Chapter 26: The Panther

February 9th, 2016

    Vladimir sat in his Laguna Beach mansion watching the news. Their plan had gone off without a hitch. Jon was in jail and subdued for the moment. While he did not expect Jon to stay there, he wanted him to stew a little, at least to teach him a lesson about who was running things.

    He meditated in his studio. His eyes were closed, and he had amazing focus, visualizing the world outside his realm. Vladimir liked to imagine that the world was a peaceful place. There were no more criminals and all his organizations had shot all the politicians to death or thrown them into a swamp where crocodiles would eat them alive. There no longer were conservatives and liberals eating each other because of power, and his organization aligned every person in the world willing to change to his vision. Vladimir was not power-hungry. He did not care to rule the world, he merely wanted to change it.

    This 2016 election for President of the United States amused him very much. When he was not watching the news on the events occurring in Orange Grove, he tuned into local news just for entertainment and it reminded him of why he never had previously owned a television. Television clouded the mind and made fools of people, and this one, with all the cable news shows, was no exception.

    But he kept a television to notice events so he could expect everything. The top two runners for President of the United States were a former reality television host and real estate billionaire and a former first lady. That same first lady had previously lost two elections, as the American people did not like her very much. But what truly amused him was the buffoon that opposed her. The man said such ridiculous, idiotic things and had half the country under his spell and the other half inciting him and calling him racist, sexist, and fascist.

    He enjoyed watching people fight amongst each other and was more confident that wiping them all off the face of the Earth was the answer. He continued his intense meditation when he heard footsteps approaching. He did not need to open his eyes to know who it was.

    "Hello Panther," Vladimir called out.

    Thomas approached and kneeled before him. "Lion. Your tactics took me by surprise."

    "But it was effective, was it not?"

Thomas nodded. "They have elected to name me intern commissioner."

"Everything is going according to my design."

"What next?"

Vladimir opened his eyes. He locked eyes with Thomas and saw for the first time that his young soldier was a little weary. Something was troubling him.

"Why do you worry?" he asked Thomas.

Thomas looked at him cautiously, picking his words carefully. There was a small tension between them. Vladimir reached out and touched his apprentice on the shoulder gingerly. The commissioner looked up at him and shook his head.

"I was growing fond of the man you killed," Thomas said somberly.

Oh, Vladimir thought. He understood the feelings that Thomas experienced at the moment, though there was an understanding of what had needed to happen.

"You saw this man as a father figure?" Vladimir inquired.

Any other leader could have scolded Thomas for feeling this way. They would have told Thomas that he could not show weakness or anything resembling it. But Vladimir knew about human emotions and knew that it was part of humanity. Although he was confident in his abilities, he wanted to make sure Thomas would remain on their side. There was no upside to the Panther changing sides, so he took the gentle approach.

"I had felt little fondness for anyone since my mother and brother were murdered and I joined your cause," Thomas said. "You are the only other person I have been able to connect with—find some understanding with.

"I just don't know anymore, Vladimir. I just don't know. Will there be a place for me in the new utopia? I am feeling distanced from your plans, especially when you don't tell me ahead of time. Do you not trust me anymore?"

"The only thing you must worry about is keeping Jon Drake locked up. When the next phase comes, I will tell you," he assured him.

Chapter 27: A New Legion of Samurai

Legion of Samurai Fortress July 18th, 2008

After Jon Drake killed Diego, Vladimir prepared his legion for a new beginning, a new organization. The murder forced him to take action and become the new leader of the Legion of Samurai.

Vladimir had his men help him carry the body out. They had chased off Escobar and his men. While they had been victorious in chasing off the largest cartel in Brazil, they paid a dear price for it. They had killed their leader. There was no going back. They did not waste time celebrating his life. It was a beautiful ceremony that Vladimir had arranged quickly. The Legion of Samurai always prepared for death, and they had a tomb already set for Diego. Vladimir found the tomb particularly appealing.

"Gentlemen," said Vladimir in Portuguese. "We have lost a beloved friend. He was a beloved leader and the man that taught us everything about what it means to be a warrior."

In the crowd, the warriors all have their heads bowed down. Among them included Thomas, flanked by Manny, Ivan, and Nubia. The teenagers stood with Thomas, looking solemn as the proceeding continued. Manny held back tears as they celebrated his father's life and mourned him. Vladimir went on.

"We must stand together and take the Legion of Samurai to heights it's never reached. The Samurai Franco Yuan and Master Diego Rivera were like fathers, and their deaths do not mean the end. It simply means the beginning."

Vladimir waited for the crowd to say more, but no one reacted. He had expected that reply, as there was now a sobering silence.

"Following the death of our beloved master, it is now my unfortunate task to take over as ranking master of the Legion of Samurai," Vladimir continued.

The crowd listened in anticipation. He had their respect, and that was the first sign of a successful leader. Vladimir had wished to be nothing but the best leader for the Legion of Samurai.

"I also have to appoint a second-in-command. A man that will be my next in line should something ever happen to me.

"This is someone who I love like a son. Someone dear to me and someone who I believe will hold the values of the Legion of Samurai the same way I do."

Vladimir looked on the crowd to see how his son Ivan would react, knowing he was being passed over. He saw some disappointment in his son, but Vladimir had always taught his son how to deal with life's letdowns. Ivan Ramirez would have his chance someday but now was not the time. Nubia looked on at her father, with her eyes focused.

"I'd like to announce my next-in-command, the Panther," Vladimir called out.

The crowd erupted in joy as Thomas slowly, stupidly made his way onto the stage. The man awkwardly stood next to him and kneeled before him. Then Vladimir raised him with one arm and lifted him off the ground. He embraced Thomas and together they began their new regime.

Chapter 28: The Breaking Point

February 9th, 2016

They booked Jon and arraigned into Orange Grove Detention Facility for holding. They were rough with him, as Freewald and Santos handled the booking. He was not sure how many officers on Hudson's force were corrupt, but he knew that there were enough for Hudson to have to worry about. Now that Hudson was dead, things might spiral out of control. There was no commissioner at the moment, but it seemed like they named Thomas the acting commissioner. The rest of the force scattered, and Jon felt that the only person he could truly trust was Ulisez. Even then, Ulisez had doubted him a little and allowed Thomas and his goons to arrest him.

An hour had passed since his arrest, and Jon had gathered himself. He had calmed down since the incident. He realized that his panicky behavior had allowed him to let his guard down and thus get himself arrested. He was waiting for the right move. There would be a time and a place for everything, and Jon could be a little patient.

The guard entered the room. He was a husky bald man, Jon knew him as Tyler Pennington. From what Jon knew, he had a wife, but Tyler was very rough with the inmates, at least the ones he did not like. Tyler stared down at Jon. "You have a visitor."

He looked up, and Tyler left before he could say anything. Vladimir arrived before him, dressed in sunglasses and a suit that made him look larger than life. Jon stood up immediately.

"You…"

"Now Jon, please let us not forget our place, shall we?"

"You bastard! You killed an innocent man!"

"Only a fool would truly believe that Frank Hudson was innocent."

"He did nothing to you, man! He wasn't responsible for anything! I am the one you want!"

"He was a symptom of a bigger problem. Did you really think I brought you back home just to destroy one man?"

He glanced at Vladimir, curiously. "What are you talking about?"

"Remember who I represent and what my master taught me."

"And what was that?"

"That evil comes in many forms and this entire town in this state… has become corrupted beyond repair and must be allowed to die."

"You sure have a funny way of defining good and evil when you just murdered an innocent man."

"The people of California have become so wrought with corruption that it's time for someone to bring it back to its former glory."

"What else did your masters teach you? That murder is acceptable as long as you believe the other person is evil?"

"They could have taught me more --- had you not killed one of them."

Vladimir's words rang off his ears and brought back horrible memories for him. Suddenly, he saw himself stabbing Diego Rivera in the heart. Everything made sense to him now, and Jon finally realized that everything came full circle.

"All this time, you were out for revenge?"

Vladimir shook his head. "I was willing to overlook your transgression, especially considering your hand was forced. But let us not make a mistake here; you took away a 12-year-old boy's father by murdering him."

He realized the irony. In a sick, twisted way, he had become exactly like Freddy Hunter. He had killed a man and took away everything that the man would ever become. Regardless of who Diego was, the man still had a child. That child grew up to become Manny Rivera, top right-hand man to the leader of the Legion of Samurai.

"Diego Rivera," he acknowledged the name of the man he killed. "He was trying to kill me. Diego was…"

"Manny Rivera's father," said Vladimir. "Now while our original goal was not revenge, you not would blame us for wanting to partake in an eye for an eye?"

He thought about it for a moment but said nothing. Vladimir went on.

"Despite all this, I still see potential in you."

"What are you saying?"

"I can make this all go away. The murder charge, the assault charge. Everything. All you would have to do is pledge your undying loyalty to me."

"You must be out of your mind…"

"Dead serious."

"What about Manny? Surely he cannot be happy about the fact that I killed his father…"

"If you rejoin us, meaning you fully turn away from everything you love and hold dear, I will handle Manuel. He will not attempt to harm you. The good of the Legion overtakes any personal vendettas."

Jon pondered this for a moment. For a moment, he considered the offer until he shook his head. He glared right into Vladimir's eyes.

"No. Not after what you did. You can take your offer and go to hell."

Vladimir smiled and shook his head. "It's a pity. We could have been extremely powerful together. We could bring balance to the world."

"We're better as adversaries. When I get out—and I will—I will look for you, I will find you, and I swear to fucking God I will kill you."

Vladimir smiled and waved at Jon as if the words meant nothing. "Good luck."

Tyler walked into the holding cell area again. "You got another visitor, Drake."

Ulisez walked into the area, and Tucker left. Jon rolled his eyes.

"Why are you here Ulisez?"

"Can't a guy visit his buddy in jail when he's been accused of murder?"

"So you don't actually believe I did it right? I mean you did nothing to stop the arrest."

"Same way I don't believe the 49ers are a talented team and will never win another Super Bowl."

"You got a way with words, you know that?"

"I honestly never thought I would see you in this situation again."

"A lot better than the last time."

"You're accused of murder. How is this better?"

"Because this time I am not in a South American jail."

"I think you'd probably be more comfortable in a South American jail."

"But the circumstances are not ideal.."

"What happened Jon?"

He paused for a moment. Then he told the story. "Frank and I were having a beer, hanging out. Vladimir and his damn Samurai warriors break-in and three of them beat me down and hold me.

Vladimir spouts off some sanctimonious crap about Frank being responsible for Caine and his crimes and letting Caine run wild all these years."

Ulisez said nothing.

"He wants to make an example of the people he sees as evil and will do anything to do it."

He looked at Ulisez, who remained silent. Ulisez held back tears, feeling a little miserable when hearing this story.

"I loved him, man. He was like a father to me. Now he's dead–because of me. I don't–I'm not sure what to do anymore."

"Stop," said Ulisez, finally breaking in. "Stop talking. Just shut up for a moment."

They stood there awkwardly for a moment, neither knowing what to say. Finally...

"What were his final words?"

"His what?"

"His last words! What were his last words?"

"Tell–he told me to tell Jessica that he loved her. Always."

Ulisez once again was speechless. Jon went on.

"I watched him die–it was terrible…"

"I don't want to hear any more."

"We have to find Vladimir."

"We will."

Ulisez nodded and then signaled goodbye.

He took a brief nap as he had to conserve his energy for what he planned to do. Tyler reentered.

"You're popular around here, Drake. You got another visitor."

He picked himself off the bed. He looked up, and in the darkness, he could see the radiant light. Jessica stood in front of him.

"Jessica."

"Tell me what happened."

"I was hanging out with your father. Everything was okay. Then they came–they came, and they killed him."

"Who killed him?" asked Jessica, despite already knowing the answer.

"Vladimir Ramirez. Jessica, your dad was innocent. He didn't deserve this. Vladimir did this to teach me a lesson."

"How did Vladimir kill my father?"

"You don't need to hear that…"

"Tell me how he died!"

Jessica had never snapped at him before. This took him by surprise. He hesitated for a moment, saw the pain in her eyes.

"As Vladimir's men held me down, Vladimir took out a Katana sword and stabbed your father through the chest, impaling him."

Jessica clasped her mouth in horror. He went on.

"It was the worst thing I have ever witnessed."

"And you have witnessed some sick shit too."

"I was powerless to stop him, Jess. Believe me. I tried so hard. I would have let them kill me over him."

Jessica nodded. "I know."

"I'm still coming to grips with it."

He hesitated. Then he went on.

"I'm sorry you had to find out this way."

"It wouldn't have made a difference either way."

"I am–responsible for this total mess."

"You didn't see this coming."

"I should have."

There was a moment of silence. Both thought of what to say next, with neither knowing the right words. Finally, Jessica broke the silence.

"Why did Thomas arrest you?"

"His two corrupt cops assaulted me and I defended myself."

Jessica shook her head and slightly smiled. "What are you going to do now?"

"I will find a way out of here. But I am worried about you."

"Me? You're the one in jail, dude."

"Yeah, and now Vladimir has a way of getting to you."

"I survived Caine. I will be fine."

"Please be careful."

"What were his last words?"

The second time someone had asked him this question today. Jon hesitated, now knowing it would hurt even more.

"It doesn't matter anymore."

"It matters to me."

He considered this, then relented.

"Tell Jessica I love her."

Jessica finally broke down. She fell against the cell bars, her eyes going watery all over. He comforted her by patting her hair and extended through the bars and kissed the top of her head. She finally regained her composure. He looked her dead in the eyes.

"Jess, you need to stay strong. Do you hear me? Stay strong."

She nodded. He continued.

"I will fight this. I will overcome this minor hurdle. We will overcome them all–Caine, Vladimir. All the evil men in the world, we will overcome them."

"It's getting harder to believe."

"You have to. For me. And for yourself. We will keep fighting and we will win."

"I hope so."

He reached through the bars and held Jessica's hand. Her hand felt warm to him, and it was perfect.

"For you, your hope is all I need."

"You will need a hell of a lot more than me."

"Trust me, Jess. I got a plan."

Jessica looked at him curiously, then nodded gracefully. They held hands for a moment, then she released and headed out. He watched her go.

Tyler entered the room again.

"You got another visitor, Drake."

He looked up to see none other than Alexander Caine standing before him. He immediately stood up and walked to the bars.

"Now this is an interesting sight. I just had to see it with my own eyes," said Caine.

"What the hell are you doing here?" exclaimed Jon.

"Seeing an illusion," replied Caine as he grabbed the bars as if he were trying to see if they were real. "It's ironic a bit, isn't it Jon?"

"Go to hell!"

"We'll both be there soon enough."

"Why are you even here? To gloat?"

"No, my boy, like I said–I had to come to see this with my own eyes."

"Hard to believe that I am in jail?"

"Hard to believe you are in jail for the murder of Frank Hudson."

He did not respond. Caine's smug look irritated him. But he had no defense for Caine's sharp words.

"You," Caine continued, this time pointing at Jon. "You would never do anything to hurt that man. You loved him like a father and he loved you like a son."

"What's your point?"

Caine laughed. "You're an innocent man. One of the rare times."

"Even you know that no one in this world is truly innocent."

"Careful. You're starting to sound like Vladimir."

His eyes narrowed. "So Vladimir left you alive."

Caine smiled. "He claimed he was warning me. As if Frank Hudson's death would affect me."

Jon slammed his elbows into the bars, startling Caine. "I am nothing like Vladimir!!"

"Did I hit a nerve? I don't believe you are like Vladimir. You and I -we're not all that different."

"I am nothing like you, Caine! I don't kill for personal gain and power."

"And you haven't? For the love of God Jon, if you're going to throw stones, at least make sure you don't have your own skeletons in the closet."

"What do you want? Why are you here?" Jon asked for the second time. He studied the expression on Caine's face to see if he could pick up on anything.

"I have a proposition for you," said Caine.

"What?"

"A proposition. Oh, I forgot you didn't get past sixth grade. Let me make it simple for you; I have a deal for you."

He was hesitant. At first, he believed Caine was here just to gloat. But now, after speaking with him a little, Jon could see that there was something else Caine wanted.

"What kind of deal?"

"I can make this all go away–the murder charges, the assault charges, everything if you agree to one little thing for me."

"What?"

"You come to work for me. Be my guard, my number one guy."

His eyes bulged. He was not sure if Caine was being serious or if he was messing with him. It was also a weird coincidence.

"You're joking, right?" he asked.

"No joke. I see a lot of potential in you," said Caine.

"What about Freddy?"

"Freddy is skilled–you and I both know that."

Those words hurt, and he instantly remembered who he was speaking with, and the anger returned. Caine went on.

"I have never met anyone with your skills. All the skills you have shown me over the last few weeks are, in no words, incredible. But you have wasted all this energy in hating me.."

"You killed my father," Jon reminded him. Caine ignored him.

"Can you think of all the potential you have? Can you think of the amazing things you and I could go together to better this world? I am mankind's true salvation, and my products will always make things better. But with you by my side, we'd be unstoppable."

"And who else would die to further this agenda?"

"Allegedly. I am a businessman with many powerful enemies. I can be as ruthless as I need to be."

He did not reply. Caine just looked at him with interest, realizing that the younger man was taking it in.

"Consider this Jon. Don't make the same mistake your father made."

The anger returned now. He scowled at Caine now. He shook his head and leaned in.

"Fuck you and your offer."

Caine leaned back, slightly amused. "Have it your way. Enjoy your murder charge."

"I will beat this on my own and then I will resume my fight to bring you down! Now with Frank gone, I am more motivated than ever to take you down."

Caine chuckled. "Good luck." He motioned for Tucker to signal that his time with Jon was over. Before he left, he turned back toward him. "You can't ever say I didn't try to work with you, Jon."

"Your work I don't need or want."

Caine smiled. He walked off, and the door closed behind him.

He had a plan, but he needed a little more time, and the right person to execute it on. A little later, the door opened and instead of Tyler making an announcement, Thomas entered the room. The Panther started clapping, and Jon just smiled.

"And finally, we get to the biggest piece of shit in the room," he beamed as he looked at Thomas, who looked around and then made a motion with his finger and mouth as if to say 'me?' but otherwise said nothing. "What do you want Martin?"

"That's Commissioner Martin to you, Drake. You never learned your manners."

"Good thing you helped kill Frank to take his job."

"Bullshit boy. That's all you are."

He grinned and could sense how it annoyed Thomas. The new commissioner just scoffed at him, and Jon shook his head.

"It's kind of despicable what you're doing, Martin."

"The Lion will not tolerate your antics much longer."

"Oh, are we doing code names again? Lion for Vladimir? White Warrior for me because you all are racist pieces of shit? What are you again? The Shit Tiger?"

"Panther. Some have called me Black Panther, but Panther will suffice just fine."

"Oh, that's right, Panther. Who the hell comes up with these names? I'm surprised Manny never got one."

"You earn your name with stripes. You did a lot of damage to get yours. Many saw you as one of the best before Vladimir even trained you."

"And how long have you worked for Vladimir?"

"I don't work for Vladimir. It's a mutual understanding. We both were disciples of the man you killed."

"Yes, I know Diego Rivera. I have heard this garbage before."

"And you don't seem to take this seriously. You are in jail because of your inability to follow orders."

"Or maybe my inability to follow an insane man's orders makes me a much better person than the loser I am looking at."

"What d'you call me?"

"You heard me. You are a loser, Martin. You always have been, always will be."

"You talk too much, white boy."

"And you cry too much. What's the matter, still crying over your dead brother and mother?"

"You still crying over your dead daddy?"

"I'm actively doing something. What are you doing, other than being Vladimir Ramirez's little bitch?"

He saw Thomas's cheeks go red. The anger was rising, and his plan was working. Thomas took out some keys and unlocked the cell. He opened the doors and entered. Thomas stepped forward, and he smiled maliciously. Jon quickly grabbed Thomas's arm and yanked it forward, surprising the Panther. Thomas yelped in pain as this startled him. He elbowed Thomas in the face, sending his head careening into the jail bars, before watching as he landed on the ground with a thud.

He dragged Thomas's limp, unconscious body into the cell. He grabbed the keys and placed them into his pocket. Then, he closed the door behind him and locked it, while Thomas laid there, out like a lamb. He slipped out the door and quietly made his way out of the station.

He made his way toward his apartment and gathered some material. No cops other than Hudson and Ulisez knew where he lived, so it was relatively easy. He had to get out of town quickly to process what he would do next, but grabbed his car and headed toward Jessica's apartment first.

He got outside her apartment and headed over and knocked on her door. She opened it and looked at Jon awkwardly.

"Jon?"

"Jess, get your things ready. We got to go."

Part 3

Chapter 29: On The Run

February 10th, 2016

It did not take Jessica long to agree to go with Jon. She believed in his innocence, and that was enough to give him the benefit of the doubt. Jessica knew in her heart that she could trust Jon more than anyone in the world, and she did not trust anyone.

They drove for miles with nothing on the horizon. Jon and Jessica packed some belongings and quickly headed east on the 15 freeway. From there, they made a turn to the Interstate 395 freeway to head up to the Sierras. Jon had mentioned to Jessica that he had a cabin in Lake Tahoe, which was technically true. The cabin belonged to Ram "The Bounty Hunter" Delacruz, a former partner of his. Ram had told Jon he could use his place anytime he needed it for emergency uses, and well, this was as big of an emergency as could be. Jon drove up the road while Jessica slept. She could tell that he slightly felt bad for dragging her into this, but he needed help and aside from Ulisez, she was the person he trusted the most. Ulisez was not exactly an option right now as he was too close to the police, so Jessica figured she was the best option.

They drove past Bishop now, as they had been on the road for approximately five hours. She slept a little while Jon drove.

Jessica rustled a little, starting to stir a bit. Her eyes flickered as she woke up a little. She looked off as her eyes finally opened. She turned groggily toward Jon.

"Where are we?"

"Almost where we need to be," replied Jon.

Jessica shook her head a little and rubbed her eyes to focus her pupils. She adjusted her body and sat up a little straighter. She turned to Jon.

"Jon, what are we doing?"

"We're doing what we need to do, Jess."

"Okay master of the vague comments."

"I have to be."

"Jon, why did you break out?"

Jon looked at her for a moment, considering his thoughts. She kept her gaze focused on him, not relenting.

"Would you rather I still be in jail for a crime I didn't commit at the mercy of corrupt cops?"

"Of course not…"

Jon turned back toward the road. "I didn't have a choice. No one believed me except you and Ulisez. And I couldn't get him because of his cop ties."

"Don't you care about what I think about this?"

"You're here, aren't you? You could have said no."

"But still. Don't you care what this is doing to me? He was my father…"

"And I heard there was a funeral. I'm sorry I missed it."

"How did you know?"

"I make it my business to know. Also, aren't you at all curious about the mysterious benefactor that paid for your father's funeral?"

She widened her eyes and wanted to ask 'how did you know' again, but said nothing.

"I could make a bet that Vladimir Ramirez paid for the funeral."

"Why would the man that killed my father pay for the funeral?"

"Because in Vladimir's mind, it was his way of making up for taking your father from you."

"Gee, that's nice," said Jessica sarcastically.

"He is a strange man in the way he hurts people but still respects them. It's the Legion of Samurai way."

There was a moment of silence that passed as Jessica processed this all. Jon looked ahead to the road, and she looked out the window.

"Jon, why did you bring me into this?"

"If it weren't for you, I wouldn't be in this situation."

"Excuse me?"

"Don't take it the wrong way. I blame myself completely."

"Then why did you just say I was the reason?"

"Because of my connection to you, Vladimir used it against me."

"You say that only because you came back to town to kill Alexander Caine. Where would that get you in the end, Jon? Your father would still be dead."

"Wow, harsh Jess."

"I lost my father too, Jon. I'm still mourning the unsolved murder of my mother, you asshole," she cursed at Jon with a harsh tone he had never heard from him. It took him by surprise.

"And I have lost my parents too! And countless others! So don't you dare lecture me, Jess," he replied.

There was another moment of silence. This was their first actual fight, as they had always been cordial with each other. Jon kept his eyes on the road now, but now Jessica's gaze was upon him. Her brown eyes studied him for a moment, and it made Jon slightly uncomfortable.

"What are you looking at?"

"You never got over your parents' deaths, did you?"

"And you did? Are you over watching your mother get shot and hit by a car, Jess?"

She shook her head sadly. Jon realized that was a low blow, but he could not help himself.

"My number one priority is keeping you safe," said Jon. "I can't–I can't imagine my life without you."

They drove in silence for the remaining duration of the trip. It was not an awkward silence, but one that felt right. They had said everything they needed to say before they reached their destination. There were harsh words exchanged, but they got it out.

Finally, they reached their destination. Jon parked the car in front of the cabin. Jessica looked at the cabin, and it surprised her. She opened the door and exited the car. She shivered as the cold air hit her like a ton of bricks. There was snow on the ground, but it was only slightly windy, if not cold.

"Why are we in a cabin in the woods?"

"We're in Lake Tahoe."

She glanced at him with shock. She processed everything, and it was as if she remembered something from long ago.

"This is the place our parents used to take us as kids."

"Well, not this cabin exactly, but yeah."

Before the bad times, their parents were friends. Robert and Natalie Drake and Frank and Rachel Hudson had vacationed together twice when all four were alive. They took their respective children, Jon and Jessica with them. Lake Tahoe was the place where they all came to take some time away from it all. Jessica remembered playing on the beach with Jon, and she remembered riding a bike behind her mother. Her father used to pick her up and run straight for the water. The water was chilly on most occasions. But it was wonderful.

Jon headed for the cabin and she followed him. They entered the cabin. It was a small cabin, as there was a living room, a small kitchen, and one small bedroom. A fireplace also on the edge of the living room. She spotted the small room. Jon closed the door behind her. He took off his coat.

"Looks like we got ourselves a comfortable setting," joked Jon.

"There's only one bed…"

"We can share it."

Jessica looked at Jon, almost embarrassed. "But.."

"I mean–unless you are afraid that you cannot resist me.."

"Don't flatter yourself."

Jon smiled. He headed to the kitchen, and she followed. He reached into the cupboard and pulled out some pasta. She stared in shock.

"How long has that been there?"

"A month. I had a feeling I'd be needing this cabin. I'm here sooner than I figured I would be."

She saw something she had never, ever believed she would see: Jon cooking. She watched in amazement as he took out the pasta and then a pot and pan and boiled some water. Jon had also turned on the heater in the cabin, which she was not even aware there was. She was pleased about that, as it was cold. The weather outside was about 22 degrees Fahrenheit. Jessica brought some clothes with her that would help stave off the cold. It still did not feel like enough. The heater being on helped a lot. She sat on the couch and waited patiently while Jon cooked up some pasta silently. She noticed a book on the coffee table and glanced at it curiously. The title of the book was "Bounty Hunting and How to Excel At It". She opened the book and read a little. Jon had told her about the cartel part of his life, but he was very vague about the bounty hunting part. This was a part of his life she was genuinely curious about. She read while Jon cooked. Finally, after about ten minutes, she finished cooking the pasta. Jon placed the pasta into two dishes, which he had available for use. Jon handed her a plate of pasta and she nibbled at the pasta hesitantly.

"It will not make you fat, you know," Jon remarked.

"It can, it's pasta."

"Pasta is good for you."

"No, it's not."

"The Italians invented pasta in the 13th century. Are you going to tell me that all Italians are fat?"

"Shut up."

Jon laughed. They ate their pasta without another word. After they both finished eating, Jon cleaned the dishes and put the pasta away in a container and placed it into the fridge. She remained on the couch and read a little more from the bounty hunting book. It was the only book in the cabin, so she figured that she might as well read it.

Jon finished up in the kitchen and then turned the fireplace on. It was about eight o'clock in the morning, which made it even stranger that they had just are pasta for breakfast. She gazed at him with curiosity.

"How did you come upon this place, anyway?"

"An old friend owns this cabin."

"The bounty hunter?"

He nodded. "He gave me access to it whenever I wanted, especially since he knew I was from California."

"Seems random for you to have a friend with a cabin up in Lake Tahoe. We are at least eight hours away from home."

"I know it's convenient."

Jon turned up the fireplace, and he sat on the couch across from Jessica. He noticed she was reading the book on the table. "You like it?"

"Bounty Hunting and Ho to Excel At It."

"Yeah, like I said. My bounty hunter friend owns this cabin."

"Is he a bounty hunter or were you a bounty hunter?"

"Well, duh–why else would he have a book on bounty hunting?"

"Well, I don't know.."

"You think a random guy who isn't a bounty hunter just randomly keeps a book about bounty hunting lying around?"

"No."

"Then you know the answer..."

"Jon…"

"Jess…"

She punched him in the shoulder. Her fist connected with his upper body, and it was rough. He looked at her in shock.

"What the hell was that for?"

"For speaking to me like I was an idiot."

"I didn't speak to you…"

"Yes, you did asshole! And I'd appreciate it if you didn't."

"Well, if it seemed that way–I'm sorry."

She looked at Jon, surprised he apologized for something. She understood how rare this was, but started laughing.

"What's so funny?"

"I have never seen you apologize for anything."

"You're right. I don't normally apologize."

"And yet you apologized to me…"

"Well, you deserved it."

"And why is that?"

"Because you're worth it."

"That was an incredibly nice thing to say."

"It's the truth, Jess."

"I'm not sure I deserve it."

Jon leaned in closer to her than he had been. He gazed upon her eyes, and she looked back.

"You are the most amazing woman I know. You're intelligent, you're courageous, and you're beautiful. You deserve nothing but the best."

"I do?"

"Jess–when I look at most people, I feel nothing but irritation and hatred. But with you, I feel nothing but…"

She saw Jon stumble over his words. It was adorable. He stared at her for a moment. She stared back and there was a moment between them, where they had forgotten all their issues for just a moment. He leaned in and kissed her on the lips. She reacted at first, not sure how to take this. After a few seconds, she fell into the kiss and embraced him. She pulled back from him for a moment and just stared at him. There was a slight feeling of uncertainty for her here. She felt so many conflicted feelings for Jon, but she was not sure about how to process them. Then, as she looked into his eyes, gave in, and pulled him into a kiss.

They fell sloppily together on the couch, their bodies pressed on each other like glue. She ripped off his shirt with animal aggression that startled him a little, but he went with it. They kissed passionately and aggressively, both engaged in a moment that had been a long time coming. She pulled Jon's jeans off and struggled slightly to get it off his body. He ripped her shirt off, displaying her bra underneath, then did her pants the same way. She brushed her fingers into his neck, lightly scratching him. Her eyes filled. Within seconds, both of them were naked and were breathing hard in each other's arms, not letting go for a single second.

They laid on the floor with a blanket over them, both of them with their eyes open, awkward. She could not bear to look at him, not yet.

"I can't believe we just did that."

"I can't believe it took us so long," replied Jon.

"I'm serious," She turned over to Jon. "What is this? What are we doing?"

"Literally? We just had sex–what else would we be doing?"

"I mean come on Jon–you are on the run and I am now an accomplice. We are both fugitives and we should both be looking over our shoulders. But we're–we're.."

"Making sweet love?"

"Cut it out. What does this–what does this mean?"

He smiled, which annoyed her. "Cut it out!"

"Why do we need labels? We both know how we feel for each other."

"I just–I am not sure I can do this–this life you have set for yourself."

He stared at her for a moment, then leaned in and kissed her. She pulled back.

"You can't just shut me up by kissing me. We still have to talk about it…"

He kissed her again. They start actively making out on the floor and he climbed on top of her and reached around to grab her thigh when a noise outside startled them. His eyes instantly became alert, and he went into another mode. He stopped kissing her, then stared right at her with a serious look.

"Someone is here."

Jon slowly picked himself off of the floor, and off of her. He grabbed his pants to put them on. She stirred under the covers and scrambled to find her clothes. An explosion ripped through the room, with debris flying across the room.

The front door blew off the hinges, and they fell back from the impact. Jon groaned. Freddy entered the area with a gun in his hand and a shit-eating grin on his face.

"Hi kids missed me," exclaimed Freddy as he stepped into the fray with a small 22-millimeter handgun in plain view. Jon looked over to her, and she looked more mortified than frightened.

"Freddy. What the hell are you doing here," growled Jon to sound intimidating. But he did not have the energy he usually did.

"Boss thought you being on the run and a fugitive was the perfect time to finish you off. That way when we finish you off.." Freddy stopped himself as he looked at Jessica and her naked body hidden under the covers.

"What?" she asked.

Freddy turned to Jon. "Is she naked under there?" He looked back at her. "Are you naked under there? Why don't you remove the covers so I can have a peek?"

"Go to hell, you disgusting pig," she snapped.

"Oh, feisty. I love that," said Freddy. He aimed his gun at Jessica and Jon moved in front of her to protect her.

"You really should reconsider, Freddy. I spared your life," said Jon.

"Spared my life while breaking my legs. I'm still not fully recovered, you dick! Least now I have the gun and the high ground," said Freddy.

"You're right," said Jon. "You do. And I will give you ten seconds to get out of here and I will pretend this never happened."

"Do you have some balls on you or what Drake," replied Freddy.

"Ten."

Freddy cocked his gun and aimed it at Jon. "No countdown, asshole. You both die now. You know it's funny. It will come full circle for both of you."

"What are you talking about?" asked Jessica.

"I killed Jon's old man ten years ago and today I get to finish the job," replied Freddy. "But you sweetheart, you will be the main kill. I finally get to finish what I started."

This anger inside her boiled over and she wanted to destroy everything in her path. She clenched her fists and rose to her feet, the blanket still covering her. Freddy reminded her he had the gun, holding the weapon close to her face.

"Uh uh," he said. "I only told you this because you will die, anyway. You're welcome for granting you an extra ten years to live."

"You need to leave now," said Jon to Freddy.

"It's over, Drake. Any last words?" asked Freddy.

"Just one; surrender," said Manny as he appeared from behind Freddy and held a knife to his throat.

"Manny?" exclaimed Jon, at the turn of events and a little shocked that Manny came by himself.

"Only one person gets the privilege of killing Jon Drake, and that's me," said Manny.

"I didn't know you care," replied Jon sarcastically.

"The man who murdered my father must pay with his life," said Manny.

She turned toward Jon. "Is this true?"

"I did what I had to do to survive," said Jon.

As she took this in, attempting to understand it, Manny knocked Freddy out quickly and swiftly with an elbow to the temple, sending him hurling to the ground.

"I was tired of holding a knife to his throat," Manny remarked.

"Manny…" Jon began.

"Hush, you will die now," said Manny. He turned to Jessica. "I have no quarrel with you, Jessica Hudson. You can get your clothes and leave. My vendetta is with Jon Drake."

Jessica put her shirt back on, and her jeans. Manny watched this carefully, and Jon watched Manny. Then, Jessica took a step forward and stepped in front of Jon and between him and Manny's gun.

"Jess, what are you doing?" asked Jon.

"No," was all Jessica said, both to Jon and Manny. She faced Manny, filled with courage and some fear. "Jon made a choice back then. It's not morally right–but neither is you killing him. An eye for an eye is not right."

"I do not wish to kill you, but do not make the mistake of thinking I will not. Move out of the way, foolish girl. Jon Drake is not worth your life."

"Yes, he is," she shot back. This moved Jon a little. Jessica went on. "He is everything to me and I cannot live without him. If you want to kill him, then you better go through me."

"You are very brave, very foolish–but very brave, regardless."

"I want you to leave us alone. Jon is not a killer anymore," said Jessica.

"That does not change the fact that he murdered my father–I must avenge my father. No?"

Jon stood beside Jessica. She looked at him, and he gave her an approving look. They stood side by side as equals now, as Jessica had shown her willingness to stand by Jon.

"I used to think I was alone," Jon began. "That is why it was easy for someone like Vladimir to come in and manipulate me into doing what he wanted. Now I realize I am not alone."

Jessica touched Jon's arm, touched by his words. Manny smiled, something rare for him.

"You are correct about one thing, Jon Drake. Because of your foolish girlfriend's actions, you won't be alone–in dying." Manny revealed his sword. "This time you both die."

"Not yet," said Ulisez as he emerged out of nowhere with a gun aimed at Manny. Jon and Jessica looked at one another and realized that they were lucky in this situation. Manny dropped his knife and smirked as he looked at Ulisez.

"You? The cop?"

Ulisez smiled. "Yeah me, the cop."

"You are making a mistake, young man. I can easily disarm you."

"Maybe–maybe not. But you will not be killing today."

Manny pointed at Jon. "He murdered my father. Vengeance must be swift."

"Yeah well, it's not happening today."

Without warning, Manny grabbed Ulisez's gun and deflected it away. He punched Ulisez in the face with a right forearm and then head-butted him for good measure. Manny grabbed Ulisez's left arm and wrenched it, causing Ulisez to scream in agony. "Foolish boy–you are no match for me or the Lion."

Manny kicked Ulisez in the chest now, causing him to cough loudly. He pulled out a dagger and Jon and Jessica watched this in bewilderment. Jon leaned in toward her. "I have a plan."

Jessica did not keep her eyes off Manny standing near Ulisez with a dagger in his hand.

"What? We're caught between a rock and a hard place," she said.

"I came prepared. Reach into my pocket."

Jessica did this. She reached into Jon's back left pocket and felt something rough and also round. The item also had a pin attached to it. Her eyes lit up in shock when she realized what she was touching.

"Are you kidding me?"

"Always be prepared."

"Do you realize what that is?"

"Yes. Now pull it out and hand it to me."

"I don't want that thing."

"Jess. Do it."

"Jon, don't make me.."

"Do it."

She slowly picked up the item from Jon's back left pocket and carried it carefully and then handed it to Jon.

Manny held out his dagger. "Now I get to kill someone that Jon Drake cherishes."

"You don't have the guts," said Ulisez.

"Oh no?" Manny fired back.

"You're just Vladimir Ramirez's errand boy," replied Ulisez.

"Watch that tongue," snapped Manny. He grabbed his dagger with his right hand and stepped on Ulisez's left leg, pinning him.

"Hey, Manny! Remember us?" Jon called out, diverting Manny's attention.

"You ready to watch your friend die?" asked Manny.

"No," replied Jon. "But I have a question for you."

"What?"

"Do you like to play catch?"

"What?"

"Catch."

Jon threw something in Manny's direction and then jumped on top of Jessica, sending her plummeting back behind the couch. Manny's eyes grew large with fear as he realized what it was. "Grenade!"

The grenade exploded instantly, sending a shock-wave of debris flying through the already destroyed cabin. The explosion was small, but enough to knock Manny out. It knocked Ulisez out too now, and Jon and Jessica peeked out from behind the couch to examine their damage. Jessica shoved Jon off of her.

"You crazy asshole," she exclaimed.

"Hey look, it worked," Jon remarked.

"Jon," She began, and walked over to check on Ulisez and realized there was a pulse. Jon helped her.

"He's fine," Jon said. He grabbed his jacket. "Come on, grab your stuff, we got to go."

"We can't just leave Ulisez here," cried Jessica.

Jon sighed, annoyed. "Fine. I'll grab him. Least I could do for him for saving our lives."

He lifted Ulisez with every ounce of strength he had and raised him over his shoulder fireman carry style. They walked outside and Jon placed Ulisez into the backseat of the car. Jessica turned to Jon.

"Where are we going to go?"

"Home," replied Jon. "I will figure this out."

They got their belongings and got into the car and headed out, leaving Manny laying there unconscious.

They drove down the 395 freeway, much of the time in silence. The scenery was beautiful on the way back as they had arrived just after a snowstorm. After a short while, they stopped. She looked at Jon, curiously.

"Why are we stopping?"

"You will drop me off here and take the car."

"What? Are you crazy? We're in the middle of nowhere!"

"Jessica—I have already gotten you into enough trouble."

"What are you doing?"

"Take my car and go."

"What?"

"Do it!"

"I won't leave you."

"You have to. We need to separate for the time being. It's the only way for either of us to have a chance. It's the only way for Ulisez to have a chance."

She looked back at Ulisez in the backseat and he was stirring. Before she looked back, the car door opened and Jon disappeared. He vanished like a ninja. She did not want him to leave, but he promised her he would see her again. She opened the passenger door and moved into the driver's seat and drove off.

Ulisez stirred in the backseat as she drove, and she glanced into her mirror and noticed her friend coming to.

"Oh good, you're awake," she said dryly.

Ulisez groaned. "What the hell happened?"

"We needed an escape–so we threw a grenade at Manny."

"You what?" exclaimed Ulisez.

"Relax–you're still alive," replied Jessica. "And I'm about 63 percent certain that Manny and Freddy are too."

"Remind me to kick Jon's ass next time I see him," said Ulisez.

She scoffed. "Good luck with that."

She continued the drive back home, more worried than ever about where Jon was and what he was doing. She had a feeling that the confession by Freddy might drive him further down the edge, and she worried more than ever about his livelihood.

Chapter 30: The Wildcard

February 11th, 2016

    Vladimir had expected Jon Drake to break out of the jail. He had known it was only a matter of time. The White Warrior was too talented to hold inside a simple jail. That is why Vladimir had sent Manny to go after Jon. He had specifically instructed Manny to bring Jon to him. A small part of him had expected that Manny might even go off the hinges and do something regretful. There were ways of reeling in his apprentice. But he also knew that Manny was no match for Jon and did not expect him to kill Jon.

    He meditated in his master bedroom. This always helped him maintain his focus. It also was something he preached to his students, and his children. His eyes were closed, and he was in another universe. There was always an intense focus when he was in deep meditation. He needed this to channel his thoughts and get to a place where he needed to be.

    The doors opened, and Ivan and Nubia entered. Vladimir had instructed his children to only bother him if it were important. So there must be a reason they were here, interrupting him. He opened his eyes and kept his gaze centered on both of them. Ivan looked stoic, maybe even a little worried. Nubia looked determined like there was a message that needed to get out. Vladimir waited patiently for them to speak.

"Yes, children?"

"Father, we have been contacted by Manuel," Nubia informed him.

"Jon got away," Ivan added.

    Vladimir shook his head. This was not a surprise. He had expected Jon to be difficult, but he also felt disappointed in himself for not training Manny well enough to at least subdue Jon Drake. So this was partially his fault. He studied his children for a moment, attempting to see what their thoughts were. A part of them felt it was a mistake bringing them here, and another part felt that they were his children and must share in his journey. The conflict within him surged, and he was not sure how to balance that.

"No matter," Vladimir replied. "We shall find him."

    His children nodded in acknowledgment. Then they turned to leave. Vladimir motioned with his hand.

"Daughter, stay a moment, I wish to speak with you a moment."

Ivan and Nubia glanced at one another as if it were a test. Then Ivan turned back around and headed off while Nubia approached her father.

"What is it, father?"

"You have become an amazing and beautiful young woman," He told her.

Nubia kind of looked at her father with confusion then stuttered.

"Thank—thank you, father. Is there anything else you need from me?"

"Yes," he answered. "How familiar are you with the city?"

He watched his daughter think about this and could tell she was searching for an answer. He waited patiently.

"I am familiar father. We have scoured the area looking for potential spots to spread our organization."

"Excellent," he replied. "I will need you to do some scouting for me. I trust you completely."

"Thank you, father."

"Now run along now. I have much to get ready for."

Nubia smiled and turned around. Vladimir saw Nubia as his favorite, and it would be a lie to admit otherwise. She was the most like him, with a mix of ferocity and sweetness. Ivan was a little distant, and Vladimir believed that Ileana's death had taken a much worse toll on him. Either that or Nubia was better at hiding it.

He made his way to the Orange Grove Police Department. There was unfinished business to take care of, and he wanted any information he could find on the whereabouts of Jon Drake. The man was becoming a bigger problem than he had expected. He needed information from his biggest confidante, and that was the Panther.

As he entered the office of the commissioner, he saw Thomas huddled at his desk behind a stack of papers. The Panther looked at least ten years older since he had taken the job. It amused him to see him aged so badly in this situation. But he also needed Thomas to focus a little. Thomas looked up from his stack of hell and nodded. That was one way he acknowledged Vladimir. It was endearing.

"Do you have news?" asked Vladimir.

Thomas shook his head.

"Freddy Hunter tried to kill Jon Drake first. Your boy Manny entered the picture. And then something happened. Apparently, well—well, they threw a grenade at him."

Vladimir looked at Thomas peculiarly.

"A grenade?"

"Yes, then they made their escape. My officers informed me that Jessica Hudson has returned to town, along with Detective Ulisez Saucedo. But no Jon Drake. Do you wish me to do anything to them?"

Vladimir shook his head. "They are not important."

"Are you sure? It might draw Jon back."

"No, Jon Drake will find his way to us, eventually. That should be no issue."

There was a moment of silence between them. The silence was common between them as they had known each other for a long time and had accepted each other's mannerisms. It was not awkward, nor was it off-putting.

"So what next, Lion?" asked Thomas.

He pondered the question. He did not believe Jon would be a problem yet. Jon had a lot more to deal with than just him. Maybe he could redeem himself. Now, Vladimir suspected, Jon would head after Caine. Potentially, he might finish his mission. Caine had put a hit on him, threatening his life and the life of Jessica Hudson. Because of that, there was a higher chance Jon might go after Caine next. It would make sense. That is what Vladimir would do.

"Remove the warrant."

Thomas stood up. "What? Why?"

"I do not wish for Jon Drake to be locked up any longer. Remove the charges and announce a man-hunt for the real killer of Frank Hudson."

Thomas hesitated, and Vladimir could see his apprehension.

"But Lion, you are the real—"

"I trust you to be creative."

Vladimir did not allow Thomas to say another word. He exited the office and made his way back to his vehicle.

The Legion of Samurai did not drive much. They rarely drove when they were in Brazil. But they had taught Vladimir how to drive. Diego had been the man responsible for his driving skills.

Because of this, he transferred what he had learned over to his children and Manny. It was something that every member of the Legion of Samurai needed to know.

When they arrived in Orange County, he had gone to a dealership and purchased three vehicles. All the vehicles they got were environmentally friendly. So they bought electric cars. Unlike the local politicians that preached about climate change and being environmentally friendly, the Legion of Samurai practiced what they preached. Vladimir made sure his entire fleet did everything within their means to protect the environment. Though the larger scale plan was to destroy and rebuild, they still practiced rituals that helped preserve their ideals.

He drove his vehicle from the Orange Grove Police Station, but he did not head home. He had some unfinished business to handle first.

Ulisez Saucedo lived farther than the rest of Jon's friends. He was the only one that lived on the other side of the 22 freeway, further north toward Fullerton. Vladimir felt that he needed to visit Jon Drake's best friend. He wanted to see what the detective offered and felt there was potential. He expected hostility, and it would surprise Vladimir to not have any.

He made his way toward the outside of the home and saw Ulisez inside watching a movie along with his two dogs and cat. Swiftly, and quietly, Vladimir made his way inside the home. He grabbed something out of his pocket and flung it toward Ulisez and his pets. Tear gas erupted into the room and Vladimir watched as Ulisez coughed, but not before shielding his pets from any harm. Vladimir found this admirable and believed that this displayed how loyal Ulisez could be. The first test of how loyal a person was to another person involved how they treated their animals.

He made his way into the room, and it was not until the smoke cleared that Ulisez realized who was in the room with him. The detective looked fearful as he stared up at Vladimir and then held his arms protectively in front of his dogs.

"Mr. Saucedo, I am glad you are back in town," he stood before the detective and brushed off his suit.

"What are you doing here? What do you want?" Ulisez inquired. Vladimir noticed that there was a hint of fear in his voice. But from his experiences with this detective, Vladimir knew him to be fearless. He suspected that Ulisez feared for his pets. While Vladimir would never harm an animal, it was to his advantage to let Ulisez continue to think otherwise.

"I am here to offer you a proposition," Vladimir informed him.

Ulisez looked at Vladimir like he was crazy. With his hand, he motioned for his dogs to leave the room and they listened. Vladimir watched as his pets obeyed their master, and even the cat followed. Now it was just the two of them.

"What proposition?" Ulisez was curious, at least, and Vladimir knew it. He observed the young man's face as he said this. There was curiosity, and that could be enough to sway him.

"Join the Legion of Samurai," said Vladimir.

Ulisez's face fell, but not in horror. The detective held back laughter, and this confused him. What was funny about this? To Vladimir, this was the opportunity of a lifetime. Who would not want to join one of the most prestigious groups in the world?

"What is amusing, boy?" he asked him.

Ulisez was still chuckling. Finally, he broke out. "You realize I could never work for you, right?"

"Why not?"

"Well for one, you tried to kill me."

"What? I never tried to kill you."

"You threw me off a cliff!"

Vladimir scoffed. "I knew Jon Drake would save you, you were never in any real danger. And I did my homework. You could swim."

"You looked me up?"

"A man does not become the leader of the Legion of Samurai without understanding the world and the environment in which he partakes."

He studied Ulisez, waiting for a reaction. The detective's refusal disappointed him, but it did not surprise him. There was an expectation that Ulisez might misinterpret their last encounter as hostile. Vladimir wanted to cleanse the world, and that would include destroying much of it. But he also wanted the right people with him by his side, and he felt that Ulisez Saucedo was a superb choice. There had to be another angle to this.

"The answer is no Vladimir. Now please get out of my home. You scared my pets."

"One thing I admire you is how you treasure your animals," he acknowledged.

"That's nice getting recognition from a psychopath," Ulisez sarcastically remarked.

Vladimir leaned in, tired of being insulted. Ulisez felt his prescience now as he hovered over him.

"You are not one to call anyone names when you associate yourself with Jon Drake and Jessica Hudson."

"What the hell is that supposed to mean?"

"Jon Drake has killed more people over the last decade than I have in a lifetime, and your friend Jessica is a drug addict that has done more destruction than anyone. So do not snipe at me detective throwing stones, especially when a great opportunity is being offered at you."

He noticed, from the corner of his eye, that Ulisez had his fists clenched. He did not expect the detective to dare hit him, but the possibility was open.

"Why did you believe I would ever join you?" Ulisez was curious.

"Because I know there is a lot of good in you. And when the time comes for the end of all things, I wish for you to be preserved."

Ulisez said nothing. He went on.

"You do not understand how the world works, despite your travels. Believe it or not, we have shared enemies in the past. I know all about your time in England and your encounter with the Deathstalker."

Ulisez's eyes rose and he knew he got the detective's attention. "How could you possibly know—"

"I make it my business to know everything about my adversaries. You are a very intelligent young man Mr. Saucedo and I want you on the right side of history."

He turned to leave. Ulisez sat there saying nothing for a moment, then called out before Vladimir could exit.

"What do you mean by that?"

Vladimir looked back while one foot was out the door. "Judgment day is coming Mr. Saucedo. Choose wisely. Some terrible people will pay for injustice."

Chapter 31: Natalie Drake

February 12th, 2016

Jon staked out the Caine Mansion. He would do it; he would finally finish Caine. But first, he wanted answers. He staked out the Caine Mansion and noticed two guards at the gate. He snuck up behind them and leveled them both with sleeper holds. They dropped like logs. He slowly and securely made his way up to the gate and climbed with ease while also being quiet.

He made his way toward the front door and unraveled a grappling hook from his bag and flung it toward the window ledge. The hook landed with precision and clung on. He used the rope to lift himself off the ground and toward the windowsill. Caine's Mansion was a four-story, 15,670 square foot monstrosity. There were two floors to this house, so Caine's bedroom was on the top. Mike Wilson had given him Intel on exactly where Caine's bedroom would be. There were eight bedrooms, and seven bathrooms in the house and Jon knew from memory where many of them were.

When he was young, his mother Natalie used to take him to the Caine Mansion. He was barely eight years old, but he remembered enough. That was around the time he met Amy Caine. They played together as children. From his memory, Caine's bedroom. The master bedroom was in the back of the house, with an unrestricted view of the tennis courts and the pool. Amy's bedroom was next to that room, and Rion's was on the other side. Scotti's bedroom was at the front of the house on the second floor. It was clear from Jon's point of view that Caine hated Scotti as much as he hated Jon. Ivy, the estranged wife, had a bedroom to herself. Jon remembered it was on the side. They used the rest of the rooms as entertainment rooms or Caine's home office.

He made the climb, steady and cautious. Finally, he latched onto the top where his right arm clung to it and used his upper body strength to pull himself up. He pried open the window with his left hand and used all his strength to press it open. The window was narrow, but accessible for an adult body. He inched through the window and was now in the hallway. The hallway was long and narrow, and there seemed to be an intersection at the end of the hall.

He slowly and steadily made his way through the hall. Memories came surging back to him as he remembered the time he had spent in that hallway running with Amy. He made his way toward the end of the hallway where Caine's office was and pressed his hand on the doorknob, feeling the pressure in his veins and the nervousness of what he was about to do. He turned the doorknob and entered the room.

At that moment, the French doors opened and he rushed toward Caine, stiff-legged and with a purpose. His expression was blank and focused, his walk powered by relentless energy. Caine instantly picked up on this and looked up. As he got closer, he took a little sidestep, cocked his arm back, and punched Caine in the face.

It was a straight shot, as his fist connected with Caine's face, sending the businessman tumbling against the bed. Freddy entered the room and had a gun in his hand. He glanced over to Freddy and took out a dagger and flung it in his direction, knocking the gun out of his hands seamlessly. Freddy whimpered from the pain, clutching his hand. He walked with a purpose toward Freddy and reared back and punched Freddy in the face. The fist connected with precision and sent Freddy staggering.

"That's for killing my father," he said with a fire that he had not exhibited in a long time. Freddy slowly picked himself off the floor. He took out a gun and aimed at Freddy and pulled the trigger. Freddy cried in pain.

"Jesus Christ!!!!!"

Freddy's leg slumped over as the bullet pierced through his skin. Jon stood over Freddy with his gun still in hand.

"That's for trying to shoot me," he spoke methodically.

He yanked Freddy by the neck and dragged him before flinging the hitman toward the door, causing him to hit his head with a large thud. Then he aimed and fired again, and Freddy yelped in more pain.

"Damn it!"

The bullet pierced through Freddy's other leg, leaving him now completely incapacitated.

"And that's for trying to shoot Jessica," his voice was nonchalant.

"I hate you," cried Freddy, almost in tears from two bullet wounds, one in each leg, and blood pouring all over the place.

While all this was happening, Caine stood near the bed, slumped down, and in shock from what he was witnessing.

"You're only alive because I am generous. Now shut the hell up or I will put a bullet through your brain," he told Freddy. He turned to face Caine. The sweat dripped down Caine's forehead, the terror rushing through him, and Jon loved it. He turned the gun toward Caine.

"You pull any more shady shit like that and I will blow you both to hell."

"You're insane," cried Caine.

"You made me that way."

Caine did not respond. He stayed quiet now, pondering his options.

"Now we will have a long talk," he announced.

"I'm dying over here," cried Freddy from the front of the master bedroom.

He turned to him. "You will be if you don't shut up." He turned his attention back to Caine, aiming his gun at him. "I have questions for you."

Caine's face fell. "What—what do you want to know?"

"Why did you kill my father?"

"But I didn't —,"

"Enough bullshit!" cried Jon, and it made Caine flinch. "The truth, I want it now."

"You want to know why your father died?"

"For the hundredth time…" His voice trailed off as he looked at Caine.

"Your father died because of your mother."

"What? My mother?" The statement confused him. Jon thought about it for a moment and gave Caine a curious glance. "All those times I visited this mansion as a child?"

"Do you remember that?" Jon nodded. Caine continued. "Now Jon, why do you think you were here so many times as a child?"

He shook his head. "No, my mother would never…"

He could not find the words to finish what he was thinking and now saw exactly what Caine implied, and he did not like it. Jon had spent a lot of time in the Caine Mansion during the summer of 2001. He remembered always coming to the Caine Mansion with his mother and hanging out with Amy. Natalie Drake died shortly after under mysterious circumstances. Then Freddy killed his father four years later.

"You're right," said Caine. "Your mother would never cheat on your father. But that didn't stop me from taking the initiative."

"Are you saying you hit on my mother?" asked Jon, repulsed.

"Yes," replied Caine. "She was the most exquisite woman I had ever known. I met her at a party I was hosting. There was the matter of her being married to your father. But that inconvenience did not matter to someone like me."

"What about Ivy?"

Caine scoffed. "Ivy was a marriage of convenience and a business transaction. But Natalie, she was incredible. I knew I had to have her. So I told her I had a young daughter, roughly the same age as her son. We arranged for our children to play together. But deep down, she probably knew what my intentions were. But that didn't stop her from bringing you to the Caine Mansion every time.

"One day we were at a park. You and Amy were on the playground and doing what kids do. I sat on the bench with her and just stared at her beautiful face. And I made my move."

"You kissed my mother?"

Caine nodded. "And she rebuffed me almost immediately. She told me she was a married woman and loved her husband, blah blah blah. You know that bullshit."

"Can you get to the part where my dad allegedly is responsible for my mother's death?"

"It devastated me. She rejected me. But I knew there was a way around it. I discovered where your parents enjoyed eating out and had them followed."

Jon saw where this was going, and he did not like it. "Are you telling me you killed my mother?"

Caine's face fell, despondent. "She drank a poisoned glass that was intended for your father."

His face filled with tears. He still had his gun aimed at Caine. But now, his rage was increasing. All these years, he had wanted revenge on Caine for killing his father. But he never suspected that he had also been responsible for his mother's death. He stayed silent as he wiped away the tears with the free hand. Caine went on.

"I hated your father for allowing that to happen and that's why I ordered his death four years later."

Jon trailed off for a moment, processing this. Finally, he came back and just looked at Caine. Jon took a moment to think about it. He took a deep breath, then another.

"You killed my mother…" He took a moment to compress himself. The next few seconds could go one of two ways. He placed his gun back in his holster, reared his right arm back and punched

Caine in the face. The businessman stumbled from the blow that connected properly with his face. Caine recovered enough to put his hands in front of his face.

"Now take it easy Jon—"

"You sanctimonious son of a bitch! You… you killed my mother!"

"To be fair, I was trying to kill your father—"

"And that makes it better?"

He punched Caine in the face again, his right hand connecting with Caine's face. His fist drew blood this time, as Caine's nose broke from the blow.

"Boss," cried Freddy from the corner and Jon had forgotten he was still in the room. He turned to Freddy.

"Not a word you stupid son of a bitch," said Jon. He put his attention back toward Caine.

"Jon… you got to calm down," said Caine with no conviction.

He lunged at Caine's throat, grabbing it with his right arm, squeezing. "I will make you suffer." He smashed Caine's head into the ground and off the bed. He stepped on top of Caine, forcing his face upward. Jon reared his right arm and connected again with Caine's face, drawing more blood from his upper lip this time. He used his left hand to pound on Caine now and unleashed a flurry of punches for the next few seconds. Freddy cried out in the corner but was helpless to do anything as Jon pounded Caine's face. From Jon's vantage point, he knew Caine's nose broke, but his jaw bled profusely and possibly shattered.

"Please—" Caine spit out blood as he tried to speak. "Stop—"

His right arm popped forward and strikes Caine again, striking him the left cheek, and knocking the wind out of him. Caine hunched over the floor, almost lifeless from the beating he has taken. He hovered over him.

"You think you can just kill people without repercussions, huh?" He sneered as he kicked Caine in the stomach with his right foot. "You think your money and your power gives you the right to do whatever the hell you want?"

"I'm… I'm —"

"Shut up!"

He reared his right arm and lunged, punching Caine in the stomach, knocking the wind out of him. Caine gasps in strides as the blow took its toll. He reared up again and punched Caine in the stomach again, then reared his right hand back and landed shots to the knuckles. Caine screamed in agony. Jon stood over Caine, who crumpled on the floor, bleeding all over the carpet, but otherwise alive.

"I should kill you…" He suggested as his thoughts trailed off slightly. He grabbed Caine's throat and lifted him off the ground with astounding force. Caine's face filled with blood, and his eyes were barely flickering, and he struggled to speak.

"Do it, it's over for you, anyway. Go ahead, kill me," Caine coughed up more blood as he said this. "It won't bring your mommy or your daddy back—"

He backhanded Caine in the face, sending him plopping to the ground. Caine was unconscious now. Jon analyzed the damage he caused. He sighed, turned around, and started for the door. Freddy noticed this and grew angry.

"Don't just leave me here, you asshole. I'm bleeding to death!"

"I hope you bleed to death. It wouldn't be enough punishment for what you've done."

"Hey! Don't leave me here. Drake! Drake!"

He walked out the door, ignoring Freddy's screams, deciding to not kill either of them as it would solve nothing.

Chapter 32: The Caine Case

February 13th, 2016

Jessica had expected some harassment when she returned to town. She believed they might arrest her for abetting a fugitive. So it took her by surprise when no one arrested or accosted her. Was it something Ulisez did? No, he did not have that power. Someone dropped the charges, and that someone was Thomas Martin. A part of her wanted to know why, but another part of her wanted to avoid that situation altogether. There was still work to do.

She walked into the coffee shop and her private investigator Patrick was there waiting for her. He had a serious look on his face as if he were about to give her some news. She was not sure she wanted to know why he looked that way, but she took the bait.

She sat down across from Patrick and waited as he sat there. He slipped a manila envelope over to her and she opened the contents. The folder contained many files, and she recognized some designs. There was something in here, something she could use. She scoured through the pages quickly, while scanning the words carefully. Jessica looked up at Patrick.

"Is this what I think it is?" she asked.

Patrick nodded. "Dates, timestamps. Photographs. All linking Caine Enterprises to both the vehicles and the bullets that were used to kill your mother."

She stared at the files in awe. She finally had the information she needed. She had the proof. Alexander Caine would go to jail for his crimes. There was some conflict in her because now she might need to hurt Amy and Scotti, and even Rion. But then she realized that they needed to see what kind of monster their father was. And they would see exactly what type of scumbag he is. She closed the envelope and grinned.

"I cannot thank you enough," Jessica gushed.

"The paycheck did more than enough," replied Patrick.

She extended her hand, and Patrick shook it. He completed his work and left while Jessica kept the contents. Now, the question was who should she give this to.

She went to the paper store first and made some copies. One could not be too safe here as she had to cover her ass. She made about ten copies of each page and paid for it accordingly. The plan now was to give some copies to Dan West to show the proof she needed to put Caine away for her mother's murder. This was what needed to happen. As she stood there, she felt a prescience behind her and turned around.

"Hi Jess," Mike stood there and waved his hand awkwardly.

She looked at her newly discovered brother and was unsure of what to say. The last time they spoke, she kicked him out aggressively. "Mike, how are you?"

"Good," he was nervous. "It's funny running into you here."

"Yeah, funny."

There was some awkward silence. Neither knew what to say to each other. What could they say to each other? Mike put his hand behind his back nervously.

"So I heard someone kidnapped you?"

She shook her head. "No, not kidnapped. I went by choice."

"Oh," he mustered out.

She could give him credit. He was trying, and she was not making it easy for him. Was she supposed to make it easy for him? Why should she? But a better part of her wanted to because he did not ask for Frank Hudson to impregnate his mother. It was not his fault, and a small part of her knew that.

"So I—" they both spoke at the same time.

"Sorry," he apologized. "You go."

She took her time. "I know you didn't ask to be born, the way you were. And I wanted to apologize for how I treated you the last time we spoke."

"It's understandable."

"No," she shook her head. "There is no excuse for how I treated you. You are my family now, you are the only family I have left. I have to treat you like a brother."

"I appreciate that." He noticed the papers in her hand. "What you got there?"

She hesitated, then held it up. "Evidence against the man that killed my mother."

"Oh wow," he was awkward, not understanding what else to say. "Cool, good luck to you."

She smiled. "Listen, let's hang out soon, just you and me. A fresh start and we can get to know each other."

"That would be cool."

"Sweet," she replied. "Take care, Mike. I'll be in touch."

After she left the store, she drove over to the district attorney's office. She sauntered through West's office without asking permission. The secretary tried to stop her, but she nudged her away. Another woman was coming out of the office, a pretty brown-haired woman in a suit. The woman gave her a dirty look as they passed each other, and she noticed her badge said 'Clayton'. The woman went on her way without incident. West was on the phone when she entered his office. He looked annoyed to see her, but she did not care. They had business to attend to, and Jessica would make sure she had his attention. She took a seat in the chair across from him and threw the manila folder over his things and in front of him. West looked at her with disdain and sneered. A part of her felt he might throw her out. It was a possibility. She smiled pleasantly as she planted her butt in the chair and got comfortable.

"What do you want?" asked West.

"Typical, you would not say anything nice about my father or 'I'm sorry for your loss'," Jessica shot back.

"Okay, sorry for your loss, what do you want?"

"Dan, have you always been such a dick?"

"I am a dick to you because you seem to think you can get whatever you want and become disappointed to find out it doesn't work out that way."

"I have the evidence I need to put your boss away."

West shot her a look. "The mayor?"

"What? No. I am talking about Alexander Caine. Look at it before you mock me. It's all there."

West scanned the contents. She could tell that it was killing him but knew he would have no choice.

"Interesting," was all the piece of shit district attorney said as he scanned through the files. She kept her eyes locked on him, waiting for some kind of excuse or even an attempt to deflect. She did not remove her gaze as she waited patiently for West to finish. He finally closed the envelope with the papers inside and sighed.

"What do you expect me to do with this?" asked West.

"Your job," replied Jessica.

She stood up to leave but then turned around. "If I discover that you have not pressed charges against Caine, I will find someone who will. And don't even think of somehow deleting those files. I made copies."

She exited West's office before he could say a word. She had accomplished what she wanted to do. He would have to press charges against Caine and his cohorts. Jessica was sure of that fact. But now, she had somewhere to go and something to do.

Later, Amy and Scotti visited her as she had invited them. The two of them walked in and she greeted them both with hugs. She loved them both, which made what she would tell them even more difficult. It was never easy learning that a parent was despicable, but they had to know.

She closed the door as Amy and Scotti made themselves comfortable. Amy was the first to turn to her, studying her intentions with her eyes.

"What are we doing here, Jess?" Amy was straight forward.

She glanced at her nervously. How was she going to tell them? She pulled out the folder immediately and unloaded the contents. She passed them over to Amy, who looked at Jessica, then at the files. Jessica watched as Amy looked over them for a moment. Scotti glanced at her sister, and then nudged in beside her, looking.

"I have the proof I need so you won't just brush me aside anymore," said Jessica.

Amy kept her eyes on the files and Scotti peeked over her shoulder. Jessica waited to see how they would react. She had a feeling it was about to get lively in a moment, and she hoped that she would not feel the Caine women's fury that she knew so well.

The tension built as the Caine sisters continued to scan the document from top to bottom. Jessica curled her lip as she waited. She was not sure why she was so nervous. Maybe it was because these women were two of her best friends and she did not want to jeopardize that? But in her heart, Jessica felt that Amy and Scotti needed to know the truth about their father. They deserved to know exactly what kind of man their father was. Amy was the first to look at Jessica, leering a little cautiously.

"Where did you get this?" Amy asked. It was an odd question and not the one Jessica expected. Scotti gave Jessica a bedazzled look as she too waited for an answer.

"I had a PI look into my mother's murder," she informed them. "I wanted to understand what happened. And that turned up."

Jessica curled her lip again. Amy placed the files back into the envelope. Scotti said nothing, choosing to stay silent. The silence worried Jessica, as Scotti was usually the lively one.

"What now?" Amy inquired.

"I have given the evidence to the district attorney and plan to press charges," Jessica replied.

"You can't do this," Scotti finally spoke up.

"He's our father," Amy added.

"He killed my mother," Jessica shot back. "He probably killed a lot more people. When will the both of you take the blinders off and realize what a scumbag your father is?"

Scotti slapped her across the face. Her open right hand flung against Jessica's face in an instant that there was no time to react.

She caressed her face gingerly as she looked at Scotti, who was wheezing, her anger on full display. Amy stood behind her sister, reserved, with one arm on Scotti's shoulder holding her back. Jessica knew that Amy was the calculating one, and also the calm one, while Scotti was the hothead. She was just like her father, and her mother, all the worst qualities.

"You have no right to judge us," Scotti bellowed out.

She kept her hand on her face, just looking at Scotti.

"I never wanted to hurt you," she reassured Scotti, then to Amy. "Either of you."

"Funny way of showing it," Scotti spat back, holding back tears.

"You realize now that once you do this, we will have to defend him," Amy declared.

Her eyes widened. She could not believe it. Even after displaying evidence of her mom's murder and Caine being the one who orchestrated it all, they still wanted to defend their father. It was ridiculous to Jessica.

"You still defend him? Even after what I have shown you today?"

"You understand that no matter what he's done, he's still our father," Amy replied.

This was not the reaction Jessica had expected, but it also did not surprise her. Caines always stuck together, even when they were trying to bite each other's heads off. She knew this from her time with Rion, and how she feuded with Ivy Caine.

"I—I don't know what to say," said Jessica.

"You don't need to say anything," Scotti hissed.

"What's done is done," Amy added.

Amy and Scotti grabbed their jackets and put them on. Jessica watched in silence as they both turned away and opened the door and closed it, leaving her standing there.

She took a walk later. She needed it. Amy and Scotti hated her, and Jon was still missing. Was he missing? Jessica was not entirely sure. She knew that she had not seen him since she dropped him off on the road in the Sierras on the way back.

Jessica stepped inside the Orange Grove Café, which was the main coffee shop in town. It was a hip place to get a cup of java, and not a large scale coffee chain like the one with the mermaid. She entered the coffee shop and it surprised her to see that there was only one person in line. The sound of coffee brewing was intoxicating, and there were also blenders going off. Although it was a small scale, people still wanted blended drinks.

As she stood in line, a woman entered the coffee shop and stood behind her. At first, Jessica paid her no attention. There was no reason to pay attention to someone coming into a coffee shop. People needed coffee. Jessica noticed out of the corner of her eye but did not look.

Jessica ordered her drink from the barista and felt the woman behind her. It was not a feeling of fear or anything like that, but it seemed familiar. She stepped aside when done and got a good look at the woman as she took her turn ordering.

The woman was beautiful. She had long raven-colored hair that flowed just toward her shoulders. The first thing she noticed about the woman was her green eyes, like a cat. The woman possessed a square, triangular face. Jessica also noticed that the woman wore all black, with black yoga pants and a black tank top. It was not anything special, but it was peculiar. The woman was pleasant as she smiled and ordered her drink. Jessica watched her without being creepy, just glancing over. There was something about this woman that was familiar, but Jessica could not put her finger on it.

She was not sure if she felt attracted to the woman, or if it was something else. The woman was an enigma, and Jessica was curious.

The woman walked over to where Jessica was and stood next to her. It was strange, and a little bizarre. Had she noticed Jessica looking at her? There was no telling, but something was off about this woman. Jessica minded her own business, just glancing at her phone, then at her drink, and then back at her phone again. Looking at her phone was what Jessica did when she wanted to avoid talking. But this woman did not seem to possess a phone. She looked directly at Jessica.

"I noticed you ordered the same drink as I did," the woman said eloquently.

Jessica turned to her.

"Huh?"

"Your drink," the woman pointed at the drink, which was not complete. "It's a Carmel Macchiato with Soy Milk. I got the same thing."

She looked at the woman curiously and was not sure if the woman was intentionally trying to mess with her, or if it was a coincidence.

"I also like the Zebra Hot Chocolate, but I needed the coffee today," Jessica replied.

The woman smiled. It was a beautiful smile with great white teeth.

"I like that too," she beamed.

Jessica studied the woman's face, still trying to figure her out. Who was this woman and where did she come from?

"I'm Jessica," she extended her hand to the woman. The woman returned the shake and locked eyes with her.

"Nubia. Nubia Ramirez," the beautiful woman replied.

The name should have run out alarm sounds in Jessica's brain, but at the moment it did not. Jessica shook Nubia's hand and looked at her beautiful green eyes, and they hypnotized her. There was something about Nubia that was interesting. She had always loved Jon Drake and even had a long fling with Rion Caine, but Jessica had experimented with women before. If she was honest with herself, Jessica would admit that women gave her a rise just as much as men. Any other woman would have paid Nubia no attention, but Jessica could not stop looking at her.

Jessica disengaged herself tactfully. Nubia snickered a little, and Jessica found it adorable.

"You want to sit?" Jessica asked her.

"I would love to," replied Nubia.

It was a weird thing. Her two best friends spurned her because she wanted to put their father away for the murder of her mother. This was after a tense confrontation with the district attorney, a man who hated her guts. So what was this after all? Was it just a coincidence, or was there some special connection here?

Nubia took a seat on the chair at the table closest to the door. Jessica sat opposite her. They decorated the walls of this coffee shop with flowers and cats, which Jessica found to be an odd mix. She had been in here once or twice before. Usually, when she met clients, it was at the Orange Grove Diner.

"So," Jessica began. "Are you from around here?"

She had noticed a slight accent in Nubia's voice, so she had to ask this question. It was more of a curious question than anything else.

"I am originally from Brazil," replied Nubia, and it sounded like 'Brazeal' coming out of her mouth.

She gave Nubia a look, still curious. Jon just came back from Brazil. Was there a connection? There could not be. Jon Drake did not know every person from Brazil. But was there something else? Jessica pondered who this person was. She remained quiet for the moment.

"My father has a business here, and I have come to visit him. My brother and me," Nubia proclaimed.

"What about your mother?" Jessica heard herself ask without thinking.

Nubia's face fell now, and the entire demeanor of her being slunk a little. "My mother was killed when I was very young."

"Oh," she answered back, then placed her right hand on Nubia's shoulder to comfort her. "I am so sorry."

"It's okay," replied Nubia. "It happened very long ago."

A moment passed, and she could not believe she had asked Nubia that question. It was very personal and not something one would ask a person they just met. Irrationality took over her life sometimes, and she let it.

"My mother was killed a long time ago too," Jessica revealed as Nubia glanced upon her curiously. "I recently found the evidence needed to put the killer away."

"That's wonderful."

It sounded like 'wanderfool' when Nubia pronounced it. She observed how her accent went in and out of traction, depending on what she was saying.

"Yeah. It's something I have been waiting to happen for a long time."

Nubia did not reply. Jessica noticed as she seemed to observe the surrounding area. Her head cocked sideways, glancing at a mother and her child. There was a sadness in Nubia's eyes that she recognized. It was something that she was very familiar with.

Nubia sipped her coffee with a pleasantness that Jessica had never seen before. She had to catch herself from staring at her for too long. As Nubia finished her coffee, she gently placed the cup down on the plate.

"Well," she began. "This has been pleasant but I really must be going."

"Okay," was all Jessica could mutter. Nubia stood up, and Jessica did the same. What was the protocol here?

"I shall see you again hopefully," Nubia beamed.

"Of course," replied Jessica. "I am not hard to find."

Nubia smiled. Then she turned and walked off. Jessica watched her go and could not understand why this felt nice. She had just had a civil conversation with an exceptional woman, after all the bullshit she had gone through that day. It felt great to be civil with someone for once.

Jessica stood up and placed the coffee cup and plate gently on the counter. Then she waved to the barista pleasantly and headed out the door.

Chapter 33: The Cleansing

February 13th, 2016

Vladimir was fidgeting. Nubia was late. She was never late. But here he was, waiting for his daughter. They had work to do. He needed his children to aid him. The hour was at hand. He had temporarily lost sight of Jon Drake, but he would locate him, eventually. That was not the only person missing.

Alexander Caine had gone missing. Someone had put a warrant out for his arrest. That little tidbit had interfered with his plans for the mogul. His resources had scoured Caine Enterprises and the Caine Mansion and reported that he was not in either location. His forces had located the daughters, but Vladimir did not mess with children. There were certain rules that he played by and attacking children was always off-limits, even if they were adults. This contrasted from his choice to eliminate Frank Hudson. He figured that the old man had lived a full life, so he ended it at an appropriate time. Besides, he did that to teach Jon Drake a lesson. It had occurred to him he had never officially met Jessica Hudson yet. It was an oddity, especially considering that she was a huge reason Vladimir had to teach Jon a lesson. It was also strange considering that he killed her father. He supposed the day was coming when she might come after him. But what concerned him the most at the moment, aside from Jon's absence, was what was taking Nubia so long.

He began his cleansing. Several people in this city deserved an ending, and Nubia was in charge of one of them. He had deployed Manny to take care of Mayor Rodriguez and used Bao and Kareem to hunt down anyone left standing at Caine Enterprises. He did not deploy Elicia for any of these missions. Vladimir had wished to take her with him when he found Caine. He felt they would need her there much more so. The plan was to take Ivan and Elicia with him, as they would be in perfect harmony when he found Caine. Vladimir figured that wherever he was, his lapdog Freddy would be with him.

He sat in his chair and waited. He did not feel like meditating. It was usually his go-to thing to gain some inner peace. But there was too much at stake. The Legion of Samurai were making their move, and he had to be a proper leader for them.

Once he finished making an example of Orange Grove, the entire state was next. Vladimir would also be ready to strike at the entire United States once he had sunk California. The entire country distracted themselves with an election between a corrupt clown that used to host a reality show and a corrupt woman that had engaged in politics her entire life. Vladimir felt that any good left in the country disappeared, and it was time to cleanse. But he had to start small. The first step was finding Caine.

The front door opened, and Vladimir stood up immediately. Nubia walked into the home, disheveled and looking horrid. Her face was white like a ghost now, and she trudged on slowly as she dragged her feet with hesitation. He walked toward her and towered over his daughter now. Nubia looked up solemnly, and it looked like she had done something horrific. Vladimir did not take his gaze off his daughter.

"Is it done?" he asked her.

Nubia nodded slowly, unsure of whether it was the right thing to do, but said nothing otherwise.

"Yes," she whispered.

"Describe it," Vladimir insisted.

Nubia gave her father a look that showed that the question was too much. She sighed, and Vladimir waited patiently. Finally, she told the story.

"I had to gain my courage to do such a feat. You must remember my father that I had never done such a thing before. I got myself a coffee before I went—"

"You went to get a coffee? We have coffee here."

"That's not the point, father. The point is I needed something, because I might back out and disappoint you, and I did not want to disappoint you."

"No," Vladimir replied. "You didn't. Go on."

Nubia hesitated. He could tell that this was tough on his daughter, but she had to learn. If she wanted to survive in this world, she had to do the things she did not want to do.

"I got my coffee and after sipping it, I departed for my mission, the one you gave me. From your notes, I knew exactly where I was going. I also learned about the defense mechanisms that this man took.

"I snuck past security. The security was not that great to begin with, just two large men who looked bored out of their minds. Had they paid attention to the slinky slender girl was near them, they might have been able to stop me. But they were useless. Incompetent. I entered the office building and searched for his office when I finally found it. The City Attorney Daniel West.

"I entered his office and took him by surprise. He was not expecting a tiny woman to enter his office, at least not without an appointment, or without sexual gratification, I gave him neither.

"I gathered myself and my courage. I took out my sword, and after a slight hesitation, slashed him across the chest. He bled and cried. It was horrific. I then stabbed him through the chest to put him out of his misery and to stop his incessant crying. He was like a large baby. I watched him fall to the ground and waited until he died."

He watched Nubia's body language as she finished telling the story of how she killed Orange County District Attorney Daniel West. He was proud of her. She had accomplished her mission despite any misgivings she might have had.

"Did anyone see you?" he asked her.

Nubia shook her head. "The cameras were taken out as you insisted. I snuck my way back out. I am positive they are about to discover his cold body any moment now."

Vladimir noticed how Nubia spoke with a slight form of regret. She did not want to kill anyone, but in time she would realize it was the right move. Daniel West was not a good man, as he had been in Caine's pocket from the very start. Corrupt men needed to perish, and Vladimir had set his daughter on this path. He felt no shame about this.

"You have done a magnificent job, daughter," Vladimir reassured her as he patted her on the shoulder. Nubia looked uncomfortable as her father did this, and a little unsure if she did a good job.

"Thanks," she replied, not knowing what else to say.

"Now go rest, there is much to accomplish, and you have played your part," Vladimir told her.

Nubia turned and walked away, likely toward her room. He watched proudly as his daughter had done what she had been told. She had passed the test. He was not entirely sure what would have happened had she disobeyed him. He might have disowned her if it had come to that. His children were his life, but they also had to believe in his values. Daniel West was dead as he should be. Now, he awaited news on the others.

Manny staggered into the home now. Vladimir smiled as his young apprentice entered the room. This was another person he had sent out on a mission. He did not have to worry about Manny accomplishing a mission.

The young man walked up to Vladimir. He looked as saddened as Nubia had, and that bothered Vladimir. Could his people be having second thoughts? Surely they must all believe in the mission at hand? He had to find out what was going on here.

"Manuel," Vladimir began. "You have something positive to report, I am sure."

Manny threw his bags down. The bags contained some of his weaponry, and the man had thrown them down as it relieved him. Vladimir read his face, and it seemed dour and maybe even ashamed. Vladimir pressed on.

"What happened, boy? Tell me?"

Manny sighed, hesitant. Vladimir could see the conflict in him but wanted to resolve it.

"I did as you asked, Master," Manny began. "I searched the mayor's office. He was not there. So I made a note of it and scoured his frequent spots. I discovered a spot he usually went to; a seedy, bereft motel.

"I made my way toward the area and searched the area. It was not difficult, but there were a lot of rooms, so it was sort of time-consuming. But I had a mission to accomplish and I would never fail you, Lion."

Vladimir noticed the weariness in Manny's voice. It was almost like the mission itself had tired him out to where he was just over it. Manny continued.

"I finally found the room our beloved mayor was located in. It was room 66. How profound. I knocked on the door because that would have been less attention-grabbing than simply breaking it down.

"Mayor Rodriguez opened the door, and the man had no shirt on and was in his undergarments. The man had a bottle of champagne in his hands and had been celebrating something. I did not hesitate Master to stab him right through the chest. It was after I did this that I realized the man was not alone.

"A woman in her undergarments screamed her lungs out as I stabbed the man. I had a choice; leave the mayor dead and a witness or eradicate the witness. I made the—the—unfortunate choice. I stabbed her right through the heart. She died instantly."

Vladimir understood why Manny looked like someone had broken his world. They had forced the man to kill an unwitting witness. Mayor Rodriguez was the target, but there was a woman with him, and Manny dealt with her. He went on.

"It was an unfortunate thing, Master. The woman was nothing but a trollop. A harlot. But that didn't mean she deserved to die. She was unfortunate collateral."

Vladimir sensed the pain in his apprentice and he understood it. But he felt like he had to do or say something to assuage him somehow.

"Listen, Manuel," Vladimir started. "It is not your fault. We have a vision, and that is a world without sin. This woman, unfortunately, was locked in sin. She willingly gave her body to a disgusting man and paid for her crimes with her life."

Manny looked at Vladimir with a puzzled look. It was as if he were trying to comprehend the words Vladimir was telling him.

"You did well, Manuel," Vladimir reassured him. "You did well. Now, will you be ready to help me on the next mission?"

Manny looked at him and then kneeled in complete obedience.

"Of course, Master."

"Good. Go rest. We have much to accomplish."

Manny left the room now, and Vladimir smiled. So now Daniel West was dead, as was Mayor Rodriguez. Someone might make a connection. The bumbling police would not be a problem, especially with the Panther leading them in a different direction. He did not need to ask Manny if anyone saw him because he knew the answer. While Thomas was his best warrior, Manny was a close second. He was one of the best at stealth and knew how to enter a room and leave without being seen. It was a quality that Vladimir had passed down on him, and one that Manny had picked up quickly.

He walked over to his bar. There was an assortment of alcohol, but the most known one was saké. The Legion of Samurai had many values, but they did not shy away from alcohol when they needed it. The old Samurai warriors used to partake in this drink, and it helped strengthen their resolve. It was the Japanese warriors and the Emperor's men that usually emphasized the drink. They usually served the drink on a special occasion, and Vladimir felt this was as special an occasion as ever.

He took the bottle of saké and a glass. He opened the bottle and poured himself a drink. The only downside is that there was no one to drink with at the moment. His warriors had either went on missions or retired to their chambers. Vladimir tasted the saké on his lips, and it was warm and savory. It also had a fruity flavor that he preferred. Whatever the case, the drink did its job.

As he enjoyed the drink, Bao and Kareem walked in. Vladimir spotted them from the corner of his eye. These were two of his greatest acolytes. He expected good news. Bao strutted in and Kareem angled beside him.

"Well?" Vladimir began. "Is it done?"

Bao nodded. Kareem grunted. They threw their equipment down. Vladimir was not sure he appreciated his warriors just throwing their possessions down like it was a boulder. But he bit his tongue.

"We eradicated every member that was in Caine Enterprises, we did a search and execution on every being we could find," said Bao.

"We made sure there was nothing left," Kareem added.

"It was a bloodbath," Bao gushed, almost proud of what they did.

"Did anyone see you?" Vladimir inquired.

Bao shook his head.

"The only thing anyone saw was two masked men in black clothing leaving the scene. There was nothing to tie anything to anyone."

"We know what we're doing," Kareem spat.

Vladimir turned his head and focused now on Kareem alone. He did not expect nor appreciate the tone in Kareem's voice.

"Do you have something to address Black Mamba?"

Vladimir towered over Kareem as he said this. 'Black Mamba' was Kareem's nickname or his warrior name. It also was the nickname of a popular basketball player, but Vladimir had never considered this when naming Kareem. He did not appreciate disrespect and had to show Kareem that he would not tolerate it. He waited to see if his 'Black Mamba' would say anything else.

"No, sir," Kareem meekly said.

"Excellent," replied Vladimir. He grabbed two additional glasses. He poured them both shots of saké. "Now we toast."

As they did this, Ivan and Elicia walked into the room. Manny joined them now and surrounded them all. Vladimir stood in the middle of the room.

"Now we have accomplished our goals. The mayor is dead. The city attorney is dead. And every remnant of Caine Enterprises is gone. We have one man left to eradicate."

No one said anything. No one dared say anything while Vladimir was speaking. The only member of their Legion absent from this meeting was Nubia. That was by design. Vladimir felt that she had endured enough and would need her for another occasion.

"Gentlemen," Vladimir began and then noticed Elicia give him a look. "And lady. Today we have accomplished a lot. Now we take down our last target before starting the Final Protocol. We find our last target, Alexander Caine, and eradicate him from this Earth."

The entire room roared in approval. Vladimir nodded accordingly and smiled. It was time to go wipe out an evil man.

Chapter 34: The Death of a Salesman

February 14th, 2016

    Jon had heard about Jessica's plan to have Caine arrested. He knew it would become a problem because now he knew Caine would run. His instincts were right when his sources told him Caine had mysteriously disappeared when the authorities went to his work and home to arrest him. He knew exactly where he would go that would be where he went too.

    If anyone would get Caine, it would be him. He followed the trail and found Caine's location at a safe house in Laguna Woods. Mike had given him the information thanks to the tabs they were keeping on Caine. Something that worried him now was that Mike was not responding to his texts. Maybe he was busy? It was a possibility, but he also felt that something might have gone wrong. It was not normal for Mike to not reply. But Jon could not worry about that right now.

    He drove down the 133 freeway to get to Laguna Woods. He had driven this route before and knew the area very well. It was the one road that connected East Orange County with Laguna Beach. But he did not need to go all the way to Laguna Beach. His destination was Laguna Woods.

    It was already dark, and traffic was a little heavy. This was the norm for Orange County and Los Angeles County. He had stayed out of sight since he returned to town. After departing from Jessica and Ulisez, he had called Mike. It was a semi-urgent call. Mike had listened to everything he had said and agreed to pick him up in the desert. He paid him a handsome reward for his silence, and Mike took it and enhanced his products. There were few people in the world Jon felt he could trust, but he was glad that he had found Mike.

    After beating the absolute tar out of Caine, he once again went into hiding. He did not go back to his old apartment. Instead, he found refuge in a place in Tustin. It was an old studio, but one that would keep him close to the action. He registered under the name Ram De La Cueva. Jon figured his old friend Ram the Bounty Hunter would not mind him borrowing his name wherever the hell he was. God, he needed a drink. But he decided not to drink and drive. He could get away with that in Brazil, but apparently, Americans did not tolerate this, especially in California.

    As he drove, he noticed a slight wind. No doubt the Santa Ana winds were roaring. It was mild since it was late February. There was a slight chill in the air, but it did not bother Jon. He drove along, hoping to reach his destination. Finally, he found a slight exit which led to the house he was seeking.

It was not a large building at all. The exterior walls were concrete, and the door was metallic. He knew it would be a little difficult to penetrate, but he had just the thing. He parked his truck about 100 yards away.

He stepped out of the truck and looked upon the building. There was a slight moment of hesitation, but he knew what he had to do. Jessica was not around to influence him, and this might be the only way to keep her and everyone else safe. He had to finish what he started. The entire purpose of coming back to town was to destroy Alexander Caine, and he would do it.

He grabbed his bag of goodies. He took out some plastic explosives and walked methodically toward the door. Strategically, he placed each explosive on each corner of the door. There was a method to this, and he had to do it correctly. Otherwise, it would come out looking stupid. Jon applied the explosive and backed away slowly. He did a silent count in his mind.

Five.

Four.

Three.

Two.

One.

The door blew off the hinges, a massive explosion. Jon smiled. He walked toward the now-open hole in the building. With anticipation, he stepped through the hole and poked his head inside. Caine and Freddy were on the floor, as the explosion must have taken them by surprise.

"Hello, boys, did you miss me?" Jon exclaimed as he stepped in front of them.

Before they could reply, Jon leaped off his feet and charged toward Freddy, who touted his gun but was too late. He grabbed Freddy and knocked the gun away. Then, he clenched his hands on Freddy's chest and flung him across the room, sending him tumbling with a thud. Freddy groaned as he laid on the floor. He walked up methodically toward Freddy and reared his right hand back and punched him in the face, causing blood to spurt out. It did not hurt that Freddy still had lingering injuries from their encounter two days ago.

He spotted Caine out of the corner of his eye, watching this in horror. He paid him no attention for the moment. The focus right now was on Freddy Hunter and him alone. Jon raised Freddy with his left hand, lifting him by the throat. He strangled him.

"Oh how I have waited for this moment," Jon gloated.

Freddy struggled to speak as Jon's arm wrapped around his throat. He released his hold and then reared back with his right hand and punched Freddy again. The hitman stumbled back a little.

"That's for my father," he bellowed.

Freddy stumbled as the fist connected with his face. Jon grabbed him again and reared back and connected once more with his face.

"My mother," he roared.

He caught Freddy after punching him to keep him from falling. He reared back and connected one more time with his face.

"Jessica's mother," Jon exclaimed with authority.

He once again caught Freddy before he could collapse and punched him one last time, and this time allowed Freddy to fall to the ground, unconscious.

"And anyone else I might have missed you scumbag piece of shit!"

He turned his head and eyeballed Caine. The businessman grew fearful as he watched this all unfold. Jon was not used to seeing any emotion come out of Caine, but all the emotions were spilling out here.

"Stop it," Caine ordered with hesitant authority. "You will kill him."

"You of all people have the nerve to tell me that!"

"Everything—it's all in the past now."

"The past? Are you kidding me right now?"

"Whatever is done is over with. You can't bring your parents back."

"Because you killed them," Jon exclaimed.

Caine took offense to this.

"I loved your mother, damn it! With all my heart," he hissed back.

"Yeah," Jon replied. "So you have said. Enough to rip a family apart."

"I wanted her for myself but Jon don't misunderstand—I loved her so much I was willing to love you."

He looked at Caine like he lost his mind. This man was out of his mind if he believed that Jon could ever accept that reasoning.

"You will never be half the man my father was."

Caine picked himself up and stood toe to toe with him. There was a slight fear in his demeanor, but the businessman hid it well.

"As I told you when you came back to town, Jon—I don't hate you."

"Funny yet you unleashed the Deathstalker on me—"

"Because you forced my hand! I have no ill will toward you. You are like—"

"Don't you dare say I am like a son to you when you don't even know where the hell your actual son is."

"I know where he is—"

"Really? Where is he? Where is Rion Caine?"

"I'm sure he is with his mother somewhere—"

"See! You don't even know where your own son is!"

"I am a very busy man," Caine insisted.

He pulled out his gun and aimed it right at Caine.

"Not for long."

Caine stared at the gun with trepidation. Jon could see the fear in his face. The older man looked tense as he had the barrel of a gun aimed at him.

"Do you realize how long I have waited for this moment?" Jon asked him.

"No, but I am sure you will tell me—"

"Ten years. Ten years. You ordered that piece of shit," Jon motioned his finger to point at Freddy. "You ordered him to kill my father.

"Do you even know where I went? Do you even give a shit? Do you?"

Caine did not reply. Jon continued.

"South America. It wasn't by choice. I was kidnapped as part of an attempted sex slavery ring. I was saved, ironically, by the leader of the largest cartel in Brazil. I was involved with the cartels, with bounty hunters and even with a maniacal eco-terrorist."

"Vladimir," Caine guessed.

He nodded. "He was there, too. He was the final motivating factor to get me to come back here and end you."

"So what's your plan, Jon? You have destroyed my businesses. Your shitty girlfriend allegedly has evidence that is enough for an arrest warrant for me. You have beaten me to a pulp. The only thing left to do is the one thing you have yet to do.

"The whole reason you came back to town. The whole reason any of this is happening. You want to kill me."

Jon positioned the gun and kept his aim. "I do want to kill you."

"Then do it already. I am growing tired of hearing you bitch about your daddy."

"Don't tempt me, Caine."

"Do it you little bitch."

He hesitated and was not sure why he did not just do it. There was something in him that was stopping him from killing Caine. Was it Jessica? Why could he not kill Caine?

"So all of this—all this started because of my mother?"

Caine sighed. "Yes."

"And you loved her?"

"I still do."

"Why couldn't you see what you were doing to her family?"

"I always loved her—even went to her funeral."

This revelation hit Jon like a ton of bricks. Jon shook his head irrationally while grinding his teeth.

"Speak," Jon ordered Caine.

Caine hesitated. Jon saw his hesitation and enjoyed it. He wanted an answer.

"As I said," Caine began. "I was at the funeral. I felt that I needed to pay my respects. I loved the woman. She was someone I had envisioned myself with. As I made my way into the church, your father approached me. He suspected nothing. He approached me and shook my hand, thanking me for being there.

"The next thing that happened was pretty bizarre. Your father and I chatted for a moment. I told him I was sorry for his loss and we embraced. It was the first time I had done that with anyone. For a moment, we grieved together."

Jon heard this in astonishment. He could not believe what he was hearing. His father and his most hated enemy embraced? What the hell was that?

"You dared to show up at the funeral of the woman you killed?" Jon asked, his voice rising.

"I was trying to kill your father—"

"And that makes it better?"

He pistol-whipped Caine across the face. He had heard just enough of this story. Caine stumbled as the gun connected with his face. Jon kicked him in the gut and the older man groaned.

"You deserve to die," Jon told him.

He once again held out the gun and aimed it at Caine. His hands trembled as many thoughts raced through his mind. He was not sure what he would do but braced his gun near Caine's temple. The mogul looked up at Jon and scoffed.

"Someone needs to end you," Jon stated.

"Then why don't you do it already?"

"You don't think I can?" Jon asked, now shaking his head. "You have destroyed so many lives."

"I am not responsible—"

"Shut up!"

His anger startled Caine, who looked at him, waiting for whatever decision he made.

"You are responsible for so much pain and death. When people are around you, they suffer. You ruin lives. And with you around, people will always suffer. You need to pay."

He clenched the gun. As he held it, what happened next would change everything.

A massive explosion!

This time, it was the walls that blew up instead of the door. The shrapnel from the explosion flung everywhere and some of it hit Jon. It knocked him to the floor from the impact, and he now laid fifteen feet away from Caine.

He groaned from this explosion. His eyes flickered, but he remained conscious. He saw Caine in his view and he was also conscious, but bleeding from shrapnel like he was. Jon tried to crawl, but the pain was too much. The walls of the warehouse had somehow blown off, so now the building looked like someone took a bulldozer and blasted right through it. The smoke from the explosion rose, and for a moment Jon feared there was a fire. It took a moment for him to realize that this was a controlled explosion. He heard footsteps and tried to focus on the noise and where they were coming from. Jon looked up and saw exactly whose footsteps those belonged to.

Vladimir entered the room methodically. With him was Manny, his son Ivan, and his assassin Elicia. His thugs Bao and Kareem were also with him. Jon recognized all of them because they were all there when he trained with them. The only one that was missing was his daughter, Nubia. Jon and she had a history of their own that was too long to get into right now.

Vladimir approached Jon first, and there was nothing he could do about it. He was too weak from the explosion to move to defend himself. The Lion leaned in and grabbed Jon by the hair and yanked it up, causing some pain.

"By any means necessary," Vladimir sneered.

Vladimir took out a dagger. Jon recognized the weapon. It was one that he had trained with when he met Vladimir. He watched helplessly now as the Lion walked methodically over to Freddy, who was stirring. Caine watched this also, and he too could not move. Vladimir presided over Freddy for a moment and waited until the hitman woke up. Freddy was awake.

"Goodbye Frederick," Vladimir told him.

Vladimir quickly leaned in and slashed Freddy's throat. The Caine associate gagged and held his neck as the blood poured out quickly. Jon saw this all and could not believe it. He looked at Vladimir's face and saw nothing but coldness. Freddy gagged for a moment, then fell dead. Caine screamed in horror as this was happening. Vladimir turned to Caine and strolled over to him. Jon could not move. He was in agony and conflicted. Vladimir had killed Freddy, and Jon watched this unfold in disbelief.

"You monster! You killed Frederick!" Caine exclaimed hysterically. Jon found it ironic for Caine of all people to call anyone a monster.

Vladimir smiled. He wiped his blade from Freddy's blood, and Caine's eyes lit up with absolute terror.

"Please! I beg you! Let me live! I will do anything!"

Vladimir pounced, slashing Caine across the throat. Jon watched silently as his most hated enemy clutched at his throat and gagged in his last moments. It took a little longer for it to hit Caine, as Vladimir made it even more painful than Freddy's. Vladimir slashed Caine again, making a second mark across his throat. This one did it, killing Caine.

Jon watched this all unfold, and it offended him slightly that Caine showed more fear of Vladimir than he did of him. He now saw both of his parents' killers slain on the floor and thoughts of terror raced through him. What was Vladimir going to do now?

Jon looked on and tried to see what Manny, Ivan, Bao, Kareem, and Elicia would do. They all stood silently on guard, waiting for their master's orders. The odds looked worse than ever. Jon was in pain, and the Legion of Samurai outnumbered him by five.

Vladimir turned toward Jon. He walked over and knelt beside him. Jon felt nervous and terrified. He had not feared death before but now feared it more than ever. It had more to do with the fact that he had something to live for now, and that was Jessica. He looked up at Vladimir. The Lion smiled.

"That is how you eradicate evil," Vladimir hissed.

"You have become the thing you claim to fight."

"I have destroyed two of the most wicked men on this Earth. Now your choice is simple; join me."

"You think I will join you now? After all you have done?"

"I did what was needed."

Jon spat on Vladimir. The saliva raced quickly from his mouth onto Vladimir's face. It was something he did not hesitate to do. Vladimir just gently wiped the spit off his face.

"I will never join you," Jon lamented.

Vladimir wiped Caine's blood off the knife. It was the same thing he did before he killed Caine. He brandished the knife, taking pleasure in this.

"I am going to enjoy this," he gloated.

BLAM!

A gunshot rang out suddenly. Jon bobbed his head, trying to locate the source.

BLAM!

Another gunshot and he could see that Bao and Kareem crumpled to the ground. Someone had shot them. Vladimir looked back at them. Manny and Ivan looked around them to locate the source.

BLAM!

Another gunshot and this one knocked Ivan down to the ground. Vladimir rushed over to his fallen son and held him. His face grew with horror. Ivan's shoulder was bleeding.

Manny had his sword out and held it in the air and then stopped dead in his tracks. Ulisez emerged out of the chaos and he had the gun. Jon now realized he had been the one to shoot Bao, Kareem, and Ivan.

"Step away from Jon, or Manny gets it," Ulisez demanded.

Holy shit, Jon thought. Holy shit. Holy shit.

Vladimir glared at Ulisez, who held his gun at Manny. Bao and Kareem clutched their wounds, which were lower-body injuries. Ivan's shoulder was bleeding all over the floor as Vladimir held him.

"You disgraceful little nobody," Vladimir spewed out.

"The way I see it, Vladimir," Ulisez began. "You have two choices; stay here and fight and watch your son and two associates bleed to death. Or you can leave and save your son's life."

Holy shit, Jon thought, Ulisez has balls of steel.

Jon tried to pick himself up and noticed Vladimir considering his options as this was happening. It was now a waiting game, the one making the important decision was the Lion. Vladimir continued to glare at Ulisez, and Jon figured he was probably thinking of a hundred ways to kill him.

"Do you really believe you can take me?" Vladimir asked as he rose.

BLAM!

Ulisez shot Vladimir, and Jon's jaw dropped. The bullet pierced through his hip. Jon watched as Vladimir flinched and for a moment admired his ability to take a gunshot and not show pain.

"You shot me, you insignificant little man," Vladimir glowered.

"That's for throwing me off a cliff and then pretending like everything was cool," Ulisez shot back.

"You will not win," said Vladimir.

"Last chance. Either stay and die or leave."

Vladimir smiled and reached into his pocket, and before Ulisez could do anything, the Lion flung something at the ground. An enormous cloud of smoke rose through the air, and Ulisez instinctively huddled beside Jon. After about fifteen seconds, the smoke cleared, and the five members of the Legion of Samurai disappeared.

Jon did not know how Ulisez found him, but he was grateful regardless. Vladimir was about to kill him. For a moment, he forgot all his issues. Then reality struck. Jon looked around and realized what had happened. Caine and Freddy's dead bodies laid there, and there was blood everywhere. Jon panicked, shaking all over. Ulisez held him up.

"It will be okay," Ulisez informed him.

Jon shook his head.

"I—I—I was going to bring Caine in; the right way," Jon stuttered. He had never stuttered before, but the sheer terror of what went on had shattered him.

Ulisez tried to lift Jon, but he shook him off.

"I can't get—I can't get blamed for this."

"You won't," Ulisez reassured him.

Jon looked at Ulisez solemnly and shook his head.

"We have—have to stop him before he does any more damage."

"We will, I promise you."

"Thanks for saving my life," Jon said.

"Anytime Jonny," Ulisez teased.

"Don't call me that," Jon shot back.

Jon and Ulisez slowly picked themselves up and staggered out the door and knew that they had a tough fight ahead of them.

Chapter 35: Jessica's Journey

February 15th, 2016

Jessica rushed over to the Orange Grove Hospital when she got the call. There had been a massacre at Caine Enterprises. There were over 40 people shot, with at least 23 deaths. It had startled Jessica when she got the call. Mike was in the hospital! She made her way there as quickly as she could.

She ran into the emergency room and could see Mike on the gurney from the corner of her eye. He was still alive! A nurse intercepted her. The nurse was a plucky blonde-haired woman with short hair and wrinkles.

"Ma'am you can't be in here," she scolded.

"Please! He's my brother," Jessica pleaded.

"You need to leave the room right now," the nurse demanded.

"Mike! Mike!" Jessica exclaimed hysterically.

They made her wait in the lobby. It was a terrible experience waiting to find out if the half-brother that just came into your life would live or die. The worst part was that Jessica still did not know what happened. She had found out about a mass shooting and that the shooters somehow escaped. How the hell could two mass shooters escape from the police? She figured it was more corruption at work. She had just got to know Mike, and now he might die. It ravaged Jessica with guilt, and she could not contemplate how all this happened.

The television in the lobby was on. Jessica heard the anchors talking and at first ignored it, then noticed it immediately.

"A terrible day for the city of Orange Grove as Mayor Rodriguez was found killed in a motel room along with a female acquaintance," said the anchor. "That was in addition to the Orange County District Attorney Daniel West being found dead in his office from a stab wound. We also got reports from Caine Enterprises of a mass shooting, where 50 people were shot, and 23 confirmed dead in one of the most horrific massacres in Orange County history—"

Jessica changed the channel. It was the same thing on every channel. Finally, she turned it off. Her entire body trembled. She could not believe the horror and chaos that had reigned upon her city. Now she worried about where Jon was. She still had not heard from him in over a week. Was he even in town? Worse, was he still alive?

She banished such thoughts from her mind. She had to think positive. That was the only way to get through this. Another thought pierced through her mind; why was Mike even at Caine Enterprises to begin with? What business could he possibly have there?

The nurse, the same bitchy one from before, walked out. She attempted to look pleasant, but that was too difficult even for her.

"You may visit him now, he is stable," she announced quietly.

Yeah, whatever, Jessica thought.

Instead, she just nodded gracefully and walked into the room where her half-brother laid. She noticed the incisions they made and how they patched him up. It did not look as bad as she feared. Someone had shot Mike in the lower abdomen. But the doctors had saved him with emergency surgery.

She sat in the small chair beside his bed. Many thoughts were racing through her mind, but it was hard to fathom anything else other than the wellbeing of her half-brother. Scratch that, he was her brother. The sooner she saw him as her brother and took out the half, the sooner she could accept him. Jessica regretted being so stubborn and not welcoming Mike right away. It was difficult to do so as he had appeared right after her father died. Her father, she thought.

They still had not caught his killer. According to Jon, who could have lied or even be dead, it was Vladimir Ramirez. Ramirez, she thought.

Suddenly, something in her memory horrified her. *Ramirez, she thought. Vladimir Ramirez. Nubia Ramirez?* Jessica shook her head.

It was a coincidence, Jessica thought, Ramirez was a common last name among Hispanic people. Then Jessica thought more about what Nubia had told her. She had told Jessica that she recently came to town to visit her father. Jessica knew that Vladimir was in town because Jon and Ulisez both had encountered him. But Jessica had never met him. He was still a myth to her, and she was not sure she wanted to meet him.

Before she could get further lost in her thoughts, she felt something in her hand. Mike's hand grabbed her softly, and she looked hopefully. Her brother's eyes flickered slowly, and it elated Jessica. He was waking up!

The machines beeped annoyingly, and Mike was still hooked to all of them. But he groaned a little and looked up and noticed Jessica.

"Where—where am I?"

"You were shot. Don't you remember?" Jessica asked him.

Mike shook his head. Then he cringed a little. Then she saw his face rise.

"You actually came to see me? Despite everything," he seemed touched.

She nodded. "It's time we put the past behind us. You are my brother. I have a brother. I have to be there for you as your sister."

She held Mike's hand and he embraced it. She continued. "Tell me what happened."

"There were two guys. I didn't know them. They walked in with swords and guns. There was a guy in front of me. He was—he—he—"

Mike stuttered. Jessica noticed this and quickly realized that he was reliving a nightmare.

"What happened at Caine Enterprises?" a familiar voice asked.

She turned and smiled radiantly. It was Jon! She ran toward him and hugged him and kissed him on the lips. After all the horror that had happened today, just knowing Jon was here and okay, it made her okay. He peeled her off him after a few seconds. She embraced him and held back tears.

"I'm so glad you're okay," she whispered.

"Okay is a relative word," Jon replied.

Jon gently peeled Jessica off him a second time. She watched as he walked past her and sat beside Mike. Jessica did not realize they even had a close relationship. But as she watched, she noticed a small bond.

"What happened at Caine Enterprises? What happened to you?" Jon asked.

Jessica knew that Jon would ask what no one dared to ask. That is part of the reason she admired him.

"It was a mass shooting. A bunch of people were shot. It was horrible dude. I saw a guy die right in front of me," said Mike.

Jon did not react. He stayed stoically for a moment. Jessica observed this and waited to see who would budge first.

"Who did it?" asked Jon.

"It was two guys," Mike recalled. "An Asian man and a black man. They were decked in all black, head to toe."

Jessica suddenly had a horrible memory. She remembered Nubia dressed in black from head to toe, and she had a bag with her. No, she thought, it could not be. She had to banish this thought from her mind.

"Bao and Kareem," Jon said as if those names should mean something to Jessica and Mike.

They all stayed silent for a moment, the three of them. Jon looked down for a moment and she was curious about what had happened to him and worried about his well being.

"This was orchestrated," Jon began. "All carefully planned and executed. Vladimir did this. He had his minions go around town and kill all these people, the mayor, the district attorney, everyone they could find at Caine Enterprises. It was a cleansing. Then Vladimir found me and found Caine and Freddy. Caine and Freddy are both dead."

She clasped her hands over her nose in shock. She had not seen this coming. Jon's news hit her like a ton of bricks. She had wanted Caine to pay for what he did to her mother, but not like this. Death was too easy for him. Now another dark thought crossed her mind. Jessica knew that she needed to ask it or else she would regret it.

"Did you—"

"Kill Caine?" Jon interrupted her. "No, I didn't kill him."

She noticed the tone he gave her and realized that she hit a nerve.

"It's not that bad a question," she suggested.

"I could have killed Caine anytime, but I didn't. I didn't," Jon told her.

"Why? Why did you hold back?"

"Because of you, Jess. All because of you," Jon replied.

"Guys," Mike interrupted. "I don't mean to interrupt but I think I need to rest, sleep off this gunshot wound. You know, so I don't relapse and die."

She leaned in and kissed Mike on the head.

"I'll be back to check on you," she said.

"Thanks, sis," he replied.

"Heal up, Mike," Jon said.

"Will do, dude," Mike replied.

They left Mike to rest and continued their conversation in the lobby. She wanted to get more information out of Jon. There was something wrong with this story, and not that she was suspicious, she just wanted to confirm facts.

As they sat in the lobby, Ulisez trudged in. Jessica spotted him and ran to hug him.

"Oh my God, what the hell happened to you?" she asked.

Ulisez looked at Jon, then at Jessica. She noticed the tension, and it irritated her. "Can someone tell me what the hell happened?"

Jon and Ulisez gave each other a look. She did not appreciate that they had their nonverbal language. Jessica was a little jealous of their relationship.

"I was there ready to confront Caine and end it," Jon began.

She listened intently. The words 'end it' rang through her mind as Jon spoke it. But she still kept going back to Nubia. Was she Vladimir's daughter? And if she was, did she have anything to do with the massacres? Jessica shuddered at the idea. Jon went on.

"I got there, blew off the hinges to the door of the warehouse where they were hiding. I beat the crap out of Freddy. Then I got information out of Caine. Apparently, after killing my mother, he went to her funeral. He told me he felt he had to be there because he was in love with her. That pissed me off. The nerve of this shitty guy.

"I hesitated because of you. I wanted to bring him in by the book like you."

Jessica took this in as Jon recounted his story. She felt some sympathy for him. They both hated the same man, and that man was now dead. He probably had his way of processing the death. Jon continued.

"As I had Caine at my mercy, Vladimir and his warriors blew into the area, literally. They caused a large explosion that knocked me off my feet. Then I watched helplessly as Vladimir killed Freddy. Then, he walked over to Caine and slashed him in the throat twice."

Good, she thought, he deserved to suffer. It was a vicious thought, and Jessica could not believe she could think such a thing. Anger made people think things they usually would not.

"What happened next?" she asked.

"Vladimir was about to kill me. His forces were around me, and I was outnumbered. But then, Ulisez blasts in and shoots three of his guys."

Jessica looked over at Ulisez, who was silent throughout the entire ordeal. He reacted like a man ashamed of being congratulated for his accolades.

"He saved my life," Jon added.

She gently touched Ulisez on the left arm. It did not faze him, as he looked on at both of them. Before anyone could say another word, Amy and Scotti walked into the lobby. Jessica looked solemnly at them and suddenly realized that she had been so concerned with Mike, that she had forgotten to check on them. But now that she saw them, she felt grateful they were okay.

"Oh my God, Jess," Amy gushed, and she grabbed Jessica and hugged her. Scotti trailed her sister and did the same. Jessica peeled them off her after a few seconds, similar to how Jon did to her.

"I'm so glad you're okay," Jessica told them. "Both of you."

"Oh my God, yes," Amy replied. She touched Jessica on the arm. "I'm sorry about our fight from earlier. I—we just didn't want to see the truth."

Oh shit, Jessica thought, they still did not know.

"Amy, listen—"

"What is it?" Amy cut her off.

Jessica glanced at Jon for reassurance and noticed his face was hard as stone. She looked at Ulisez and noticed the same expression on his face.

"Amy, Scotti, we have something to tell you," Jessica began.

"What is it?" asked Amy.

"Your—your—your—"

"Your father is dead," Jon finished.

Amy and Scotti's faces fell. Jessica glanced at Jon, irritated. She supposed that she could thank her lucky stars that the truth was out, but she had planned to break the news gently and Jon just gave it out without hesitation. Jessica watched as Amy stumbled, horrified at the news. Scotti's face watered.

"No," Amy started. Jessica noticed how tough she was, not letting the news break her, yet. Scotti broke down in tears, and she was crying. Jessica caught her as she fell and embraced her friend. They were friends again because friends forgave each other.

Amy held it together while shaking her head. Finally, she broke down and melted into Jon's arms, and he reluctantly held her.

Ulisez watched uncomfortably as this entire ordeal occurred. Jessica and Jon simultaneously peeled the Caine girls off of them. Amy wiped her tears and now remembered who she stood in front of. She put up a defense.

"What happened?" Amy asked.

"I was confronting Caine about everything he had done. He had been on the run, and I found him. I had him cornered."

Amy and Scotti listened carefully as Jon told the story. They wanted the truth, and Jessica figured Jon would give it to them.

"A man named Vladimir Ramirez walked in and killed them both in front of me. They had incapacitated me."

"Why were you there?" asked Scotti with a tremor of anger in her voice.

"I was there to bring him in. We are going to arrest him for his crimes," Jon replied.

Scotti wiped away her tears. Jessica realized that she was still angry. Amy stood silently as Jon had told the story.

"But they were both killed," Jon went on. "And now there is nothing any of us can do about it."

Jessica pondered something now. She needed an answer to her terrible thoughts. She stepped between Jon and Amy.

"Jon, does Vladimir have a daughter?" she asked.

Jon nodded. "Nubia Ramirez."

Jessica's face fell. It could not have been a coincidence. She befriended Vladimir's daughter before she went on her way to kill someone. Her face fell and Jon noticed.

"What's wrong?" he asked her.

"I ran into her in a coffee shop," Jessica informed him.

"Nubia is here in town?" Jon asked her.

Jessica nodded. "She told me she was visiting her father. I did not put the pieces together until now. I haven't met Vladimir."

"I'm sorry," Amy cut them off. "But who the hell is Vladimir and why did he kill my father?"

Jon and Jessica turned to Amy. For a moment, they had forgotten anyone else was in the room.

"Vladimir was the man that goaded me into coming back into town and taking your father down," Jon informed her.

Amy just stared at Jon for a moment. Then she reared back and slapped him across the face. Jessica cringed as she watched this unfold. Amy's face was grim. All of her anger was on Jon now.

"You brought this monster to town," Amy hissed at Jon.

"Yes," Jon replied. "And I am sorry."

Scotti said nothing, and Jessica noticed that she had handled the news better, which was unlike her. Amy still had that look on her face. She turned to Scotti.

"We have to go reclaim dad's body," she told her.

Amy dragged Scotti and then within a few moments, they were both gone. Neither said goodbye to them. Jessica understood it on some level. Their father was dead, and they were angry. The three of them were the only ones left now. A lot of damage occurred, but Alexander Caine was dead.

Jon and Jessica looked at each other soberly. This was not what either of them expected. Jessica touched Jon gingerly, her way to comfort him.

"Well, that went well," Ulisez interjected. "What are we going to do now?"

They both looked at Ulisez, and to be honest, neither knew the answer. They were both so traumatized by everything that had transpired.

"Now, we figure out what Vladimir's next plan is, and we stop him," Jon said.

The three of them left the hospital. They all went back to Jessica's apartment and hung out for a while. They spent some time just talking and reminiscing about life. Ulisez was the first to leave. It was getting dark.

She and Jon sat together on the couch. She knew in her heart that she loved him, and even accepted him, despite all his faults. There was also a common ground as they both found a weird closure. It was not the ending that either of them had seen coming, but it was an ending.

"Jess, I know you wanted to arrest him by the book," Jon began.

"It's okay," Jessica cut him off. "It's not your fault."

"Why does it feel like it is?"

"Because you have been dealing with guilt for a long time," Jessica explained. "But you have shown me, you changed. But don't change for me, Jon, change for yourself."

She could see Jon pondering this as she said this. He sighed, and she placed her hand on his hand, holding it gingerly. She leaned in and kissed him on the lips.

"I love you," Jessica told him.

"I love you too," Jon replied.

It was bizarre how easy it was to say that to each other. Jessica could honestly admit that she had never felt love for anyone before. She had lusted a lot. The thing with Rion was lust. Her weird attraction to Nubia was lust. But now she felt a little horrified knowing that Nubia was Vladimir's daughter. Maybe Nubia was not like her father.

Jon stood up to leave, and she stood up with him.

"I have to go do some work, I will check on you tomorrow," Jon informed her.

"Be safe," Jessica said to him.

They kissed again. Jessica held Jon's hand softly for a moment. She wished she could freeze time and just be here forever. Something in the back of her mind told her that this was far from over.

Jon released his hold on Jessica. She pecked him on the cheek. Jon exited the apartment, closing the door behind her.

Later, Jessica slouched on her couch. But as she did this, there was a knock on the door. Jon had just left so it could be him. Had she been more on her guard, Jessica would have realized that Jon would never come right back after leaving. It was not his style.

She stood up and hustled to the door and opened it with a joy that she should not have displayed.

"Did you miss—"

She did not finish the sentence. Jessica stopped in her tracks. The man standing before her was large, with a thick black beard and a long black mane. He reminded her of a lion with the way he looked. With no introduction, Jessica knew instantly who this was, and she grew fearful.

"It is about time we met Ms. Hudson. I guarantee you that you will enjoy our little chat," said the large man.

Jessica felt a chill run down her spine as she stared at the large man in front of her. He advanced on her and placed a cloth over her face. She struggled mightily but soon got drowsy. It was about ten seconds of fighting before everything went black.

Chapter 36: The Lioness

February 16th, 2016

Vladimir took Jessica Hudson by force. She was the last piece of the puzzle. This woman, the one whose spell Jon Drake was under, was the reason everything had come as it was. Now he would finally have the long-overdue talk he had been wanting with this young woman. Taking her had not been difficult. Vladimir had not wanted to hurt Jessica, so he used chloroform. It was cheap, and it was not the style or the ways of the Legion of Samurai. But he needed to get her to come to his home, and he succeeded.

Vladimir had Jessica on a chair in his master bedroom. Getting her here was easy, as she did not weigh much. She was still asleep at the moment, and Vladimir watched her for a moment. He understood why Jon Drake loved her. She was a beautiful woman, and she had given him a slight fight.

But what Vladimir wanted to know was what made this woman tick. He had known her father, briefly, before he killed him. Frank Hudson was a spineless man who let Alexander Caine run amok for an entire decade, and that was a recipe for punishment. It forced Vladimir to end both of their lives. He did it and would do it again. There was work to do, and everyone would understand that no one could mess with the Legion of Samurai. They would eradicate evil and rebuild the world.

He did not want to rule the world, but he felt the responsibility toward the world. He was qualified, and he would ensure that everyone in his new world understood the importance of a balanced environment. There was no one else in the world as qualified as he was to bring order and balance to the new world and utopia he would create.

Jessica remained asleep for the moment and he observed her. Vladimir was not sure what his next plan was. He wanted to discuss what he would with the young lady and see what could transpire of such a conversation. Despite the situation, he had no genuine desire to kill this woman either. Vladimir had deployed his warriors to conduct some research on Miss Hudson, and it saddened him to learn all that she had endured in her 22 years of life. Freddy Hunter had killed her mother as a way of getting back at Frank Hudson. Jessica also had developed a heroin addiction at 14 and was in and out of rehab. She had become entangled in an affair with Rion

Caine, the wayward son of the now-departed Alexander Caine. Her recent loss included the death of her father. He almost felt bad about being the chief person responsible for that. He stopped feeling bad once he remembered how incompetent Hudson was. His death would make Jessica stronger, or he would find a way for that to happen. He noticed she had stirred.

Her eyes flickered, and she groaned. She shuffled a little, and Vladimir waited patiently for her to realize her surroundings. She looked around the room, scanning her environment. There was a bit of drowsiness in her demeanor and he had expected that given the chloroform he gave her. Finally, she looked up at Vladimir and made eye contact. He had expected some fear. But she did not show any of that.

"It is about time you woke up, Miss Hudson," Vladimir beamed.

She did not respond. Instead, she shook her arms to free herself of the binds that held her. He had tied her hands to the chair with a parachute cord. It was effective in holding someone down. She would not leave her binds unless he allowed her to. Besides, he had some words to have with her.

"You still look lovely despite your current predicament," Vladimir told her.

"Go to hell," she hissed at him.

He shook his head. "That's not very ladylike, you have much to learn."

"Where are we? Why have you taken me here?"

"We are at my home in Laguna Beach, my dear. It's very private and remote, I assure you."

"That doesn't answer the why part."

"It's simple. I have taken you because I wanted to meet the alluring Jessica Hudson who has Jon Drake wrapped around her little finger."

"That's not exactly accurate."

"I take you that know about Alexander Caine's passing correct?"

"I know you killed him."

Vladimir just smiled. Jessica did not remove her gaze, and he had to admit he admired her spunk and her courage.

"I did. You should thank me."

She scoffed. "Thanking you? Did you forget that you killed my father, you psychopathic nut job?"

"That was unfortunate. I regret that more than anything I have done. But it had to be done. Your father was a coward who allowed evil to run free in this cesspool of a town."

"He was my father. He was innocent—"

"A man that allows Alexander Caine to run free is not innocent!"

He stared her down for a moment. She was magnificent, especially the way she showed no fear. He wondered if Jon Drake had inspired that in her, or if she already was that way.

"You are an incredible woman, Jessica," he complimented her.

"And you are a hypocritical piece of shit, Vladimir."

"Ah, so you know who I am?"

She nodded. "How could I not? The way you preach, the long hair, the mane that makes you look like a lion. I knew who you were the second you drugged me with chloroform."

"I apologize for that," Vladimir said. "But I needed to have this chat with you."

"So what now? You plan to kill me too?"

"No, my dear. My intention is not to kill you. I believe that you would make a valuable piece of my organization. I believe you are one of the kind souls that deserve saving."

"What? You can't be serious—"

"Dead serious. I admire your many qualities and I believe I could channel some of that anger into something constructive."

Vladimir picked up a glass and Jessica watched him like a hawk. He poured himself a glass of saké and drank it. Jessica watched him as he did this.

"I once had a wife, beautiful like you," Vladimir began. Jessica observed silently as he sniveled. "She was everything I could ever dream of. She was beautiful, intelligent, and sharp. She was the love of my life. Ileana was my entire being; my wife.

"We got married and had two young children. One of them was a boy named Ivan, and the other was a girl named Nubia."

Vladimir did not look at Jessica or else he would have noticed her eyebrows rose when he mentioned Nubia. He paid no attention to it yet.

"We were happy and in bliss. We lived in a small village in Brazil and were relatively humble. I ran a small store, and my wife helped me. One day, a man approached us. His name was Saul Salgado. He told us he represented the Great Command of the Capital, which was the largest and most dangerous cartel in Brazil. He offered protection services for a cost. I refused. I did not want to be at the mercy of the cartels.

"Later that night, Salgado and a few other men stormed my home and attacked us. Ileana and I made sure the children were safe. Ileana made her way to the car, with the hope we could drive off. As soon as she turned the ignition, I knew it was too late. The car exploded. My wife was killed instantly. I did not have much time to mourn, as Salgado and his men continued their attack. I ensured that my children would survive by running toward the forest. And that was the last time I ever was helpless."

He poured another shot of saké into his glass as Jessica sat there in silence. He did not know what was going on in her mind, but she seemed to be perceptive of what he told her. He did not want to gain her sympathy or anything of that nature. He wanted her to understand.

"So you dedicated your life to eradicating evil by creating an organization of samurais?"

He shook his head. "I did not create the Legion of Samurai. I merely took it over when my master was killed," He stopped himself, then resumed. "By Jon Drake."

He observed as she took this in. Vladimir was not sure if Jon had told her this little detail, but he did not care.

"Jon told me he was forced to do it," Jessica replied.

"Ah yes," Vladimir sighed. "He did a good job of playing the victim. Jon Drake has always had that fire, the ability to take a life at an instant. He had no qualms about killing Diego Rivera, and he had no issues killing any of Caine's men when he returned to town."

Before Jessica could react, the front doors opened, and Nubia walked in. Vladimir was a little annoyed. He had not expected Nubia to interrupt him and did not appreciate the disrespect. Nubia walked in and glanced at her father, then saw Jessica tied up.

"Jessica?" she asked.

"Nubia," replied Jessica.

"Ah, you two know each other," Vladimir did not show his irritation, instead choosing to act direct and calm. As the leader of the Legion of Samurai, he had to avoid showing his emotions, especially in front of his subordinates.

"I met her at the coffee shop," said Jessica.

"She was very kind to me father," Nubia added. She glared at Vladimir, and this took him by surprise. "Why is she here? And why do you have her tied up?"

He did not answer her. Instead, he grabbed Nubia's arm and dragged her out of the master bedroom and into the hallway. He closed the door behind him and gently released his daughter, who kept her balance. She turned around and got in Vladimir's face. This was unusual, and not the way he raised her.

"Why do you have Jessica? Why is she here, father?"

He slapped Nubia across the face. It was a backhanded hit, and one he rarely dished out. But his daughter had disrespected him in front of Jessica, and he has to teach her a lesson. The impact of his backhand pressed against her face and flung her backward. She pressed her face with her left hand and looked more ashamed than hurt.

"I am your father! You should never question me!" roared Vladimir as he towered above her.

Nubia gained her footing and stood face to face with her father. He admired her courage as he did Jessica. But this was his child, his baby. She was his daughter, the one who might carry the legacy someday. Surely, she understood his reasoning.

"Father," Nubia tried again. "Why do you have Jessica? What did she do to you?"

To be honest, Jessica did nothing. Vladimir had spared her. There was something about her that caught his eye. It was not a romantic attachment either; he was and always would be a widow who pined for his lost wife. Also, Jessica was the same age as his daughter, so that would be wrong on his part.

"What is she doing here?" Nubia asked again.

"I do not appreciate your tone, daughter."

"Answer the question, father! Why is she here?"

"She is here because I wanted to see what Jon Drake saw in her."

Vladimir noticed something off in his daughter. He had not mentioned Jon Drake's name since she came to town, for obvious reasons. She flinched at the sound of his name, and he understood why.

"What does Jon have to do with this?" she asked him.

He hesitated. When he trained Jon Drake for those few weeks in Brazil, he had purposely kept Nubia away. For Jon to be efficient, he needed to avoid any distractions. Nubia, his beloved daughter, would be a distraction for Jon. So he gave her a diplomatic mission that would take a few weeks. That would also ensure that the two of them did not run into each other while Jon trained.

"I sent Jon Drake back to his hometown so he could help us get rid of Alexander Caine. It did not turn out exactly as I predicted, but we got the job done."

Nubia did not respond. She waited to see what else her father would tell her, and Vladimir appreciated the patience.

"But I also knew about the unpredictability of Jon Drake. I had known this since he killed Diego Rivera, and since you and he had an affair behind my back."

Vladimir watched as his daughter shrunk, possibly from shame or dishonor. Jon and his daughter had somehow found each other a few years ago. Vladimir was not sure exactly on when it happened, or how, but he knew about it. He had stayed quiet about it all until now.

"How did you know?" she inquired.

"I know all daughter," replied Vladimir calmly.

They were at a standoff. Neither wanted to budge and for a moment, he realized how proud of her he was. She was truly his daughter. If Vladimir was the Lion, then Nubia surely was the Lioness. That might be her new Legion name.

"What do you plan to do with her?" Nubia inquired.

The nerve of my daughter, Vladimir thought.

"No harm will come to her," he replied. "I plan to take her in and offer her an opportunity."

"And if she refuses?"

He had not thought of that. He was not sure what to say to that. There were too many variables. He did not expect a refusal. Sure, Jon turned him down, but he sensed Jessica was smarter than that. Or at least, that is what he thought.

"She won't," was all Vladimir said. "Now, daughter, if you will excuse me, I need you to go off to your quarters and prepare for what's next."

"Father, you cannot just brush me aside," she rebelled.

"Yes, I can," he shot back.

He nudged Nubia away and then headed back into his bedroom and closed the door behind him. As he walked in, he noticed Jessica just sitting there apathetically. She again did not show any fear, and it was interesting to Vladimir.

"So what, did you put Nubia in the corner for daring to speak up to the great Vladimir Ramirez?" asked Jessica sarcastically.

Vladimir walked over to Jessica and leaned in close to a point where he made her a little uncomfortable.

"What occurs between me and my daughter is my business, understood?"

"Whatever."

Vladimir observed her demeanor a little. It amused him. Her feistiness inspired him, and he loved her never-ending fight.

"Have you considered my offer yet?"

"Kind of hard to consider anything with my hands tied up."

He nodded. She had a point. He took out a small dagger and watched her eyes light up, glaring at the dagger. Her eyes remained steady on the knife. He walked over and knelt beside her and cut the ropes restraining her. Jessica's arms were free, and she held one gingerly with the other.

"I have untied you with the basic premise that you won't foolishly attempt to escape," Vladimir informed.

"Oh, why wouldn't I want to escape some creepy man's mansion in Laguna Beach?" Jessica quipped.

"You know people like you have such a shortsighted view of things. You think, because your father died, that it allows you to spew the vile hatred you have done? Do you think you know loss? You have not understood what loss feels like.

"Do you know what I did to the man that killed my wife? I found him and executed him. That way, he would never hurt another person ever again."

"Did that bring your wife back?" asked Jessica.

Vladimir said nothing. She had rendered him speechless, for the moment at least.

"No, it did not," Jessica went on. "Eye for an Eye keeps the violence going. It does not make you feel any better."

"Oh, but it did young Jessica," Vladimir spat back. "It did."

This was an entertaining back and forth he was having with Jessica. She was intelligent.

"You should know that Orange Grove is just the beginning, Miss Hudson. There is still more evil to destroy. The world is filled with corruption that must be destroyed. Politicians, actors, doctors, police officers—everyone is concerned with stepping on each other to get what they want.

"What do they want, you ask? Power! The power that is utilized and has corrupted every single entity where the world has become overpopulated with entitled narcissists."

"So what are you going to do?" asked Jessica softly.

"The cleansing will begin in Orange Grove. Then we will continue throughout California and then the United States of America. Then, when the time is right—the world."

"You're a fucking psychopath," exclaimed Jessica.

"No, Miss Hudson. The real psychopaths are the people who consider themselves good while continuing to spread hatred and negativity throughout the world. We are the Legion of Samurai, and we are here to restore the balance! No misguided visionary or a young brat with an attitude will stand in our way.

"Like your father, you lack what is needed to truly be a savior. I was wrong about you. You are not Legion of Samurai material. At least your mother died a hero. Too bad she wasted her last act on your pathetic life."

Vladimir scoffed and walked off, leaving Jessica sitting there stunned. He knew it would only be a matter of time before Jon Drake found them. He was expecting it.

Chapter 37: The White Warrior

That Same Morning

Jon knew something was wrong when he went to Jessica's apartment and discovered she was not there. Her car had been there, but she was not, and her phone was also there. That meant she had not ordered an Uber or Lyft. She also would not just walk off without her phone. That was not her style.

He investigated the place and then discovered he would not need to do much more sleuthing. Someone left a clue behind. It was an envelope. Jon used his Swiss Army Knife to cut the envelope, and there was a letter inside.

White Warrior,

The moment has come. I have taken your beloved Jessica Hudson. I do not intend to do any harm to her. I merely wish to know her as you do. But I seek one last counsel with you, and I will give you a chance to prove yourself to me for the last time. The Legion of Samurai will destroy the wickedness in this world and rebuild it in our vision. Your choice is simple: join us or do not, and then we destroy you.

-The Lion.

He looked at the back end of the envelope and there was an address listed. It surely must have been the address. Vladimir's mansion was somewhere in Laguna Beach, and that was where Jessica would be.

He drove over to Ulisez's house. He had texted him briefly that he would head over but did not state why. The driveway was empty, as expected. Ulisez kept his vehicle in his garage. Jon waited patiently for his friend to come out. He really did not have the time to go inside and did not feel like contending with the dogs, maybe the cat, despite actually liking them.

Ulisez walked out and looked staggered a little. He had told him to wear some protection because they had to go accomplish something but did not go into detail. His friend stepped into the car.

"What's the big emergency, Jonny?"

"Jessica's been kidnapped," Jon sugarcoated nothing.

"Again? Who was it this time?"

"The man that threw you off a cliff."

He saw Ulisez freeze for a moment as if he were having a dreadful nightmare. His face was ghostly white, and he appeared to be reliving it all over again. It was like something out of a movie, and his friend had to hold his balance. Jon snapped his fingers in front of Ulisez's face.

"Snap out of it," exclaimed Jon.

"Sorry just reliving getting thrown off a cliff."

"I texted you because I needed you," said Jon. "I could do this alone, but it might get messy. It will be us against the entire Legion of Samurai that Vladimir has waiting for us."

"And how many people does he have?"

He started counting with his fingers.

"Manny, Elicia, Bao, Kareem, Ivan, Nubia—"

"Six people! We will have to fight six people?"

"You're not including Vladimir too."

"How the hell are we going to get into his house without being killed?"

"That's where we ask your favorite person."

Ulisez shook his head. "No."

"Yes."

"No."

"Yes. Saucedo. We have to do this. We have to ask good old Commissioner Martin AKA the Panther."

Ulisez sulked. Jon could tell that his friend did not want to do this, but they did not have a choice.

They made their first detour. They knew that Thomas was not at work yet, so the plan was to go after him at home. It would be tricky because he was essentially the second in command of the Legion of Samurai. He was an expert in combat and mind games. Vladimir taught him well and Jon knew about how tough that training was so he knew what to expect.

Thomas had a pleasant home for someone on a commissioner's salary. It was a two-story townhome in Costa Mesa, with three bedrooms and two bathrooms. The house was peach on the exterior with an orange roof. There were two trees in front of the home and a garage at the back of the home. The townhome was rectangular, going straight up, unlike a normal house. The areas to get into the home would be very difficult, as there were only two ways in, not counting windows. There were two windows in the house's front on the first floor, and two on the second floor. The plan was to go through one window, and Jon felt he could do the top window. But he was not exactly sure what Ulisez was capable of. There had been stories about his own adventures.

Ulisez had told him briefly about running into the Deathstalker while vacationing in England. They had formed a small friendship until Ulisez discovered who he really was. From what Jon understood, that was what motivated Ulisez to become a cop. He had asked Ulisez how he felt about A.J. Walker being shot off a cliff, and his first reaction was to make sure he was dead. Things had been so chaotic that neither had time to search for a body if one actually existed.

The townhome would be very difficult to get into, without alerting Thomas. From Mike Wilson's notes, Thomas had a bedroom on the top floor. But he also had a working office he liked to stay in for a while. The living room was on the first floor and there was a small kitchen next to it.

They arrived on the street just outside the home and glanced at each other and took this in mentally. What they were about to do was the first of a dangerous journey. They had to take a breath. Here we go. It was time to get to work.

They slowly exited the car and stood outside the vehicle for a moment. They looked at the townhome and scanned the building for a moment. Jon looked around and tried to see if there were any witnesses and realized there were none. It was still early morning, so no one was awake yet. Early morning and nighttime were obviously the best times of the day to break into a home.

Jon had been at this for a long time. He knew the positives and negatives of every situation, especially ones that involved monumental risk. But they were not just breaking into any house. This was the home of a police commissioner, and one of the best warriors in the Legion of Samurai.

He grabbed some rope and a grappling hook. He attached the hook onto the rope and swung for the window and watched as it latched onto the edge. Ulisez watched this in awe and attempted to see what was going on. He gave Ulisez something he pulled out of his pocket. His friend held the item in his hands and analyzed it for a moment. It took Ulisez a moment to realize he was holding a LockAid lock pick gun. He gave Jon a curious look. Jon did not respond. He just smirked at him and motioned for the front door. Ulisez rolled his eyes and then ambled toward the front door and began using the LockAid. This made Jon smile, knowing his buddy knew how to use one of these fine gadgets. He had not used it in a while but was glad he had it ready in his bag.

He climbed the rope, making his way slowly and steadily up the way. He used his feet to balance himself against the wall as he pressed his upper body up. The rope was stiff, but also very sturdy. It would not break. It held firm as he latched his arms around and pushed forward. Finally, he reached the top where the grapple hook was. He took out a pick and unlocked the window. He looked down and noticed Ulisez had already entered the house.

He squeezed himself through the window, and then quickly realized he was in the bedroom. There was no sign of Thomas. He looked around and then noticed a shadow in the hallway. From the corner of his eye, he noticed it was Ulisez.

Stupid idiot, Jon thought, be careful.

He followed Ulisez from a distance and peered out into the room and saw Ulisez slowly enter the other room. Then what happened next went so fast.

There was a loud thump. Some shouting occurred next, and he instantly realized Thomas, who had spotted Ulisez. Some glassware, or something of that nature, broke as a scuffle took place.

He still snuck by and realized that he could still use stealth. Thomas may have spotted Ulisez, but he had not spotted Jon yet.

He made his way toward the working room and peaked in and saw Thomas holding Ulisez roughly with his left arm, then saw him rear back and punch Ulisez in the face.

"Boy, you made a big mistake coming here," he heard Thomas say arrogantly to Ulisez from behind the wall.

Ulisez did not respond. Jon could tell from the corner of his eye, he was still conscious. That was a good thing. While he was confident he could take Thomas by himself, having Ulisez as a backup was more beneficial.

"Why are you here?" asked Thomas.

He noticed that Thomas's back was to the door as he held Ulisez down by force. The Legion of Samurai warrior, and police commissioner, was strong. He was roughly the same size as Ulisez, but a little taller. That gave him somewhat of an advantage. Jon could kill Thomas from this angle, but he needed him alive. They needed his information, his resources. Jon placed his right foot partially through the door. Thomas faced a distraction, or he would have heard him coming a mile away.

Thank you, buddy, Jon thought.

"I'm here to visit my friend," Ulisez shot off sarcastically.

Thomas punched him in the face again. It appeared their working relationship did not prevent him from assaulting his fellow officer.

"Why are you here?" Thomas asked again.

Jon made his move. He quickly snuck up on Thomas and clobbered him on the back of his head with his forearm. This caused Thomas to stumble back and Jon reared back and punched Thomas in the face, causing him to tumble to the ground with a thud, unconscious. Jon checked on Ulisez.

"What took you?" asked Ulisez.

"I had to let him beat the shit out of you for a while to truly distract him. Thanks for being a good sport," replied Jon.

He bent over and checked Thomas's pulse. The commissioner was still alive, so they could definitely use him.

"You asshole," Ulisez sneered at him. Jon smiled.

"Help me tie him up," he commanded. Ulisez complied.

They worked together to hold Thomas up and then placed him in a chair. He used a special rope to restrain Thomas because he was a special hostage. He knew exactly what the Panther was capable of and used a strong rope that would bind him well. Ulisez grabbed the rope and tied his hands, while Jon tied his feet.

He walked down to the kitchen and grabbed a pitcher of water. The kitchen was modest, yet very nice looking. There was a pleasant set of china plates, and the rest of the silverware looked police. The stuff also looked like Thomas had not used it for a long time. The table in the kitchen was modest, with two chairs. The fridge was stainless steel.

He made his way back up the stairs with the pitcher of water. People said that you should never wake up an unconscious person with cold water. Well, Jon thought, he would care more if he liked Thomas.

He shot up the stairs and reentered the room where Ulisez stood next to Thomas, who sat there unconscious like an innocent angel. He unleashed a water assault on Thomas and smiled as he coughed his lungs out.

"Wakey wakey Panther," Jon beamed.

Thomas gathered his senses and finally realized who was in front of him. It was not fear on his face. Instead, his face resonated with annoyance.

"White Warrior," Thomas muttered. "I have been looking for your ass for a while."

"Well, you found me," Jon replied. "And today you will help me."

Thomas laughed. It was an annoying laugh that went on for a few seconds. Jon and Ulisez shot each other a glance, both trying to understand what the hell was going on.

"You think I will help you? Boy, have you lost your mind?" Thomas said this while still laughing. Jon was getting annoyed. He slapped Thomas across the face. It was so quick it even took Ulisez by surprise. The palm of Jon's hand clapped against Thomas's face with such a force that it jerked his entire head.

"Typical white boy," Thomas spat out. "A bitch slap from a bitch."

"I got more for you if you don't help us," Jon shot back.

"I'm Legion of Samurai, I can take anything you throw at me," Thomas roared.

It peeved Jon. He knew that Thomas would be difficult, but had hoped he would listen to reason at least. The man was a stubborn asshole and one that needed to be humbled. He reached into his bag and pulled out some blue gloves. Thomas eyeballed him the entire time curiously. Jon put the gloves on.

"What are you doing to do? Molest me?" Thomas was overconfident. That was a good thing. Jon would take advantage of it.

"Not exactly," said Jon. He pressed a button on the gloves and the electrical currents rose and flew throughout the air. Ulisez instantly knew exactly what Jon had planned to do. Thomas still did not pick up on it.

Without warning, Jon slammed his electric glove down on Thomas's leg and he screamed in agony as the electrical currents surged through his body. He released his hold on Thomas's leg after several seconds. Thomas puffed out, breathing slowly after the shocks. Ulisez's jaw dropped in horror as he witnessed this taking place.

"Give me the address to Vladimir's home," Jon commanded.

Thomas recovered and spit on Jon's face. He wiped the spit off and then pressed his electrical gloves onto his left leg, shocking him even more. The jolts resonated from him and Jon kept his stare hard at Thomas, who shrieked a little from the pain.

"An address!" Jon roared.

"2529 South Coast Drive," Thomas gave in.

"Tell me the layout of Vladimir's Mansion!" ordered Jon.

"Jon, what are you doing?" asked Ulisez.

"Shut up," said Jon to Ulisez, not taking his eyes off of Thomas. He spoke to his hostage. "Tell me how to get in without issues."

"Go to hell," spat Thomas.

"You first," shot Jon. Then, he reared back with the electric gloves and again clenched it on Thomas's leg. The Legion of Samurai warrior screamed hysterically from all the pain. Ulisez watched helplessly, conflicted at all this going on. Jon released his hold. Thomas breathed heavily, taking breaths slowly. The shocks were wearing him down.

"It's pretty simple, Martin," Jon stated. Thomas continued to pant, his breaths sounding like he had just run a marathon, not been shocked nearly to death. "Vladimir took Jessica. He is trying to draw me out. He sent an invitation. I know I'll be walking into a trap. I want to be prepared.

"I figured who else would know the layout of this house better than the second most important member of the Legion of Samurai. So we came here to ask for your help because beneath all that asshole exterior is someone who truly wants to do good. And you know, deep down, that killing thousands of people—well, that's not very good."

Thomas looked at him for a moment, and Jon could tell that he was processing the information. There was a sly smile on Thomas's face.

"Well, that seems to be her problem, not mine," Thomas gloated.

Jon shook his head. "Have it your way." He unleashed his glove again, this time on Thomas's chest. The shock felt worse this time, as Thomas screamed in absolute agony. He held onto his chest longer this time.

"Are you tired of being a dick? Or do I need to cause a heart attack?"

Ulisez watched helplessly as this went on, and Jon secretly worried if he would do something. But he trusted Ulisez to trust him.

"Tell me what to do!"

"All right, all right," Thomas shouted. He released his hold on Thomas. As he looked at Thomas, he realized that his electric gloves had made a tremendous impact now. The commissioner looked distraught, heaving a little. It looked like he was having an anxiety attack. He released the gloves immediately. He knew that Thomas could withstand torture, so he did not have an issue with unleashing it. Earlier, he had shocked him on the legs. But this blow was to his chest, which was near his heart. Jon was careful to not give him a heart attack, though that was a possibility.

"Speak now, or I will send you to the grave," Jon held out his glove like a gun. He did not enjoy using torture tactics, but they were effective. Ulisez stood there silently, and Jon knew that there was a lot going through his mind.

"Vladimir has a large mansion," Thomas began by stating the obvious. "He has seven bedrooms, seven bathrooms. One room is his training room, where he meditates. The large room is only accessible via the hallway door inside the home. The exterior is a 40-foot drop into the ocean, so you won't be able to sneak into that as you did mine.

"The other five rooms are for his warriors and children. Ivan has a room, Nubia has a room. Elicia has one. Bao and Kareem share one. Manny has one."

Jon did a visual count in his mind of the names Thomas mentioned, and it matched up with his notes. Vladimir had extreme confidence in his warriors. He did not need to put overwhelming odds on his side. That weakness was exposable. There were hundreds of Legion of Samurai warriors still in Brazil. Jon wondered who was monitoring them. There had to be a second-in-command down there. But he brushed aside all thoughts of that for the moment.

"Anything else?" asked Jon.

Thomas heaved. Jon made a face. The commissioner looked worse for wear. His face was rough, like a catcher's mitt now. The electric shocks had taken a toll on him, and he looked at least 10 years older now. Jon held Thomas's face up and they were inches apart.

"I'm waiting," Jon added.

"Vladimir will send out Bao, Kareem, and Elicia first. He'll have Manny hiding by the stairs. I don't know what he has planned for his kids, but I am sure they will be in play too."

He released his grip on Thomas and watched as he wheezed helplessly. It was a pathetic display by a guy who once threatened to whoop his ass. Thomas was bent over now. Jon turned to Ulisez.

"Let's go."

"Wait, aren't you going to untie me?" asked Thomas.

"Oh I'm sure you'll find a way out of those," Jon quipped.

He packed up all his stuff into the bag and he and Ulisez headed out the door and he heard Thomas growling in anger.

"Drake! Drake! Get your white ass back here! Drake! Drake!" Jon heard Thomas screaming as he ran down the stairs, and then out the front door.

They drove in silence for the first twenty minutes. There was a sense of conflict in the air between them, especially after Ulisez watched him shock the hell out of Thomas. They made their way south down Pacific Coast Highway or PCH as the locals called it. It took about forty minutes to get to the southern part of Laguna Beach. Traffic was heavy as they were doing this during rush hour. What made it worse was that it started raining. It was winter after all and they had to get some rain sometime. While most knew Southern California for its sunshine, the rainstorms were spectacular. Usually, because of the terrible conditions of the roads, every time it rained, the streets would become flooded.

It had been dry when they broke into Thomas's home. The weather took a turn for the worse right when they exited. The light drizzle turned into a full-blown rainstorm. Jon used his windshield wipers on fast mode. Ulisez stayed quiet throughout the entire ordeal, and Jon preferred it that way. There really was no point in talking about what happened back there. They had accomplished their goal, and that was the only thing that mattered.

They continued driving down PCH. The normal rush hour traffic continued and Jon wondered how many people worked down by the beach, especially on a rainy day. He heard a roar of thunder in the background and felt it to be symbolic.

They were within a block from the coordinates where Thomas had said. It was a straight line down the coast, and Jon could see the home from the distance on the right side of PCH. The traffic was clearing out now, and it was about ten o'clock.

They had packed light clothing, maybe a small hooded sweatshirt for each of them. There was no time for comfort. They were on a rescue mission. The home was massive as they approached it. Even in this fledging storm, he could see how large this place was and how difficult it might be to scour it. They stepped out of the vehicle together. Ulisez had not said a word to him about what had transpired back there, and that was for the best. They needed to focus.

As they stepped outside, the front doors opened. Bao and Kareem walked out, with each man holding a sword. He smiled. It was so on. He glanced over at Ulisez, who had a look that showed that he was kind of hesitant. Jon motioned with his eyes it was time to work.

Bao and Kareem charged toward Jon and Ulisez separately. Bao slashed left and right at Jon, attempting to slash him. It was more difficult to fight a man with a sword in the rain, as Jon was learning. He evaded all his slashes and even caught the brunt of the sword with his hand, then head-butted Bao in the face. Bao staggered back, and Jon knocked him over with a right elbow to the face. Jon kept on the attack, stomping Bao in the neck with his boot, sending him to the wet pavement. He had knocked out the assassin.

Ulisez was not faring well. He staggered backward as Kareem laid into him with constant swipes. Their fight was sloppy too, as Ulisez tripped on the pavement and Kareem did the same. In the chaos, the sword slipped out of Kareem's hands and now neither man had a weapon. Kareem sat on top of Ulisez and strangled him with his enormous hands. Jon ran over and clonked him over the head with a baseball bat. Kareem was down for the count.

Jon picked Ulisez up and nodded. They looked back toward the front of the house and saw a figure standing in the doorway. It was Elicia. The beautiful assassin smiled maliciously, with two swords in her hands. Jon and Ulisez glanced at one another, both contemplating the next move.

Elicia decided on her own. She charged toward both of them with a ferocity that neither of the other two warriors had. This would be a lot tougher than the other two. She swiped erratically at Jon and Ulisez, who evaded every single shot. Her sword was swift and could cut through anything. They avoided getting stabbed throughout the entire first few seconds. The rain made it difficult to see anything, and it also changed the outlook on the way they prepared for battle.

When Elicia realized her effort was not succeeding, she did something odd. She retreated. Jon watched as she headed back inside the mansion and closed the door behind her. The rain continued to fall, generating even more pressure.

"You know it's a trap, right?" asked Ulisez.

"Oh, I am absolutely counting on it."

Together, they cautiously made their way toward the front porch of the house. The structure looked very eerie, and if they had not seen Elicia enter, they would not have been able to believe anyone was actually inside. This was the Legion of Samurai's Southern California fortress.

Thunder pounded in the background as Jon slowly and methodically made his way toward the door. Ulisez trailed right behind him.

He cautiously pressed his hand on the doorknob and turned it all the way around. There was no lock on the door. That was not a surprise. They looked at each other for a moment, then stepped into the home and closed the door behind them.

Without warning, Jon felt a kick to the stomach. Elicia had laid out to prepare for this. Her feet knocked him back against the wooden door, and he felt the pain of the wood as he crashed against it. Ulisez reached into his pocket to draw his gun, but Elicia quickly deflected it away with her sword. With her blade, she applied pressure on Ulisez, causing him to tumble to the ground. She applied her boot on his chest and held her ground.

"First, I kill you, then Jon Drake," she told him.

Elicia raised the blade to stab Ulisez. Jon bum-rushed her before she could make the last strike. He tackled her to the ground and then looked back at Ulisez.

As Jon picked himself up, he noticed something off. There was blood on his hands. He panicked, but then checked his body and found nothing. This was when he realized whose blood this was. Jon looked over and saw Elicia laying on the ground with a sword in her abdomen. He kneeled beside her, forgetting that she had tried to kill him a few seconds ago.

"Elicia?"

Despite a giant sword in her abdomen, and lots of her own blood rushing out, the assassin laughed.

"It doesn't matter," said Elicia weakly. She grinned hideously before softly closing her eyes. Jon picked himself up and turned to Ulisez, who recovered now.

"She's dead, let's go."

They moved alongside and away from the dead body. They could make sure that Bao and Kareem were out of it, but the beating they took could keep them out long enough for what they came here to do. They came here to stop Vladimir and save Jessica.

There was a long imperial staircase. Vladimir had gone all out on this house. There was dead quiet in this house. The Legion of Samurai had sent out three of their best, and they had overcome them all. But the question on Jon's mind was where Ivan and Nubia were? Could Vladimir be saving them for something? Or was he a decent enough father to shield them from what would come?

But as Jon looked up the stairs, he wondered what he would do when he saw Vladimir. Would he fight him to the death? Was he prepared to go all out?

He glanced over at Ulisez to check on his wellbeing. His friend was okay. He had taken a small beating from Kareem and Elicia, but no wounds of any kind. They were lucky, so far.

"Do you know where we're headed?" asked Ulisez.

"The first floors are pretty standard. If anyone else was down here, they would have attacked us by now," replied Jon.

"What if we're walking into a trap?"

Jon rolled his eyes. It was the second time Ulisez had mentioned a trap. This entire mansion was one large trap. They pressed on.

The imperial staircase was intimidating, especially since they were practically blind to whatever could be up there. Anyone or anything could come out of nowhere and strike. Jon was counting on it.

They made their way up the left side of the staircase. As they made their way to third to the last step of the top of the staircase, a shadow appeared. Manny emerged. Jon could see the pain in his face, the anger. He had felt that anger once. He still felt that anger. To Manny, Jon was just like Alexander Caine or Freddy Hunter.

"Before you do anything stupid, remember it's two on one," Jon informed Manny, who took out two swords and held them in his hands. "Well, that should help you."

Manny smiled. His silence was a little worrying and everything went nuts as he swung the sword in his right hand at Jon, who blocked it with the blade in his glove. Manny skidded left, breathing a little hard. Jon took this opportunity to leap over the top step, positioning himself on top of the staircase. This was still not a good place to be.

Ulisez also made his way to the top of the staircase. Without admonition, he charged at Manny, who was ready for him. He struck Ulisez with his right elbow, slamming his neck. Jon picked himself up and ran toward Manny, who threw something at him.

Jon's eyes stung. Whatever the hell Manny threw at him caused his eyes to swell up badly. It was agonizing, almost like an itch that did not want to go away. He yelped in pain. Manny smiled.

"That should hold you for a while, murderer," Manny gloated.

"What the hell was that?" Jon loudly asked.

"Metsubushi," was all Manny said, which did not explain a damn thing.

"That's not very honorable," Jon cried.

"Actually," Manny began as if he were some professor getting ready to make a correction to a student getting a wrong answer. "Old Samurais used this technique in ancient Japan to subdue and restrain criminals."

"You're such a little bitch, Manny," Jon shot back. "Can't fight me man to man."

"Doesn't matter how I kill you," Manny replied, raising his sword. "Just that I kill you."

Manny was about to strike, but Ulisez once again tackled him. Jon watched helplessly as this occurred.

Ulisez grabbed a taser and attempted to shock Manny with it. The Samurai warrior blocked his attempt to do so. There was a hint of subtle anger in Ulisez's demeanor as he struggled with Manny.

"Your anger will not change the fact that you cannot win," Manny roared.

Ulisez pushed Manny back with his free hand. The warrior attempted another strike with his sword, and Ulisez rolled over to evade the swipe. Then, he slid underneath Manny's legs and grabbed his nightstick from his holster. He spun around and struck Manny in the left leg with the stick. Manny leaped into the air and Ulisez caught his foot and slammed him back to the floor, dangerously close to the edge of the staircase. Ulisez thrust his nightstick against Manny's chest.

"It's over Manny," Ulisez let him know. "Tell us where Vladimir is."

Manny shook his head. "You have not won yet, you have left yourself open for an easy strike."

Jon watched in horror as Manny grabbed a knife he hid in his pocket. With a wave of anger like no other, Manny slashed Ulisez's left leg with the dagger, drawing out some blood. Ulisez screamed in agony as the knife sliced his leg. Manny stood up, with Ulisez now on the floor, clutching his wounded leg.

"Now is the time I take my revenge," Manny exclaimed. Jon picked himself up.

"Manny, what happened to your father was—"

"Was what? You murdered him. You killed him in cold blood."

It was true. Jon did not argue the fact. All this time, he had attempted to change into someone else, or something else. Despite all that, the truth was right here staring him in the face. He had to face his sins.

"Yes," acknowledged Jon. "I was young. Filled with anger. It was my initiation into the Great Command of the Capital. They saved my life, I owed them that much."

"But he was my father," Manny roared, holding back tears. It was rare to see any member of the Legion of Samurai show emotion. "I was just a boy when you took him away."

"You were the same age I was when I lost my father."

"Then you see now why I must avenge my father."

"Your father was in an organization of vigilante psychopaths."

"And what are you?"

Jon blinked. It was a good question. The stinging in his eyes had slowly dissipated, but Manny's words had a harsher effect. Manny went on.

"Ever since you came into this town, I have watched as you acted reckless, angry, and violently. You killed many lives in your quest to avenge your father, and for what? All to watch the man who murdered your father be killed by another."

"I wanted to kill Caine so badly—"

"But you did not. We killed him."

"You took the decision out of my hands and stand there casting stones. You're as bad as I am." Manny tightened the grip on his sword. "You are correct. Only this time, you will pay with your life!"

Jon took out his own sword. Manny rushed him and they tumbled together. This resulted in both men losing their swords. Manny grabbed Jon's head and smashed it against the wall. It all happened so suddenly and randomly that he had not expected it.

The assassin moved in for another strike, but Jon caught him, literally caught him as he charged at him, and used his momentum to fling Manny back at the wall. He pressed quickly, striking with brutal forearm strikes to the chest and the lower neck, finally putting him on the ground. Manny bellowed in pain as this happened, but was still conscious. There were now some cuts on his face. Manny would not be doing any modeling soon.

He placed his knee on Manny's chest and held down. Manny thrashed like a cat attempting to escape a human's hands.

"Last chance, Manny," Jon warned him. "Stay down! Tell me where Vladimir is."

"You might as well kill me because I will never tell you where my master is."

He kept his grip on Manny, but somehow, he used his elusiveness and slid out of his grip. Manny grabbed him by the hair, a bitch move, and slammed him down against the ground.

"Now you die," Manny exclaimed. He took out a gun, also not something the Legion of Samurai usually advocated for, and jammed it in Jon's face. "Vengeance is mine!"

He squeezed the trigger when a loud shot let out. Jon must have been hallucinating because there was no pain or force that entered him. Also, he was not dead. He looked up and saw blood pouring out of Manny's stomach.

But what he visualized the most were his eyes. Manny's eyes loomed large as he reacted to the giant hole in his stomach. He slowly flickered his eyes, then struggled to keep his balance, and then finally fell over backward, landing with a thud.

He looked sideways and saw Ulisez holding a smoking gun. He crawled over and now saw Manny's dead body. Ulisez still clutched onto his leg and it was bleeding profusely. He picked himself up and attended to him.

"Are you going to be okay?"

"Get my bag," Ulisez said.

He did as commanded. Ulisez had brought a bag with him and it turned out to be useful. He took out some long clothed bandages and Jon grabbed it and wrapped it around the wound. This stopped the bleeding.

"Go get him," said Ulisez.

He nodded in acknowledgment and left Ulisez there, in horrible pain, but okay. Cautiously, he made his way down the hallway and made a left. Finally, he could see it.

The largest room in the home was visible from this angle, and Jon walked toward it. Ivan and Nubia had not attacked, so they either must not be here, or they were in there with Vladimir. He would find out.

He approached the door. If there was a trap, he would be ready for it. There was no going back now. Jessica was there and he had to save her. He would save her. There were no other possibilities. She was coming back with him alive, or he was not coming back at all.

Chapter 38: The Fight of Our Lives

Jessica watched Vladimir's demeanor change drastically. There was a gunshot, and they both had heard it. But something in Vladimir's body language showed that it had to be someone he cared about that bit the bullet. He looked distraught, almost heartbroken. She noticed that he had been looking at a monitor which appeared to display the rest of the home.

Now, Vladimir had his face in both hands, and his long hair was covering his face. Jessica realized there was no movement with him as he stood still. Then she realized something. He was silently sobbing. Vladimir Ramirez, the man with plans for destroying the world because of, in his opinion, deep wickedness, was actively sobbing.

She inched a little closer. She knew that she should not have done that. He had untied her, but he was still a dangerous psychopath who could snap at any moment. She privately wondered how he could be the father of such a sensitive soul. It now made her sick to her stomach to know the truth about that. What else had he hidden from her?

Her eyes glanced at the bedroom door for a moment. She could sprint and make a run for it while something distracted him. But then, there were potential traps all over his house. It was probably not the smartest idea. Then something else occurred to her. If Vladimir was sobbing over someone close to him potentially being harmed, then that meant that Jon was in the house.

His sobbing was silent but still sad to see. The man had drugged her and kidnapped her, yet she still felt some sympathy for him. Jessica was not sure why she felt this way. Maybe this was likely because of her encounters with Nubia.

"Manuel, no," Jessica heard Vladimir whisper out loud. The man was in despair and Jessica knew she had to either console him or take advantage. Out of nowhere, Vladimir slammed his hand on the table next to him in frustration. Jessica was in awe as she looked at the smashed wooden table. It startled her.

She inched closer. This was probably not the smartest idea in the world, but her curiosity was getting the best of her. Vladimir's back away from her as he hunched over the monitor. As she crept up behind him, they were both alerted by a noise coming from the hallway.

She saw his eyes loom large. Then Vladimir turned to her. His eyes were large and scary now, like a wolf. For a moment, he looked like the big evil wolf. He marched toward her with a ferocity that she had never seen before. He extended his large arm and grabbed her by the throat. She gagged for a moment and struggled to breathe as Vladimir's large arm choked her. His arm was like a giant claw wrapped around her and there was no getting out. Still, she struggled and slapped his arm to no avail.

"I may change my mind now! I may just kill you after all! Jon Drake is coming, and he is going to witness it," exclaimed Vladimir.

Vladimir released his grip and then pressed her face with his palm and pushed her backward. She lost her balance and fell on the ground. While the fall stung a little, the humiliation from being pushed over by some guy's palm. Jessica grunted in anger. It pissed her off.

As she picked herself up. Jessica looked around the room and did not see Vladimir anywhere. Where could he have gone? Before she could process anything, the door opened and Jon walked in.

Her gaze rose from the floor to his, and she could tell he had been in some struggle. There were bruises all over him and cuts. He locked eyes with her and just stood there for a moment.

"Jon?"

"Jessica?"

Jon took a few steps and closed the door behind him. It was at that moment that Jessica attempted to let out a scream, but nothing happened. Vladimir whacked Jon in the back of the head with a crowbar. The hit forced Jon to the ground, moaning as he was in a lot of pain and Jessica knew it looked bad.

She watched in terror as Vladimir emerged and stood above Jon. He pressed his boot on top of Jon's chest.

"I have been expecting you," Vladimir said to Jon.

Jessica watched as Jon groaned.

"A crowbar, Vladimir? You insult me," replied Jon.

Vladimir shrugged, and she watched as Jon's pulse quickened.

"You should have known me better than that," roared Vladimir.

"We'll see about that," replied Jon.

Jon sprung to his feet immediately. He moved his fist to smash Vladimir, but the Lion caught it and wrenched it, causing Jon to wince.

"Skilled," Vladimir commended Jon. "But still not a match for me."

Vladimir used his other hand to club Jon across the back. Then, he catches Jon before he falls, grabbing him by the hair and yanking him up. She watched in horror as Vladimir smashed Jon's face across his forearm.

"I will be the one to end you," Vladimir whispered in his ear.

Jon lashed out at Vladimir, and they separated for a moment. Jessica watched in confusion as this happened.

"You are weak, pathetic," Vladimir goaded Jon.

Jon hurled himself at Vladimir, recklessly. They both landed over the table next to the closet. He relentlessly punched Vladimir in the face and Jessica could not see exactly what was happening. The angle obscured her view, but she knew that Vladimir was not moving.

Vladimir's arms shot up. Jon went flying backward as Vladimir's right arm took him by surprise. The Lion got to his feet as Jon staggered. She noticed that he was bleeding now, from the mouth and a little from the hand. Vladimir walked toward Jon with purpose.

"You cannot beat me, I am your better."

Jon touched his face and realized he was bleeding. Jessica stood silently, out of either fear or shock. She was not sure what to do. Her mind was racing for the options in what she could do. Her mind raced, searching for an idea on how to help Jon.

Her eyes scoured the room, looking for something, anything. She did not even know what she was looking for. All she knew was that she had to help Jon. Somehow, someway, Jessica had to prevent Vladimir from killing Jon.

Jon reached into his pocket and Jessica could see it was a gun. She watched in amazement as Vladimir reacted quickly, stepping on Jon's hand and deflecting the gun away. Jon yelped in pain as Vladimir's enormous foot crushed his already injured hand. The gun went flying on the floor and conveniently landed near Jessica's feet.

"Foolish to think that a gun could stop me," Vladimir taunted him.

God, he was so pretentious, Jessica thought.

She watched as Vladimir kicked Jon in the face, sending his cheekbones moving in one direction that looked so unnatural. The panic inside her rose by miles. Time was running out and she knew that she had to do something. Her eyes glanced at the gun below her feet. There was a moment of clarity here. She knew that there was only one thing she had to do, but she was not sure she dared to do it.

"Why don't I show you how to truly break a man?" Vladimir lifted Jon off the ground with one arm showcasing his amazing strength. "Crashing Down."

Vladimir palmed Jon's face into the ground. He twisted his large hand around Jon's neck and smashed it again. The blood was spewing all over Jon's face, and it was becoming unrecognizable.

Vladimir stood above Jon and shoved him with his foot. She still looked down at the gun, contemplating what to do.

"I will complete my mission," Vladimir hissed. "I will burn this world to the ground and you and everyone else in this city, this county, this state, this country, they will all suffer for their sins.

"You will all perish as I destroy this world and give it a rebirth in the new paradise that I will grow."

Jon looked up at him, and Jessica noticed him cough up some blood. She still had her eyes on the gun and at that moment realized that neither of these two men paid any attention to her. This was her opportunity.

"You sick fuck," Jon shot back. "You think anyone will want to live in your world?"

"They will not have a choice," Vladimir roared.

Jon and Vladimir just stared at each other for a moment. It was the weirdest thing in the world, and she could not help but stare. Regardless, she slowly inched toward the gun.

Vladimir leaned in and reared his right hand and slapped Jon across the face. More blood shot out of Jon's face as his right hand made contact. Jessica felt her hands on the gun now, and it felt like ice. She had touched a gun before. Her father had taken her to the shooting range a bunch of times. But she had never actually used it against anyone. It was something she had never expected that she would ever have to do.

Vladimir suddenly turned toward her. His hair covered half his face and thunder roared in the distance at that very moment. It was surreal, and Vladimir seemed like a man possessed. She had her hands on the gun but kept it concealed for the moment. She was far enough from Vladimir that she might get off a shot without being attacked. But she was also far enough that a gunshot would not be one hundred percent accurate.

Vladimir walked methodically toward her. Out of instinct, she backed off a few steps, trying to keep the distance between herself and the Lion.

"Now my dear Jessica Hudson," Vladimir glowered. "You will watch Jon Drake die. A lesson to you that wicked people must always pay the consequences."

"Start with yourself ass wipe," Jessica spat.

Vladimir roared with laughter. Fuck this guy, Jessica thought. He seemed amused at her, and that was even more insulting than any actual harm he could cause to her.

"Say your goodbyes," Vladimir stated proudly. "I will end him and make you watch. Then, because you rejected my offer, I will mercifully end your life."

Vladimir turned his attention back toward Jon. Jessica kept the gun close to her body, not revealing it yet. The opportunity had to be just right. She had her right hand on it and just waited. Vladimir was blissfully unaware of her plans. He took out a large knife.

"Now, time for you to die," Vladimir spoke to Jon with an arrogance Jessica had never heard before.

Vladimir brandished the knife and held it gingerly. She immediately took out the gun and took the safety out. He heard it and turned around, surprised.

"Drop the knife, you piece of shit," Jessica exclaimed.

Vladimir looked at her with bemused contempt. He still thought of her as weak, and that was exactly what she wanted.

"What are you doing to do? Shoot me?" he asked.

She hesitated. She was not sure what she had wanted to do. The only thing on her mind was that she had to save Jon. If that meant shooting a man, then that was what she had to do. But was she ready to shoot a man?

"Take one more step and I will," Jessica almost mumbled the words.

"You would do nothing. You're weak. You're a pathetic drug addict. You are nothing more than a loser.

"You would never shoot me. You are Jon Drake's pathetic little angel, the recovering addict who will amount to nothing but being a pathetic waitress."

"You've driven me to this point. YOLO bitch!" she exclaimed.

"Do you realize how many men have tried to kill me?"

"I am no man!"

"No, you're not, you're a weak little girl. Just like your father. You don't have what it takes to take a life. To make the world a better place. You cower like a woman hiding from the world."

"You don't know me—"

"But do I not? Just like the rest of society, you have no real morals. This generation of arrogant, narcissistic people and you have the nerve to call me mad? People like you, like him, like your father, you created this world."

"You are mad," she finally realized that Vladimir had completely lost his mind.

"And you always need a hero to save you."

"Do I look like I need saving?"

"A madwoman with a gun, pathetic," Vladimir said.

"Jessica," Jon called out weakly. "No."

Vladimir glanced briefly at him, then back at her. "I am tired of this. You are about to die, you pathetic fool."

"Not any closer," she threatened. "I will shoot."

"You don't have the guts!"

She proved him wrong by shooting him in the chest.

Chapter 39: Shattered Glass

Vladimir felt the bullet pierce through his chest. It was so unexpected, but he felt like a fool for allowing it to happen. He looked down at the blood that seeped down his coat jacket and felt more embarrassed than injured.

Others had shot before him, but never to the extent of it being life-threatening. That was mainly because he was always quick to disarm his opponent. Rarely had he ever allowed anyone to shoot him multiple times. But usually, gunmen or someone from a cartel shot him. It had never been a woman, let alone a former drug addict.

He realized the blood was seeping down and felt the sharp pain the bullet had caused. He realized at once he needed to put a stop to this before it went any further. The pain was quickening, and he had to react accordingly.

He advanced toward Jessica, but she fired once more, shooting him in the abdomen. This shot hurt a little more, making another hole in his body. Blood rushed out from this shot, but he kept his balance. He knew he had no other choice. There was no other way. He had to get the gun from Jessica. He had to disarm her. Another thought crossed his mind.

There was glass behind him, and he was staggeringly close. He had not intended to stand right in front of it, but it was where he was. The sound of rain continued to fall, but he heard nothing at the moment as the pain from the gunshots overcame anything he might hear or see. The roar of the thunder pounded in the backdrop and Vladimir found it charming to be happening on this day of all days.

He took a glance at Jessica's face for a moment as he saw her with the gun in her hand. She had become someone else, something else. The woman who was sarcastic and witty no longer stood in front of him. In her place had risen a madwoman with a gun, willing to do anything to get the job done. Her hair fell in front of her face. Her face scrunched up angrily. It was at that moment; he knew that underestimating her had proven to possibly be a fatal mistake.

He held his balance temporarily and for a second glanced over at Jon, who was helpless on the ground, practically crippled from the injuries he had suffered. There was no going back now. He attempted with his last will of strength to lung toward Jessica.

"Die you piece of shit!" she bellowed as she fired off another shot from the gun. This time, the bullet flung into his upper chest and now he felt his eyelids slide back. His balance was no longer there for him, and Vladimir felt himself losing his ability to stand still. Without realizing it, he stumbled backward and into the glass that separated his bedroom from the cliff below.

He felt himself flying backward. There was no stopping it now. He was falling off a 50-foot cliff.

At least I will be reunited with my Ileana soon, he thought.

The fall seemed like it happened in slow motion, and he saw his entire life flash before his eyes. He saw his wife, his son, and his daughter. The memories of his life in Brazil rushed back, and memories of the Samurai and Diego Rivera. He remembered meeting Thomas for the first time.

As his body nearly reached the water, he made peace with the fact that at least his children would live. They would finish what he started. They would complete his goal.

He felt his body nearly close to hitting the water and knew that it was almost the end. It was okay. This was a fitting way to die. This was a proper way to exit this cruel world. He closed his eyes and made peace with what was about to happen.

Then, within a few seconds, he felt his body hit the water, and it crushed his ribs instantly. The impact crushed several of his vertebrae immediately. It felt like an explosion occurring within his body. Everything inside him got crushed. His body sunk further and further down below, and at that moment, he realized it was over. Finally, as he plummeted further down, he allowed the darkness to consume him.

Chapter 40: The Consequences

Jon picked himself off the floor now. Everything had happened so fast he had not had time to process it all. How the hell could get Vladimir get the best of him? Worst of all, how could he leave Vladimir alone with Jessica? All those thoughts and more rushed through his mind as he slowly got to his feet. He had one thing on his mind and that was making sure Jessica was okay. Vladimir had not touched her, but she just shot him out a window. That was something he had not seen coming.

The blood dripped from his body. There was a lot of pain, but he ignored it for the moment. It was a matter of importance. Jon glanced over at Jessica and tried to get a visual of her face. She seemed to freeze in place.

"Jessica?"

He stood in front of her and noticed her eyes had not moved. It was like she was in a catatonic state. Her hands were still on the gun and she watched the broken glass that she had caused by shattering it with Vladimir's body.

He moved in front of her and tried to lock eyes with her, but she was not budging. Jessica's eyes followed the trajectory of the window. The wind had picked up from the new gaping hole in the shattered glass, and the rain.

"Jessica?"

She did not respond. It was surreal. Jessica stood still. Jon moved closer to her, a little cautiously. It was not like he was afraid that she would do anything. But what terrified him was Jessica harming herself. There was still no movement on her part. He reached toward her and slowly grabbed the gun from her, and she allowed her fingers to release the hold. He picked up the gun and gently put it away. At the moment, he did not even think of covering his hands. His fingerprints were all over the gun. But then again, Jessica's fingerprints were also on the gun. It did not matter. He was not thinking about that right now. His focus was on making sure she was okay.

He slowly placed his right hand on Jessica's shoulder. This was his attempt to find something, anything to reach her. Without warning, she turned to Jon. Her eyes watered and she finally let it all loose. Jessica broke down bawling her eyes and he held her close, not wanting to let her go.

He shielded her from the rain. But at that moment, neither of them cared about that. It was about a minute of crying, which would normally annoy Jon. But this was Jessica. She had every right to bawl her eyes out or bitch about anything after what she had just endured. Jon gently placed his hand on her face and softly forced her to look at him.

"Are you okay?"

She did not respond verbally. Instead, she softly nodded. He placed his arm around her hips, and they used each other for support. The pain in his entire body was deafening, but he would not allow that to consume him. Together, they exited the room slowly. As they left the master bedroom, a terrifying thought crossed his mind. Where were Ivan and Nubia? Surely they still could be in the house. Why would Vladimir bring them to California just to send them away? That worried Jon because after what they went through, he was in no shape to face either of them, especially Nubia.

They held each other. His injuries hurt physically, but she was probably worse for wear. The strain of shooting Vladimir to death was possibly having a profound effect on her. He felt the pain constantly as he drifted with her, as she still had not said a word since she shot Vladimir. It was an eerie quiet where she appeared to lose the ability to speak. He remembered the first time he killed a man and how traumatic it had been for him. Though Escobar had been around to snap him out of it by threatening to kill him. He never got to fully process the idea and learned to block it out completely. He did not want that for Jessica. That would be terrible if that happened to her.

They moved through the corridor and as they passed the corner to the top of the stairwell, Ulisez was sitting down bandaging his wounds. He looked up when they arrived.

"You're alive," Ulisez pointed out the obvious.

They moved closer to him without saying a word until they stood in front of him.

"What the hell happened in there?" asked Ulisez.

Jon and Jessica looked at each other, and water dripped on the floor. They noticed that the rain had soaked in and wet their clothing. It did not seem to bother them. The blood on his injuries seemed to wash away, thanks to the rain. It dripped on the floor from their clothing, and now the nice rug was wet. Ulisez groaned in pain as he tried to pick himself up, but it proved to be too difficult. Manny had done a number on his legs, and it was showing.

With every ounce of strength Jon could muster, he bent down and lifted Ulisez from the arms. They both struggled and Jessica hugged herself with her arms crossed over as if comforting herself. After Jon could secure them both to stand up, they staggered down the stairs carefully, taking one step at a time. It was a challenge, and something that would have been easy had it not been for their injuries.

Manny's corpse remained out on the stairs, and seeing it again was difficult. Jessica's eyes shot up and she almost let out a scream but held back at the last moment. Jon would have almost preferred her to scream. It would have meant there was some feeling.

They stepped carefully over Manny's body and walked gingerly down the stairs. It took a lot longer than expected, as they were essentially two cripples and an emotionally damaged being. From the corner of their eye, they saw Elicia's dead body. Her corpse was still fresh, and the lifeless look on her face simmered. They walked around her and made their way to the front door.

They walked outside and immediately became alarmed. There were no signs of Bao or Kareem. Jon got his guard up now, thinking an attack might happen. Where could these two have gone? Were they planning a sneak attack?

He knew that none of them were in any condition for a fight right now. He kept his eyes open for anything, but that proved to be difficult in this rain. There was not a soul in sight. The heavy rain had kept everyone inside. It made everything even more difficult, especially the walking part.

The three of them made it to the car safely. They all stowed away inside, with Ulisez in the front seat and Jessica in the back. Jon worried Ulisez might pass out and die if he left him in the backseat, so they had made a silent agreement.

They drove in silence as they took off from Laguna Beach. There were no ideas on what to do, and no one had said anything. The rain continued to pound on their windshields, and Jon used the wipers to get them away.

After about 30 miles, they had arrived at their location. Ulisez looked out the window and appeared confused, and Jessica said nothing. She still had not spoken since the incident. That worried Jon a lot.

"Why are we stopping here?" asked Ulisez.

They were in Dana Point now. Jon had driven them down PCH to the wharf where the boats docked. This wharf was where the tourists and anyone else in Orange County came to see the whales and any other sea animals.

He had not been to Dana Point since he was a child. He always found the city comforting in its way. His mother had taken him there many times to see the shops and watch the whales. His father had taken him there to ride a jet ski. This was before all things went to hell in a hand basket.

"We have to talk about what happened back there," Jon's voice was grave.

His injuries were still debilitating and his sides hurt like someone was constantly punching him. He figured he would be used to the pain, but that never feels the same even after all this time. A sane person would have gone to the hospital. He was not a sane person. His experience in South America had also taught him how to heal his injuries with no modern medicine. That was why he always kept the basics in his bag, and he privately thanked the Command of the Nation, and Ram the Bounty Hunter, for teaching him how to heal injuries.

Ulisez had used the antibiotic ointment in his bag from earlier to treat his stab wounds, but he would not be running any marathons soon. Now, Jon worried about the long term emotional scars they all might have.

"I asked you what happened back there, and you guys didn't say anything," Ulisez pointed out.

He was right, Jon thought.

But the only thing that mattered was getting out of there. It was important to escape the house and make sure everyone was okay.

"Vladimir's dead," was all Jon said.

There was a moment of complete silence. He expected Ulisez to ask how he died, and that was a question that would probably happen. He was not sure if he should answer it or if Jessica should. But Jessica was not talking.

There was also the matter of the other dead bodies. Manny was dead, as was Elicia. Bao and Kareem had vanished, and what the hell happened to Ivan and Nubia?

Those were some things that went through his mind as he sat there in this car with his best buddy and the woman he loved. The only problem was that the woman he loved seemed to be catatonic, or at least acting like it. Her face was grave and looked blue. Jessica sat there in the backseat with no movement or a hint of a word since they left. Finally, the elephant in the room came out.

"What happened?" Ulisez asked.

Jon turned back to Jessica, attempting to see if she would say anything. She stared at the back of Ulisez's seat, her lips not moving. Something was wrong, and Jon could not understand it. For now, he had to take on the role of protector, and it was not one he wanted to do much of, anyway.

"Well, Vladimir and I fought and I—"

"You killed him?" Ulisez cut him off. "Did you shoot him? I heard glass break."

"Well, I—"

"I did," Jessica had finally broken her silence. She was stone-faced, looking straight in the windshield's direction at no one in particular. Ulisez turned around in his seat gingerly and looked at her. She turned to him and gave him a blank look. "He would have killed Jon, so I shot him three times, the third time pushing him out his glass window onto the rocks below, which likely killed him."

Ulisez turned back to Jon, and he grimaced at the idea. Jon gave a nod as if to say 'don't do anything' and there was a new tension in the car. They were both worried about Jessica and the way she just reacted to what she did.

"I didn't have a choice," Jessica went on. "He would have killed Jon. He wanted to destroy him and the entire world. He was insane and gave me a maddening speech about how we were all terrible humans and how he would euthanize us like animals. It was terrible to endure, and I am glad I shot him. He deserved to die.

"I had to do what I had to do. I had to save us, save you, save the world. I didn't want to do it, but I had to do it. Now you can either be my best friend and stand by me, or you can be a bitch cop and attempt to arrest me for saving Jon Drake's life by shooting a man in cold blood. It's your choice."

She simmered down now, and that was when Jon realized that was all they would get out of her. He glanced back at Jessica and noticed how cold she sounded and wondered if she had lost some of her sanity, or even her humanity. He felt incredible guilt at this moment because he felt that coming back to town had done this to her. Had his coming back set this all in motion? Was he a monster? What had he done to Jessica?

It was something that tugged in the back of Jon's mind as he sat there contemplating what to do and where to go. He looked at Ulisez to see if he could give him any sign, and there was none. His friend seemed as lost as he was.

There was a feeling of uncertainty toward what everyone would do now. The three of them were all fractured emotionally from everything that had happened. They also had endured a hell of an experience in trying to fight a group of assassins who could have killed a normal man.

"What are we going to do?" asked Ulisez.

"They can't turn us in without exposing themselves," replied Jon.

"What?"

"The Legion of Samurai wasn't exactly conducting legal business. They kidnapped Jessica and we have her word as proof of that, plus other documents I got from their estate. When I confronted Thomas, I also swiped some materials from him."

Ulisez gave him a dumbfounded look. Jon knew he had to explain this to him. He continued.

"We have leverage. If Ivan and Nubia ever attempt to come after us legally, we have leverage. The Legion of Samurai has been crippled, and without their leader, it may fall. Ivan and Nubia may be trained, but neither of them is as good as their father. Let them try."

There was more silence for the moment. None of them knew what to say. Jon started the car back again. He did not know what else to do. So they drove. They drove as far as they could just to get out of town. Eventually, they would have to return home and face the repercussions of their actions. That day would come, and they would be ready for it. Together, they would figure it out. When that day came, they would be ready.

The End

www.ingramcontent.com/pod-product-compliance
Lightning Source LLC
Chambersburg PA
CBHW042113100526
44587CB00025B/4036